SEXY,

SPIRITED,

AND STRONG:

BECOMING A POSITIVE ENERGY WOMAN

Dear Priscilla —
Thank you for
shining your beautiful
& bright light!
The world is a better
place because of you!
With love —
Maloney

SEXY,

SPIRITED,

AND STRONG:

BECOMING A POSITIVE ENERGY WOMAN

Meloney Hudson

Illustrations by Meloney Hudson

Cover art by Tim Shullberg

iUniverse, Inc.
New York   Bloomington

Sexy, Spirited, and Strong
Becoming a Positive Energy Woman

Copyright © 2009 by Meloney Hudson

iUniverse books may be ordered through booksellers or by contacting:

iUniverse
1663 Liberty Drive
Bloomington, IN 47403
www.iuniverse.com
1-800-Authors (1-800-288-4677)

ISBN: 978-0-595-48082-1 (pbk)
ISBN: 978-0-595-60181-3 (ebk)

Printed in the United States of America
iUniverse Rev Date 01/29/2009

TABLE OF CONTENTS

ACKNOWLEDGEMENTS

I thank all of the women and men in my life for being my teachers and guiding me to be the best I can be.

Thanks to all of the spiritual adepts, scientists, archaeologists, historians, scholars, feminists, and healers before me, who provided pathways to human evolution, and from whom I have learned, and drawn information for this book. Tremendous thanks to my dear parents, Martha and John B. Hudson, for being my primary teachers and for supporting me in so many ways during my life, and through the process of writing this book. Thanks to my sister and brothers, Betsy, Benjamin, and Todd, who also provided love, support and enthusiasm for my path.

A gigantic thanks to my intelligent and brilliant editor, Barbara Ardinger, who helped me transform rough ideas and concepts into a book of substance, and who beautifully challenged and supported me to become a more mature thinker and writer. Thanks to my teacher Bodhi Avinasha, for guiding me to become a positive, energetic being, and for encouraging my growth in the path of Tantra.

Thanks to Donna Read for her mentorship in filmmaking, and for introducing me to the world of women's history.

Thanks to the many healers and personal growth coaches who helped me gain clarity in my life's direction and heal the mindsets and wounds that stood in the way of self-love, making the writing of this book possible.

Thanks to my dear women and men friends who rallied, supported my efforts, and understood my need for space during the writing of this book, and who provided an intelligent and heartfelt forum for discussion so that I may gain clarity on my writings, including my dear fellow writer friend, Mark Watson, Tiffany Knoeck, Jamie Weiss, Divina del Sol, Shakeh Herbekian, Jane DeMente, Sonya Chapnick, Marielle Taylor, John Petrie, Tim Schulberg, Xia Moon, Elliott Segal, Coleen Call, Cameron Dougan, Jeff McKay, Roxanne Steiny, Lulu and so many others.

Thanks to Kianti Murphy for his research assistance on quantum physics and philosophical discussions on women's history during the writing process.

Thanks to God/dess for all of the blessings of my life and for the inspired thoughts that created this book.

INTRODUCTION

What started out to be a simple task of compiling a guidebook of exercises for women took me for the ride of my life by insisting that I grow it into a full-fledged book. My original intention was to create support material for my Aphrodite's Secrets sexuality and spirituality workshops for women, which I've presented off and on over the years. But as I cobbled together bits and pieces that I've learned from many teachers, healers, and other wise people, I began to interject my own theories and ideas. Soon the workshops fell away to make room for a writing effort that would absorb all of my spare time and attention and expand my soul. My mission became to provide women with information to help them feel confident, proud of their feminine bodies, and build exuberantly positive energy. This mission has driven me for more than two years, and I have succumbed to my soul's urgent push to get this information out into the world as soon as possible, as women, men and the planet can benefit from it more than ever.

My journey as a teacher began when I recognized women's desires to feel good about themselves. What seemed like natural instincts— self-love, joy, inner strength, and positive attitude—were actually huge achievements for many people, especially women. I have met so many intelligent, beautiful, and accomplished women who have struggled in their lives, feeling satisfaction only fleetingly, feeling unfeminine while striving to succeed in a man's world, or not able to compete and not liking who they were. I was surprised at the number of women who on the outside appeared to be successful and "together" but who were internally highly critical, judgmental, and impatient with themselves. Having suffered from the insidious effects of low self-esteem myself in my own life, I could relate to all who had a devalued sense of self. (You'll read about bits of my life in the book.)

Luckily, I was divinely guided to work through my self-loathing. For many years, I have explored a variety of spiritual paths, especially Tantra, both Eastern and Western healing practices, ancient women's history, and quantum physics. My studies and practices taught me to love myself as a woman and create the life that I desired. My energy became more vibrant and I felt more positive in my attitude. People complimented me on the positive energy I exuded. I began to see the subtle affects my endeavors produced in my internal and external energy, and to feel the various nuances of energy. I became aware of the effects of one human's energy on other's and on what some call the "quantum field" of energy that surrounds and penetrates everything in the universe. Recognizing my own vibration and the positive results I receive from radiating positive energy, I wanted to share the things that I learned.

In my personal practices and research, I discovered the three essential energetic areas that contribute to a woman's (and man's) sense of well-being and wholeness: sex, spirit, and power. When we have sexual energy that is awake and balanced, an active connection with the inner and omnipresent divine, and inner and outer physical strength, the result is heightened self-love, which gives rise to feelings of joy and confidence and either manifestation of the things we most desire or joyful acceptance if we don't get them. Until a woman's three energy areas are alive and balanced, her self-esteem and self-love, and thus a joyful life, will elude her. I believe that luminous self-love not only helps a woman to live up to her potential and create a life that she enjoys, but also makes her a positive, potent, energetic force on the planet. I believe an increase of feminine energy in each woman will contribute to the collective feminine, which will positively affect the energetic field of the planet, and potentially balance the masculine energy that prevails today.

In my Aphrodite's Secrets workshops, I share the many practices and techniques that help a woman to increase her energies of sex, spirit, and strength. My workshop participants leave the workshop feeling several degrees stronger in self-love, confident of themselves as women, capable of creating the lives they want, and radiant with positive energy. In other words, they are sexy, spirited, and strong!

My path to teaching was a multi-dimensional one. While I had studied various religions and spiritual paths for most of my life, I became interested in the principles of human energy in the mid-1990s when I began to study the sacred path of Ipsalu Tantra with my teacher Bodhi Avinasha, from whom I continue to learn today. Tantra is a rich path that opens the energy pathways in the body so that we become an unobstructed conduit for spiritual energy. The most powerful energy in the body is sexual energy, and it is this electricity that we are taught to encourage and harness for healing and expansion. It is a beautiful practice that greatly honors Shakti, or feminine energy, which exists in every woman and man, as well as in the quantum field, or "universe." Sensual exercises stimulating sexual energy entice the rising of the Shakti energy within and invite Her to merge with one's own masculine, or Shiva, energy. Most practices are performed solo to raise and move our energy. They can also be performed in partnership, traditionally with someone of the opposite sex. The energetic union of Shakti and Shiva promotes feelings of ecstasy, love, and soulful expansion. Through Tantra, my connection with Universal Spirit became stronger, and my own inner goddess awakened.

But as my inner goddess became more vibrantly apparent, I began to see the need to be grounded on the earthly plane. There were many "earth goddesses" out there who were having difficulty supporting themselves in the earthly realm, and I didn't want to be one of them. I had been making a living, but was not "successful" financially. I wasn't even sure I was in the right career. So I pursued information and practices to empower the "earth body vehicle" that housed my inner goddess. As I learned that I had created obstacles to success with limiting mindsets and beliefs about myself, I sought teachers to help me change those negative beliefs.

Perhaps the greatest contributors to my personal growth and empowerment were John Freedom and his "Feeling is Healing" sessions, and Christopher Howard's personal power seminars. John helped me heal old childhood wounds with my parents, an exercise of diligence that caused tremendous healing in my relationship with them and with myself; these healings spurred a tremendous increase in my self-esteem. Chris Howard provided the framework through which I could reprogram negative beliefs about myself. He guided me to discover those moments in time that shaped my concepts of myself and helped me change them for the better. He also guided me to discover my life's purpose, which I believe is one of the strongest driving forces of every human being. John, Chris, and many other personal growth experts helped me to believe in myself and thus become confident, self-assured, and courageous. With this knowledge of empowerment, coupled with my spiritual and sexual practices, I discovered the formula that has translated into self-love and high self-esteem, yielding accomplishment, satisfaction, and joy.

With my desire for all people to possess positive energy, I have compiled simple, yet powerful, exercises from my spiritual practices and personal growth endeavors. If you try out the exercises and techniques designed for each energetic area—sex, spirit, and power/strength—

you'll have an enjoyable practice that makes your path to becoming a sexy, spirited, and strong woman more pleasurable. I suggest many resources, teachers, healers, books, and films that you can explore on your own to deepen your growth and empowerment.

You'll also find notes on ancient women's history here and there in this book. I believe that an acquaintance with our past will help us to understand our current state of being. We can see how traditions were formed and endure in today's culture. My discovery of women's history began concurrently with my studies of Tantra, when I began to participate in women's spiritual groups, or "goddess" groups. At these community gatherings, I learned about the goddesses of various ancient cultures, and performed rituals to connect with the earth and the Goddess. As my interest in ancient women's history was piqued and I began to read and study it on my own, I discovered that as I learned about the goddess cultures and high status of women in ancient times, my own self-esteem increased. To learn that women were revered for their mysterious abilities of bleeding and birth, were the conduits for divine magic as tribal shamans, and were credited for many contributions to the development of civilization instilled in me a sense of intense pride and feelings of worthiness that I hadn't felt before. It was as if I had opened a door to a secret room. This new knowledge completely shifted my ideas about women and myself.

During the late 1990s and early 2000s, I was blessed to participate in the production of a documentary by filmmaker Donna Read (director of the *Women and Spirituality* documentary series) and Starhawk, a global peace activist and leader in women's spirituality. The film we produced, *Signs Out of Time: The Story of Archaeologist Marija Gimbutas*, opened my eyes. Marija Gimbutas, who was a professor of archaeology, was highly influential in the world of women's history and women's spirituality. Her expertise was the study of cultures of Neolithic Europe, which archaeological evidence indicates was egalitarian and goddess-worshipping. Her work fueled the women's spirituality movement and confirmed the ideas embraced by many scholars and theologians of women's spirituality. On that documentary project, I was introduced to several brilliant scholars of women's history and related disciplines, including Vicki Noble, Riane Eisler, Miriam Robbins Dexter, and Elinor Gadon. These brilliant and powerful women and their insights on women's history inspired me so much that the study of women's history became of primary importance to me. I am not a scholar or a student in a formal educational institution, but I have read numerous books, attended lectures given by our most celebrated scholars, and engage in lively discussion with others interested in the topic. I love sharing what I learn. I feel that learning about our glorious past will increase your self-esteem, too.

In my studies, I was initially incensed by the ancient events that dethroned women from high status to wide-spread "second citizen" status. I blamed men for the enduring negative attitudes toward women and in my writings often accused men of "putting women down." But after discussing my viewpoint with a few wise women and men, my stance changed. I learned that I was perceiving women as victims and men as perpetrators, that "women were innocent" and "men were bad." I was presented with the possibility that women are as responsible for their history as men. Like a woman who remains in an unfulfilling relationship, women throughout history have had choices to accept the status quo, change it, or leave it, often at the risk of societal disapproval, or even death. And whatever her decision, she must accept her fate and do whatever she can to adapt and empower herself to make the best of her situation. I learned that anger and blame toward men will only feed the negative energy of oppression. When a woman understands her responsibility in a situation, this understanding actually empowers her to make a change. It may subtly effect a positive shift in the attitudes of more women. Often I struggle to accept women's responsibilities in our history, but only by acceptance will I become motivated and strong enough to enforce change myself. The basis of this book is to effect positive change, so I strive to present our history factually, and with as much objectivity as possible.

As vast and varied as this book may seem, with mystical secrets and common sense information, I hope it appeals to all women, from those who live conventional lives to those who follow alternative lifestyles, from corporate executives to stay-at-home mothers. My wish is that you will use this book as a guidebook, a resource guide, and source of inspiration. I want you to become the positive being that I feel I have become. The brighter your light shines, the better for you and for all of us.

Part One:

POSITIVE ENERGY

1

CALLING THE POSITIVE ENERGY WOMAN

A Call for Feminine Energy and Values

As if awakened from a millennia-long slumber by a cosmic alarm clock, women are rising to the universe's urgent call for renewed feminine energy and values. Consciously or instinctively, women are beginning to recognize their feminine energy as a source of positive influence for humanity and are cultivating their strengths to assist in our evolution. Many women feel the call to step out of the traditional roles formed by the masculine ideal centuries ago and engage their innate powers as wise and productive (not just reproductive) women who contribute to society and the advancement of humankind. As women's support and activist groups emerge around the world, feminine energy is permeating the collective consciousness. In more and more areas around the planet, the status of women is rising, and their contributions to society respected and accepted. This recent rise of feminine energy is but a tiny nudge in the shift of a paradigm, but it is a monumental hint of what is possible.

Our goal is not a feminine takeover. It's not for women to rule the world. It is to be accepted as equal partners with men in the name of progress. This rise of feminine energy isn't just a frivolous feminine experiment for women to "get their way," but an urgent push from the depths of the universal soul, the force that has inspired every step of human evolution, to unify the feminine and masculine energies for the survival of the species and the planet.

The Positive Energy Woman

Women hold tremendous responsibility for the evolution of humankind. But before women can raise their collective energy enough to truly make a mark in the world and influence a paradigm shift, each woman, individually, needs to cultivate her own feminine energy. This requires a conscious revival of one critical element, our self-esteem. Self-esteem is a belief in oneself and self-respect. It is recognition, acceptance, and love of every aspect of ourselves and our potential as human beings. High self-esteem is the foundation of our confidence, the fuel that motivates us to create a joyful and fulfilling life. Most of us are born with high self-esteem, but because of many outside influences, by the time we are adults it has lowered to often debilitating levels.

I believe women can regain self-esteem by vitalizing three energetic areas that are essential to a woman's being, which through the centuries have been most challenged by cultural traditions: sexuality, spirituality, and strength. This combination of refined energies will help create confidence and increase the innate capabilities that women were discouraged from exhibiting. It's still going on. I call this new breed of femininity the *Positive Energy Woman*. As an advanced being, the Positive Energy Woman has the abilities to create an outstanding personal life and also enforce beneficial change to the planet.

A Positive Energy Woman is easy to identify. She is a positively radiant, loving, and joyful being. Filled with self-love and appreciation for her feminine body and soul, she fully accepts those around her and exudes love toward them. She cultivates her gifts and pursues her dreams and strives to rise to her highest potential as a human being. She harnesses a positive universal power and uses it as a source of inspiration, guidance, and love. With an expanded consciousness, she sees the "big picture" of life and enjoys all of life's twists and turns. With high-caliber and bright energy, the Positive Energy Woman becomes a beacon of goodness that shines on those around her and out into the universe. Just by raising her own energy, one Positive Energy Woman contributes to raising the vibration of the entire planet.

What Is Energy?

To become a Positive Energy Woman, we need to first understand human energy and, specifically, feminine energy. Human beings are much more than flesh, bones, and organs. We are walking energy fields. We generate and express energy, and are made capable to take action by energy. This energy is present at several centralized areas in the body. Seven invisible energy centers, called chakras, are located one above the other along the spine, and each energy center generates energy of a specific quality. These energetic qualities are survival, sex, power, love, expression, intuition, and spirit. A healthy, empowered person possesses energy centers that are healthy and balanced.

Human energy comes in two forms, feminine and masculine, and is typically defined by its human package. Feminine energy is correlated with the female human being, and masculine energy is associated with the male. Our physical forms, including glands and organs, and hormonal functions, and even our genetics, can influence our energy to be more masculine or more feminine. Like the human bodies they reside in, the qualities of masculine and feminine energies are different, if not opposite.

Some schools of thought associate pure feminine energy as being receptive, cooperative, emotional, intuitive, and nurturing. Pure masculine energy is associated with qualities of brute-strength, competition, aggression, logic, and goal-orientation. Even the dictionary stereotypes feminine as "having qualities regarded as characteristic of women: gentleness, weakness, delicacy and modesty, etc," whereas "masculine" is defined as "qualities regarded as characteristic of men: strength, vigor, boldness, etc." While the physical and chemical makeup of the female and male bodies may drive them in different ways (specifically, testosterone in a man may compel him to be more aggressive, whereas the estrogen of a woman may influence her to be more emotional), women and men inherently contain both feminine and masculine energies, and their organs and energy centers regulate the amount of each energy they contain. So, typically, women are capable of generating more feminine energy than masculine energy, likewise with men. The goal is to balance those energies within us.

The laws of nature illustrate the need for a balance of polar energies, both in individuals and universally. The earth itself provides an illustration. Earth is surrounded by an electromagnetic field that becomes stronger and more concentrated at the North and South Poles.

The equal and opposite pull of the electromagnetic fields at these poles creates our earth's axis and maintains earth's steady rotation around the sun. This electromagnetic field, balanced by polar opposite energies, is vital for the planet's survival. Should the energy of one pole diminish, disaster of epic proportions could occur.

Batteries provide another illustration of opposite energies. A battery stores electrical charge and furnishes a current of energy to power any number of mechanical devices. Batteries contains a negative electrode (-) on one side and a positive electrode (+) on the other. To create an energetic charge, the energy of both the negative and positive electrodes must be harnessed. To power up a flashlight, for example, two batteries must come together, with the negative end of one battery touching the positive end of another. If two negative ends or two positive ends connect, there is no flow of energy. Only when the opposite sides are connected is an electrical charge formed.

Like night and day, female and male energies are equally critical to a balanced world. At one time, women and men lived as equals, and the world was in harmonious balance. Then the balance was tipped as masculine energy predominated the planet. As feminine energy and women's principles and contributions are accepted and respected, we can regain balance in the world.

Sexy, Spirited, and Strong

While the energy of each of our chakras is critical for health and wholeness, I believe that three are key energy centers that empower a true Positive Energy Woman: sexual energy, spiritual energy, and power, or strength, energy. Because of centuries of cultural conditioning, these vital centers have withered, causing modern women to feel powerless, unsexy, and disconnected from their own souls and higher powers. The good news is that with focused effort and awareness, we can vitalize these energy centers and raise our overall energy, which will cause us to feel positively radiant with sexual health, spiritual fire, and inner strength. Our self-esteem will rise, and we will more confidently express ourselves in the world. We will contribute to the balance of the planet's energy with a dose of our feminine charge.

When the energies of sexuality, spirituality, and strength are cultivated and developed into equal potency, they form a powerful triangle of feminine energy in which the energetic whole is greater than the sum of its parts. As the vital components of sex, spirit, and strength merge, this triangle becomes the powerhouse source of positive energy. Sexual energy is the fount of feminine energy and the commander of our womanly body and its functions. Spiritual energy expands our consciousness and strengthens the connection to our soul and to the universal spirit. Our power energy and strength amplify our presence in society and on the planet as we confidently bring our gifts to the world and manifest tangible results for our efforts. A Positive Energy Woman attends to all aspects of her energetic being. If any one of these areas is neglected, her effectiveness as an influential being on the planet is reduced.

Let's explore each side of the energy triangle and its importance to a Positive Energy Woman.

Sexual Energy

Sexual energy is the ingredient that makes a woman a *woman*. Sexual energy is the most fundamental essence of the human female. It is her "juice," her "fire." It is a source of feminine beauty, and the regulator of her female functions. It is a delicious energy that influences the feminine qualities in a woman. The Positive Energy Woman embraces her feminine qualities and unabashedly exudes feminine energy.

The source of our feminine sexual energy is our sexual chakra, located in the area of our reproductive organs. On a fundamental, primal level, the function of sexual energy is to influence mating and procreating. Sexual energy inspires a woman to attract a potential sexual partner and influences her to create a connection with him to increase the sexual energy in both parties.

But for today's Positive Energy Woman, sexual energy is not entirely about attracting a mate and engaging in sexual intercourse or procreating. For her, sexual energy is the source of radiant health, feminine beauty, and feminine energy, which she sends out to the world to balance masculine drives. She appreciates her feminine body and all of its female parts and functions and feelings and recognizes the benefits of healthy sexual energy to her physical and emotional being. Sexual energy contributes to her feelings of overall womanliness, raises her appreciation of her feminine body and drives without shame or embarrassment, and allows her to maintain a positive perception of herself as a woman.

She enjoys feeling sexy and while she may do things to make herself physically attractive, she knows that sexual beauty is much more than skin deep. It's beyond coy expression. It is a powerful exuberance that comes from deep within and far outshines superficial expressions.

Female sexual energy was once regarded as a sacred energy, but over time a number of cultural influences deemed it sinful and bad and conditioned women to fear it and hide it. Today, women are called to remember and reawaken their sexual fire for their own sake and to create balance in our masculine world.

Spiritual Energy

Spirit is a multidimensional concept of personal and universal energy. Spirit exudes from the soul, around which our body and entire being is built. It is the cosmic energy of the highest realms of love and peace. It is an expansion of consciousness that transcends ego and takes us beyond the three-dimensional world. In the context of the Positive Energy Woman, spirit is the expression of her soul, a conscious awareness of her true and divine nature, and a connection with the universal energy that supplements her soul.

A Positive Energy Woman acknowledges that she is a unique, divinely created being with gifts and purpose on the planet. She also recognizes everyone around her as divine beings and honors them for their talents and ideas, even if they differ from hers. She is grateful for the planet and recognizes the multi-dimensional vastness of our universe. She acknowledges a loving and benevolent Higher Power— often called Goddess, God, the Universe, or what I refer to as God/ dess—that is greater than her, that surrounds her and exists in all that is. Her habits and practices connect her own spirit with the love and light of the God/dess, so that her own spirit increases in strength, love, peace, and increased energy. As her connection with the God/dess increases, a Positive Energy Woman becomes an open channel for inspiration and intuition, which heightens her creativity and leads her, like a divining rod, in the right direction and to the greatest opportunities.

As a result, she is a spiritualized being whose body becomes a conduit for divine spirit as it connects with her own soul. She is constantly infused with love, joy, compassion, and inner peace, which she radiates to the world. She becomes a beaming light of love, joy, and peace. This has a positive affect on those around her and on the planet itself.

At one time, women were the center of worship and goddesses were celebrated as the vessels of divine power. Earth-based religions honored our planet. But certain cultural and religious influences replaced the divine female with divine male, and woman lost sight of her spiritual roots. Women are now asked to reconnect with the feminine spirit and integrate it into our imbalanced world.

Strong Power Energy

Strength is defined as physical, intellectual, and moral heartiness and power, will, and competence. Energetically, this mix of attributes dwells in our power energy center, which is associated with energy and vitality. Power gives life and rules the ego, and fuels our *abilities* to be strong.

As with our sexual energy, women's expression of power was suppressed by various cultural conditions, starting perhaps as early as 4,000 BCE with the rise of the Indo European and other warrior cultures. But even deprived of social power, women have always been strong, raising families and working inside and outside of the home, supporting husbands, families, and friends. Now the planet is demanding female strength to come forth. Women must fully express themselves and their ideas to add balance to the masculine power of the world.

The Positive Energy Woman has a new kind of strength that empowers her to break out of culturally-defined female roles and take on new roles and responsibilities that contribute to the evolution of society and humankind. She has a healthy body, a keen mind, and a solid stance on the earth. Her strength and power contribute to her effectiveness in life, her authority over her destiny, and her influence over others.

Strength refers to a physical body that contains healthy organs and highly functional muscles and bones, to a mind that is fed and stimulated and which thinks logically and creatively, and to emotions that are balanced and under control. The Positive Energy Woman is strong because she knows who she is. She knows what she needs to do to fulfill her dreams, and she dreams BIG. She strives to be the best she can be and live up to her highest potential in this lifetime and allows very little to stand in her way.

A Positive Energy Woman is a leader in a feminine way—through community, caring, creativity, and compassion, not force, domination, or aggression. She is driven to do what she can to make the world a better place, whether it is raising healthy, intelligent children or leading an activist group.

A strong woman is self-confident, courageous, and self-assured. She has the fortitude to persist, and if faced with an obstacle, she'll figure out a way to get around it. She is a "Yes" woman, and for her anything is possible. It is only with strength that woman will be able to determine her mission and truly make an impact on an evolving race.

Becoming a Positive Energy Woman: The Energetic Triangle

Through conscious awareness of the three aspects of your energetic triangle and a commitment to nurture and cultivate each aspect, you can become a balanced source of energy. It is important for each side of the triangle to be attended to equally; if not, your overall feminine power and influence will be reduced and unbalanced. If, for example, you have strong sexual and spiritual energy but uncultivated strength, you may bless the world with your feminine beauty and feel all the love and peace you've dreamed of, but you may live an ungrounded life and not be motivated or empowered to bring your ideas and gifts forth into the world, not be able to make a living. Likewise, if you are very strong, but your sexual and spiritual energies are low, you may get the job done, but in a manner that doesn't leave a feminine fingerprint on the world. This may leave you feeling unfulfilled as a woman.

By becoming energetically full and complete women, we can create fulfilling lives for ourselves and contribute to the positive energy of Earth. We may create a positive shift in the collective consciousness of women as a whole, planet-wide, and help increase self-esteem among the female population. Perhaps as we become more energized and empowered, our input and ideas will make Earth a kinder place, where we support each other to live to our highest potential and create the most fulfilling lives possible. Perhaps we can continue to raise our status and influence in the world and become equal partners with men in the advancement of civilization.

As one individual woman, you have much to gain from vitalizing your energetic triangle. The results of becoming sexy, spirited, and strong will spill over into your entire being. Here are a few results you can expect:

- Your confidence and self-esteem will be raised.
- You will feel happy and joyful most, if not all, of the time.
- You'll attract other positive people and exceptional relationships.
- You can bring your grandest dreams to life.
- You will become the best you can be and live to your highest potential.
- You will radiate beautiful, youthful energy and remain youthful throughout your life.
- You will positively affect those around you and the entire planet.

The mission of this book is to provide you with the tools and practices that will help you strengthen each side of your own energetic triangle so that you will become a Positive Energy Woman. As multi-dimensional, energetic beings, we can benefit from a variety of approaches, from logical to mystical. Exercises that focus on each side of your energetic triangle are presented. By practicing them and becoming aware of your body, energy, and potential and taking action to become the best you can be, you can make positive changes in your life and your world. Your mission, if you choose to acknowledge it, is to become a Positive Energy Woman.

Enjoy!

2

SELF-ESTEEM

Could our dream of a peaceful and healthy Earth—where no one goes hungry, everyone acts consciously, and loving respect abounds for all—become a reality? While this idea may sound like a utopian dream, it does fall within the realms of possibility. But in order for planetary peace and health to prevail, every person must embody an attitude and a sense of being that exemplifies perhaps the most valuable of all human conditions: *high self-esteem*. The inhabitants of Utopia have no need for power, approval, or attention, for these qualities are easily accessible within themselves. Because they embody high self-esteem and respect their own unique qualities, they can also appreciate and honor the uniqueness of everyone else around them.

Esteem is derived from the Latin word *aestimare*, which means "to value, appraise, estimate." High self-esteem, then, is defined as having a high value or estimation of the self. Some call high self-esteem self-love, self-respect, or belief in one's self. Self-esteem is the essential ingredient we need to create a life that is joyful, satisfying, and fulfilling.

When we have high self-esteem, we truly value ourselves and see the value in others. We don't need extraneous exhibits of wealth and power to feel good. We are not driven to put down, overpower, or harm others to feel superior, not driven to shrink in the company of those who hold a higher position. We don't judge our personal value by our material riches. Our feelings of power and value come from our riches within. They are expressed in our contributions to the world. And thus we are motivated to create a world that yields the greatest benefits for all.

If everyone on the planet had high-self esteem, we might act more cooperatively in the common cause of creating and maintaining a healthy existence on the planet. We would respect each other's ideas and confidently bring our own ideas to fruition. High self-esteem among men would inspire a greater respect for women, along with an appreciation of feminine wisdom and the feminine perspective. High self-esteem in women might help us advance to a new position of equality where we could become valued contributors of ideas and solutions. With abundant self-esteem in a society, women and men would work in partnership, respecting each other's strong suits, to create a better world.

I think we can see that we were all born with high self-esteem. As babies, we were fascinated by our fingers and toes. We loved our reflection in the mirror. We asked for (if not demanded) our basic needs, fully expecting to receive them. As we grew, we explored and experimented without hesitation. As learning machines, we consumed voluminous information, and spit it back out in our own personal style, without inhibition or need for approval (although we loved it when we got it). But as many of us grew older, our self-esteem slowly diminished. This happened for a great number of reasons. Unfortunately, women with high self-esteem seem to be a minority on Earth. Even in the United States, the so-called land of opportunity and the wealthiest nation on the planet, low self-esteem permeates the female population like toxic waste.

Symptoms of Low Self-Esteem

The signs of low self-esteem in women are numerous, some, obvious, others, insidious. They fester deep inside us, hidden beneath our façade of success. Some symptoms of low self-esteem include the following:

- Feelings of worthlessness and not belonging
- Entering into abusive relationships (romantic, professional, and social) and remaining in them
- Depression
- Dependence on others to feel good or secure
- Need for approval, for which we will do just about anything
- Poor self-image, with negative thoughts about our abilities, no matter how skillful or talented we are
- Negative self-talk, calling ourselves "dumb," "lame," or a "loser"
- Underachievement on the job, job-hopping
- Eating disorders

- Addictions to alcohol, drugs, food, sex, work, even religion
- Sexual promiscuity
- Busyness and the Super Achiever style of living, which is how we avoid facing our demons
- Harm to self, self-mutilation
- Thoughts of and attempts at suicide
- Fear of judgment, which stifles our every expression.

A *New York Times* article, "Personal Health: Girls and Puberty: the Crisis Years," by Jane E. Brody, reveals that the symptoms of near-universal feminine self-loathing are evident as early as school age. Brody reports that depression has increased in high-school students, with more girls entertaining suicidal thoughts than ever before. Cigarette smoking is also on the rise in young women, who say they smoke to settle their nerves or as they succumb to peer pressure. Alcohol consumption among young women rivals that of young men, with high school students reportedly drinking at least once a week. For girls, engaging in casual sex with no regard for their bodies or reputations has become a high-school sport, with more than two thirds of high school seniors surveyed having experienced sexual intercourse. The result is almost one million teenage pregnancies a year, with 85 percent unplanned.[1]

As girls become women, these symptoms only grow more pervasive. Women think their bodies are ugly. They hate them and spend fortunes to become "prettier." So ingrained is our attitude that thin is beautiful, that according to the National Institute of Mental Health, five to ten percent of girls and women in the United States suffer from eating disorders.[2] Self-esteem, whether it's high or low, is deeply embedded in the core of the self. It is much deeper than our state of mind. It is a full-body experience that affects our bodies on a deep cellular level.

But most of us don't even pay attention to self-esteem. Worse yet, we don't recognize or understand the symptoms of low self-esteem. I, myself, had low self-esteem and didn't even realize it until I was in my thirties, when I realized that I wasn't nearly as successful in my career as I wanted to be and that I was enduring relationships with men who were unappreciative of me and border-line abusive. I went through bouts of workaholism, moved constantly from city to city, taking jobs and quitting them, looking for the right place and the perfect thing to make me happy. I was an emotional wreck, experiencing depression and symptoms of Attention Deficit Disorder. It wasn't until I began to see a counselor that I even heard of low self-esteem! It was then that I began to see how my lack of self-esteem caused detrimental effects in my life. It was then that I began to take action to learn to feel better about myself, but it took years to raise my self-esteem to healthy levels.

The good news is that we can improve and increase our self-esteem. Numerous methods and modalities are available to us to help us see our own beauty and love ourselves. This book is filled with practices and information to help you see how magnificent you are.

Causes of Low Self-Esteem

If you suffer from low self-esteem, your first order of business is to stop blaming yourself for not being filled with a sense of total self-love and power. You are not to blame. If you have low self-esteem, you had plenty of help getting it.

This insidious, negative condition of the psyche exists in a majority of women. Why do so many beautiful, accomplished, smart, sexy women not like themselves? Why are self-doubt, self-loathing, self-mutilation, depression, and disrespect for the self rampant among women in America? A woman doesn't just decide to have low self-esteem; she is conditioned by her family and society. One study has even found that self-esteem is a moderately heritable trait.[3] Our lack of self-love is learned and perpetuated in us by the attitudes of society. For thousands of years, women have been barraged with messages that demean them as human beings. Our history, family, society, and media are to blame.

Awareness is the first step to healing. In my endeavors to raise my own self-esteem, I learned as much as I could about its sources. I believe that until our culture recognizes the source of low self-esteem in women, we will continue to perpetuate it.

Parental Conditioning

Low self-esteem begins in childhood, even when a child is surrounded by a loving family with abundant love. Parents and/or guardians may unwittingly chip away at a girl's blooming self-esteem, as can teachers, friends, siblings and other family members who unconsciously use damaging words. A child who is frequently told that she is dumb or stupid and gets frequent "what is *wrong* with you?" messages will believe what she hears. The impact of being ignored or neglected can give the child signals that she isn't important. These messages are absorbed in a girl's brain and program the way she will think about herself for the rest of her life.

A young child definitely detects a parent's favoritism of a sibling, and her self-image is often reduced to "less than." This perception can carry into adulthood. Siblings can also make a major impact on a young person's self-image and self-esteem. Big brothers and sisters that are bullies and teasers can damage the delicate psyches of their younger siblings. Parents are often either unaware of the damage of this seemingly innocent child's play or don't believe it has any impact on the child. Thus, they seldom step in to control it.

Parents who have low self-esteem can pass it down to their children. The messages that parents send out, verbal or through subtle action, can be detected by the child and engrained into the child's psyche. Children are thus programmed with negative messages and soon come to embody them. As a child growing up, I witnessed my own parents' struggle with self-esteem. My father, unconfident in his highly-proficient business and managerial skills, was apprehensive to assert himself to his employers, fearful that a wrong move would mean the end of his job. With four kids and a homemaker wife, he knew that could lead to certain disaster. He worked seven days a week most of his life and rarely took vacations, thinking it would keep his employers happy. My mother didn't acknowledge her many gifts and allowed the struggles of motherhood to diminish her sense of self. She was an accomplished singer with a highly-intelligent mind, as well as a fabulous cook and seamstress, but she constantly put herself down and felt powerless to make change. Unfortunately, the seeds of low self-esteem sowed by my parents were planted early in my life, and I was unaware of it until I was an adult.

Cultivating high self-esteem in a child is a parent's duty, and is best begun the day a child is born. Parents need to become conscious of their actions and words and take care not to criticize, but rather to praise. They must display a genuine interest in their child's daily life and celebrate a child's achievements and milestones, such as birthdays and graduations. They must recognize a child's gifts and skills, and encourage their development. When parents suffer from low self-esteem, they must take responsibility to heal themselves, not only for themselves, but for the sake of the child.

Our Educational System

In 1991, Gloria Steinem's book, *A Revolution From Within: A Book of Self-Esteem*, was published and became a number-one national best seller. The book brought to light the cultural practices that undermined women's self-esteem. Part of the book describes our educational system, perhaps the second most influential aspect of a child's self-esteem (following parental conditioning). Below are a few of the statistics presented in her book.

- A 1991 study commissioned by the American Association of University Women found that as nine-year-olds, 67 percent of girls and 60 percent of boys were "happy with the way I am." By high school, the percentage of boys who felt that way dropped to 46 percent, whereas in girls, the percentage dropped to 29.[4]
- In a 1981 study of male and female high school valedictorians entering college, 23 percent of males described themselves as "far above average"; by their sophomore year, this dropped to 22 percent. At the same time, 22 percent of the females described themselves as "far above average", but by sophomore year the number dropped to only four percent.[5]
- A study of college undergraduate women showed that women reported a major increase of "self-criticism" between the time they entered college and graduated, whereas male students' self-esteem was maintained or strengthened, even when their grades were lower than the women's.[6]

What are the reasons for these woeful statistics? Steinem cites studies that indicate that teachers perceive boys differently than girls. They treat boys with greater respect, choosing boys more often than girls when hands are raised. Boys are interrupted less frequently.[7] Tests are more geared to masculine logical thinking. School textbooks, especially history texts, glorify male heroes and kings, but barely mention women. Early childhood books are more boy-centered than girl-centered.[8] Boys are more often praised for achievement than girls, who are more often praised for interacting well with others.[9] Men are more often school principals and hold higher positions than women, so there are few examples of accomplished women for young girls to look up to. In colleges, there is even less presence of authoritative women for girls to model themselves after.[10]

In her book *Throwing Like a Girl*, Iris Marion Young observes the different styles in which girls and boys throw a ball—boys move their whole bodies, bending backwards and thrusting their arms forward, while girls stand practically immobile, except for the throwing arm, which extends forward and releases the ball—and perform other physical tasks. She explains that because they lack trust in their bodies, girls are often intimidated, uncertain, or hesitant when faced with a physical challenge that boys confront with ease. Girls are divided by paying attention to their body, and saving it from harm and often feel frustrated or self-conscious and don't want to appear too strong. They will often fulfill their own prophecy of not accomplishing the task they believed to be beyond their capability. From a young age, that is, girls learn that they are girls. Unlike boys, girls are not encouraged to use their bodies in free and open ways. They aren't often asked to perform tasks that demand physical strength, the way boys are. They are told not to get hurt or get dirty. Seeing themselves as "feminine," girls begin to assume they are fragile and immobile. The girl "enacts her own body inhibition."[11] This lack of confidence in her body will often endure throughout her life.

Young people who are not aware of the damage that verbal abuse and negative body language can have may also harm their classmates. Cliques are as old as time, along with nasty comments about the way someone dresses or her or his ethnicity or physical attributes. Such negative messages from her peers can lower a girl's self-esteem. Teachers, overwhelmed with poor classroom conditions, are not likely to notice and do not step in. Often, peer pressure will detour a girl from following her own instincts, and she will find herself in compromising positions that are dangerous or damaging. Working parents are often too distracted to give their daughter real attention and overlook her discontentment. The girl is on her own.

Other studies indicate that female athletes are often ridiculed by their fellow students. Labeled "unfeminine" or "lesbian" by her classmates, a young female athlete may quit the team and set aside her desire for sports or athletics to halt the name-calling. *Young Children's Social Construction*, by C.A. Hasbrook, reports that athletic girls are often perceived as "inappropriately masculine" girls who invade the male territory.[12] *Sociology of North American Sport,* by Stanley Eitzen and George H. Sage, states that teachers instruct girls to contain their energy and refrain from jumping, running, and yelling because "it isn't ladylike," whereas boys constantly move and learn physical skills by throwing, kicking, and climbing.

Young women in America suffer from low self-esteem. They don't like themselves. They want to hide their bodies and play down their feminine shape. But they may also dress in inappropriate ways for their age, wearing too much makeup and revealing clothing. With little to no sex education, and now no physical education, girls don't learn about their bodies. They feel embarrassed about their bodies and their bodily functions.

Fashion Magazines

Psychologist Emily Hancock, author of *The Girl Within,* discovered that female self-esteem peaks at the age of nine, and plummets thereafter. Hancock writes that girls "lost their prepubescent strength, independence, spirit and lucidity, and became riveted to the issue of how they look."[13]

Fashion magazines may be the biggest offenders in toying with girls' self-esteem. Beauty magazines don't make you feel beautiful. They make you feel unbeautiful. Such magazines largely influence a culture's standard of beauty, and unfortunately, women (and men) buy into this standard as something to live up to. The movie and television industries put gorgeous women in their leading roles. Models, considered the most beautiful women on earth, adorn nearly every magazine cover, catalog, and advertisement.

Most women love to feel beautiful and love to look at beautiful women. That's why fashion magazine publishing is a billion-dollar industry. They encourage us to buy the fashions and makeup and hairstyles that will make us look trendy and fashionable. Ironically, though, in her quest for beauty, a woman's self-esteem can be subtly challenged by the same magazines that claim to be making her more attractive.

In a survey on self-esteem conducted by Dove, respondents said they felt pressure to be a "perfect" picture of beauty. In fact, 60 percent strongly agree that society expects women to enhance their physical attractiveness.[14] According to advertising standards, the perfect female face has alluring eyes, impossibly full lips, a small nose, a defined chin, high cheekbones, and flawless skin. Rapunzel hair spirals across the shoulders of an exotically tall, thin body that is wearing lush, rich garments. We admire great beauty, but many women believe that if they don't rise to the advertising standard of looks, they aren't attractive. When we compare ourselves to the fabulous creatures in the magazines, we feel fat and ugly. Many women don't realize that perfection is rare, even in models. Oftentimes, these photos are manipulated, touched up, airbrushed, and PhotoShopped to make the woman as perfect as possible. It never occurs to many readers that magazines define beauty to get us to buy their products.

Unfortunately, by accepting Madison Avenue's standard of beauty, a woman disconnects from her own beauty. So she does everything she can to become as "beautiful" as the model she sees on the magazine cover, spending untold fortunes on clothing and beauty products, starving herself, and undergoing surgeries. She depends on her looks to raise her self-esteem.

Body image issues are plaguing America's women. According to a study released in 2007 by the Social Issues Research Centre, located in the United Kingdom, up to eight out of ten women are dissatisfied with what they see in the mirror, and more than half of us see a distorted image of our beauty; we see ourselves as much heavier or less attractive than we really are.[15] Brene Brown, Ph.D., L.M.S.W., discovered in a study that 90 percent of women experience shame about their bodies. Women are not only critical of their torsos, breasts, buttocks, and faces, but also their pimples, moles, freckles, teeth, and more. Our shame about our appearance may hold us back from expressing who we really are. We fear criticism.[16]

This sad commentary on our society and our perception of ourselves must be changed. If we are to have high self-esteem, we must have a healthy perception of our bodies and our selves. A woman with high self-esteem knows what true beauty is—joy, confidence, and an exuberance for life. She already feels beautiful on the inside. She appreciates and honors the body and face she was born with. She does not compare herself to models, but accentuates the beauty she has. A woman with high self-esteem can look in the mirror without makeup or clothing and see her radiance. She *knows* she is beautiful.

History Books

In the timeline of the development of civilization, many events occurred that greatly influenced the traditions and roles of women and men, some which may have shaped the collective self-esteem of women. Impacting our consciousness and ways of life were the development of weapons during the Bronze and Iron Ages and the subsequent rise of patriarchal societies, the demise of goddess-worshipping cultures, the definition of the proper functions of woman as mother and wife, and restrictions on education and careers for girls and women. Though these milestone events happened centuries ago, their effects echo and resound in our modern civilization today. Though women sometimes reigned as queens, participated as warriors, and invented tools that moved civilization to the next level, men defined themselves as the dominant force in society. We can see how this hierarchy endures today in our religious traditions, family structures, the work place, even medical research, where the "norm" for the human being is the male human being.

One thing is for certain. The standard textbooks that describe the history of humankind can also be held responsible for a modern woman's limited sense of self. The history books I read during my school days in the 1960s and '70s had very little to say about the contributions of women to civilization. Those books were filled with stories of powerful kings and their epic, territorial battles. But where were the women? At home, cooking and bearing the king's children? Was the shaping of humanity strictly a male endeavor? Were women too weak or preoccupied with domestic concerns to do anything but have babies and tend to their husbands? The fact is that the version of history we have adopted as standard was written and reported from the male perspective. Our original historians, as far as we know, were men like Herodotus (484-425 BCE), who is called the father of history; Titus Livy (59 BCE-17 CE); and Plutarch (45-145 CE). For centuries, the historians that followed their footsteps have been predominately male. With a primary focus on male victories in war, little was reported on queens and female warriors, religious figures, and other characters who played roles in the evolution of humanity.

In recent years, however, the old history has been reexamined from a new perspective by female archaeologists, historians, and scholars, whose new data and interpretations are shedding light on the old stories. They've discovered that women have played a much greater role in the development of civilization than our old history books suggested. Women have been religious and community leaders, they have invented new technologies, they have been great teachers. In fact, some of our most famous men, like Socrates, had female teachers. I have read many of these newer books, some of which are now used in Women's Studies programs. What I learned gave me new ideas about women through time. I highly recommend some of the following books, which illuminated me and spurred my interest in history.

Merlin Stone's *When God Was a Woman*, first published in 1976, was one of the first popular books to present history with a new, feminist point of view. Stone delivers in rich historical detail a more complete picture of the flourishing and the fall of women in early civilization, from the Paleolithic era to the rise of the patriarchy (*ca* 1500 BCE). Stone describes ancient religions of the Near and Middle East with their prevalence of female deities and the high status of women in those societies. Respected and honored, the women held high positions in families and communities. They were active in temple business and functioned as priestesses. Women were attributed with the invention of clay tablets and the art of writing.[17] In Egypt, around 3,000 BCE, women headed the family and worked outside of the home, while their husbands stayed home and wove cloth.[18] In Babylon, around 2,000 BCE, women owned and managed their own estates[19] and acted as judges and officiators during times of conflict.[20] Further investigation led Stone to describe how women lost or gave away their power. Examples are the invasion of the aggressive Indo-European tribes into the peaceful culture of Crete and the takeover of the egalitarian societies of Canaan by the Jehovah-worshipping Hebrews. Reading this book elevated my sense of self-esteem. How wonderful to learn that women had once been respected and influential. When I learned how power flowed to men in the past, I gained a greater understanding of our relative positions in society today.

The work of archaeologist Marija Gimbutas, who in the 1960s and '70s studied the ruins and artifacts from Neolithic villages throughout Europe, has led to a storm of controversy, mostly among traditional historians who cannot believe that ancient societies were egalitarian and peaceful, and by all indications, worshipped the Great Goddess. Gimbutas's books, *Goddesses and Gods of Old Europe* (1974), *The Language of the Goddess* (1986), *The Civilization of the Goddess* (1991), and *The Living Goddess* (edited by Miriam Robbins Dexter and published posthumously in 2001), all reveal the results of her study of the hundreds of goddess figurines and artifacts she discovered. Fashioned from terra cotta, bone, and stone, designed in female form, some with animal heads, and most with patterns and designs, these relics provided Gimbutas with evidence that the feminine was respected and revered as creator and nurturer of life and steward of the dead. In her studies of this ancient, female-focused society, Gimbutas theorized that its demise occurred with the rise and spread of aggressive Indo-European tribes, which she named Kurgans, that swept out from the steppes of Eurasia, wielding bronze weapons and traveling on horseback. The Kurgans infiltrated and conquered the peaceful societies of Old Europe in several waves from around 4,400 to 2,800 BCE.[21]

Riane Eisler's *The Chalice & the Blade* is another must-read. Based on her studies of ancient societies, Eisler identifies two models of social relations and women's roles in each. In the "partnership" model, everyone works together as equals, whereas in the "dominator" model, one part of society (the male part) is ranked over the other.[22] From the Paleolithic era (one million years ago to around 10,000 BCE) through the Neolithic era (7,000 BCE to 2,500 BCE), societies were nature- and goddess-centered, peaceful, and mostly egalitarian. Women and men held equal status and contributed equally to the civilization. There is little evidence of warfare in this "partnership" model of society. In later societies, formed during the Bronze Age (3,500 BCE to 1,100 BCE) and the Iron Age (1,200 BCE to 550 BCE) and beyond, a "dominator" social model has emerged, in which the strong men of aggressive tribes ranked themselves higher than all women as well as weaker men and the men of other tribes. With weapons and horses now a part of the human tool box, these alpha males took forceful control. Formerly female-oriented practices became male. To counterbalance the problems associated with the dominator model of power, which endures throughout most of today's world culture, Eisler offers solutions based on the practices of a partnership culture.

Other outstanding authors have contributed important studies of women's history. I recommend *Shakti Woman* and *The Double Goddess* by Vicki Noble; *The Book of Goddesses and Heroines* by Patricia Monaghan; and *The Rule of Mars: Readings on the Origins, History and Impact of Patriarchy*, edited by Christina Biaggi. These are new readings of old history that will awaken your mind. You can find more such books by searching on the Internet.

As I learned how early cultures venerated woman for her mystical powers and connection to spirit, I also learned to honor myself more. Understanding that women contributed greatly to the development of culture and civilization on all levels, from the arts to business and beyond, I began to feel capable and validated for wanting to make my own contributions to the world. Recognizing and understanding the world events that purposely or unconsciously subdue women, as well as the origins of certain perceptions of women, I began to understand why women are considered to be supporters of the men rather than the stars of their own destinies, as mothers and wives rather than history-makers.

Until the 1970s, books on women's history were rare, but today more and more are being published. Only four decades ago, you'd have been lucky to find a university course in Women's Studies, but now many universities offer entire curriculums and academic degrees in the subject. I believe this surge of, and urge for, new information on our past reflects our collective need for a new truth about ourselves as women. Understanding our past touches on a visceral level, heals us, and awakes glorious parts of ourselves as spiritual, sexual, strong beings. By remembering our long-forgotten, multi-dimensional greatness, we can recreate ourselves, expand our ideas of what is possible, and increase our potential as human beings.

Religion

Perhaps the strongest greatest influence on the world's perceptions of women today was the development of patriarchal religions, especially Judaism, Christianity, and Islam. With an intention to uplift "mankind" with guidelines for a positive life on earth and a heavenly afterlife, these religions established rules and practices to define the proper actions of women and men. These three "religions of the book" were, however, founded by men and had a single, male god as their focus. The concepts, symbols, and stories appearing in their sacred texts defined the roles of women and men, placing men in the authoritative positions. Perhaps at the time when these religions were founded, patriarchal tenets were necessary to bring societies into order. As humans have evolved, however, we have outgrown many of the old rules. Unfortunately, these ancient definitions and guidelines have become integral parts of civilization, and these old ideas about women have remained in our consciousness.

Before the emergence of the original patriarchal religion of the Hebrew tribes (about 1,500 BCE), millennia of worship of the divine feminine had prevailed. Archeological evidence from nearly every ancient culture indicates that the earliest spiritual entity worshipped by humans was feminine—the Cosmic Mother or Great Goddess. Sculptures and cave drawings of female figures and symbols of breasts and vulvas, some from as early as 40,000 BCE, indicate a reverence for the mystical powers of the female body and spirit. The Great Goddess was the giver of life and the regeneratrix of the dead. Venerating the power of feminine sexuality and the creation of life, ancient cultures called upon the power of the Great Goddess for abundant crops, easy births, safe passing of the dead, the healing of the infirmed. The Great Goddess had many forms and names. In India, she was known as Shakti. In Mesopotamia, she was Ishtar and Innana. In Egypt, Isis and Hathor. In Islam, the triple goddess Al-lat, Al-Uzza, and Manat. In the Middle East, Asherah. In Japan, Amaterasu. Widespread reverence for Goddess influenced respect for the mortal woman and shaped societies that were matrifocal or egalitarian.

The patriarchal religions demanded the worship of a single male god. Intolerant of any other gods or idols, the followers of the patriarchal religions destroyed goddess cultures and damned the female followers.[23] Women with so-called mystical powers were also viewed as evil and destroyed.[24] Sexual expression by women, held in goddess cultures as an auspicious function that activated blessings from the Cosmic Mother, was transformed by the patriarchs into an expression of which men should be wary.[25] Sexual activity outside of marriage was considered a sin, worthy of dire punishment, at least where women were concerned.[26] Goddess cultures held women in high esteem, and many viewed women as equal to men, but the fathers of our churches deemed women to be subservient to men, especially the husband, and unworthy of speaking in church.[27] Menstrual blood, held sacred in goddess cults, was repositioned as "unclean."[28] A woman was blamed for the Fall of Man and deemed worthy of punishment that has lasted through the ages.[29]

Perhaps the greatest offense toward women was the crusade against witches, endorsed by the Roman Catholic Church from the late 1400s into the 1700s. The witch hunt craze was set aflame with the circulation of the *Malleus Maleficarum* (The Hammer of Witches), written by two friars around 1485. Essentially a manual for witch hunters, it illustrated the traits of witches and instituted the system to destroy them. Witches were considered consorts of the devil, and capable of causing impotency in males, sickness, death, blighted crops, and abortions, with a single glance. Suspected were those who healed with herbs, danced or performed fertility rites in the fields, who were sexually attractive or highly emotional, or who were old and unmarried, establishing women as the primary target.[30] Suspects and often their families were tried, tortured, and burned at the stake or hanged, in the name of the Church. Some estimate that over a hundred thousand people, mostly women, were killed, while others estimate over a million were exterminated.[31]

Over the centuries, as the patriarchal religions took over nearly every society in the world, these views of women as sinful were established and solidified. I believe that for many women through the ages, their views of the feminine contributed to feelings of diminishment, fear, loss, and shame.

Fortunately, in recent years, as we have evolved and finer spiritual concepts have become integrated into modern society, these old ideals are beginning to fall by the wayside. But those who were caught in the old patriarchal paradigm were not so lucky.

Whereas for millions of Christian, Jewish, and Muslim women, their religion has provided a strong and fulfilling relationship with God, innumerable other women have felt the stifling control of the patriarchal rules and suffered the repercussions of dogma that opposed their feminine nature, dogma that alienated them from their sexuality, made them feel guilty about sex, made them believe they were less than any man, and severed them from their independent spirit. The patriarchal dogma is the "fact" that a woman's primary purpose and greatest value is to marry and bear children. This has been so much a part of our basic belief system that, as recently as the 1940s and '50s, women (and their parents) felt panicky if they approached eighteen years of age unmarried. Even in the 21st century, in a world of vast opportunity for women, many urgently seek a husband "to take care of them" and feel "incomplete" until they marry.

The women's spirituality movement is beginning to bring the scales back into balance as more women learn of our spiritual origins through good books and participate in women's groups and rituals that celebrate the feminine aspects of God/dess and self. Followers of the patriarchal paths can still enjoy the traditions of their religions, but I believe the recognition of the Divine Feminine will enhance a connection to spirit and invite us to explore our glorious feminine roots. This will help us feel more complete and powerful as women.

Basic Nature of the Female Gender

Louann Brizendine, M.D., the founder of the Women's Mood and Hormone Clinic in the Department of Psychiatry at the University of California, San Francisco, has studied the effects of brain states, neurochemistry, and hormones on a woman's mood. She has published her findings in her compelling book, *The Female Brain*. Her years of observation have led her to see several differences between the female and male brains.

Women have eleven percent more neurons than men in the brain's center for language and hearing. The hippocampus, the center for emotion and memory formation, is larger in women than men, making women, on average, "better at expressing emotions and remembering details of emotional events."[32] A woman's value decisions are shaped by hormonal effects on the brain, which compel her to be social and communicative.[33] She becomes invested in preserving harmonious relationships.[34] Brizendine states that the female brain has outstanding verbal agility and the ability to assess the emotions of others by reading faces and hearing tones of voices. Women are also able to connect deeply in friendship and diffuse conflict.[35]

Men have two and a half times the brain space devoted to sexual drive, causing them to think about sex several times a day, unlike women, who think about sex only once a day.[36] Men also have larger brain centers with processors that register fear and trigger aggression, which is why some men will fly into a fist-fight on the slightest provocation.[37] In fact, on average, men are twenty times more aggressive than women.[38]

Have the innate differences between the female and male brains played a part in women's place in the world? When man asserted his masculine dominance, with weapons and horses, over egalitarian or matrilineal societies, did women fully accept the new paradigm, no questions asked? Or did they yield to the aggression to spare their lives and keep peace? Did women fight ferociously against the invasion of demeaning ideas? Or did they run to escape from this negative force and establish new communities far from the invaded lands, only to be discovered again and plundered?

We don't really know. But women are innately cooperative creatures, and so chances are good that woman acquiesced to the forceful man, maybe allowing him to subvert her power and let him take charge, perhaps to spare her children, her sisters, and herself. Could one meaning of *cooperative* be *submissive?* Even today, a woman will acquiesce to a man, even if she doesn't agree with him, if only to "keep the peace."

Peggy Reeves Sanday, author of *Female Power and Male Dominance: On the Origins of Sexual Inequality* and other books, points out the differences in the ways women and men respond to stress. "Men respond to stress with aggression though not necessarily with dominance [whereas] women seem to respond to stress by striking a conciliatory note."[39] Brizendine's studies of women's brains confirm that women, especially those with children, respond to conflict and potential danger differently than men. She calls their response "tend and befriend," as opposed to the more masculine "fight or flight." She writes that "tending involves nurturing activities that promote safety and reduce distress for the self and offspring," and befriending creates the social support she needs to accomplish this.[40]

My hope is that early women put up a good fight. Some may have done so. In her archaeological research during the 1980s, Dr. Jeannine Davis-Kimball explored burial mounds in Mongolia from the Eurasian Nomadic era (*ca.* 800 BCE to 200 CE). She discovered the remains of women buried with iron daggers and swords, arrowheads and (occasionally) iron armaments. Kimball theorizes these women were warriors who helped to protect families during conflicts with other tribes. Data from the mounds indicated that warrior women were fifteen percent of the population.[41] Dr. Tara Kneller, a professor at Syracuse University, researched the queens of the African nation, Nubia (during the years 3,100 BCE to 540 CE) and discovered that they not only wielded significant control, but they also led their armies into battle when confronted by invading forces.[42] Other studies help us see that women warriors who stood against invading forces were not a rarity at all. Samurai and other warrior women of Japan were experts in the martial arts.[43] Arabian queens rode horseback into battle.[44] While our physical and neurological makeup may present women as less aggressive than men, women do have within them the spirit of combat when provoked.

Can women today be both peacemakers and warriors? Yes, we can. In fact, I believe this balance is essential if we are to become powerful, self-loving women and more positive influences on the planet. Self-love means standing up for what we believe in, without the use of guns or daggers, but with diplomacy and self-assuredness. We can successfully confront challenges when we combine our emotional strengths of compassion and nurturing with our physical abilities through strong, energetic bodies. We have the chemical makeup to "tend and befriend." Let's groom our physical being. I believe it is beneficial for women to maintain good health and fitness, not because we expect to be overthrown by a tribe of aggressive warriors, but because it empowers our entire being, including our will and spirit. I believe emotional and physical balance will amplify our self-esteem, and in turn, our self-esteem will make us stronger women. When all humans attain this balance within, perhaps then our world will function more harmoniously, and humanity will thrive in a healthy manner.

Domestic Violence and Sexual Abuse

When considering the collective self-esteem of women, I think it is important to touch on a subject that few like to talk about, something that affects millions of women in our culture today: sexual abuse. Over the years, I've met a great number of women who have been abused in some fashion by a husband, father, boyfriend, date, or stranger. As I investigated the subject, I was disturbed to learn the numbers: One in six American women is a victim of sexual assault, but only one in 33 men is a victim [45] Sixty-two percent of rape and sexual assault victims knew their perpetrator.[46] More than half of all rapes of women occur before the age of 18, with 22 percent before age 12.[47] Thirty to forty percent of abused children under the age of 18 were violated by a family member.[48] These are only statistics from reported incidents. Many women don't report being raped or abused.

Nothing wounds a woman's self-esteem more deeply than violence, and sexual abuse is the most traumatizing of violations. The symptoms a woman suffers after being raped are similar to those of Post Traumatic Stress Syndrome: anxiety, guilt, phobias, and intense shame. Without psychological treatment, the damage can be long-lasting, often resulting in substance abuse, depression, sexual dysfunction, sexual promiscuity, and even risk of future victimization.[49] When a girl or young woman is overpowered and harmed by an irrational, mentally unstable adult, parent or peer, the trauma will often instill messages of powerlessness of being deserving of pain. Often the victim will withdraw from relationships or form more strained relationships. Most definitely, her self-esteem will plummet.

Studies indicate that boys who witness acts of violence performed by their fathers are ten times more likely to engage in spousal abuse than boys who don't witness abuse.[50] Abusers have often been abused themselves, and boys who were victims are more likely to victimize others.[51] While women have been the target of sexual aggression for centuries, men are also the victims of violence of many kinds. Sexual abuse is an ugly fact of life and represents the pain and damage that festers in our world. Until we can implement massive change of consciousness and work together toward healing ourselves and others, we will not acquire the respect for human life necessary to sustain and evolve our civilization.

Collective Consciousness

Quantum physics proves that everything in the universe is energy and that everything and everyone is connected by an energetic web. A group's collective consciousness is a common attitude or belief held by that group. As more people adopt an attitude or belief, the collective consciousness grows. If it grows large enough, soon it takes off in a population and spreads as if it has a life of its own. The quantum web, filled with the energy of the common attitude, spreads to many others who unconsciously adopt it. When a vibration is strong enough, it silently penetrates us in a process like osmosis. When a large portion of the general population experiences a certain vibration, such as joy at the end of the school year, or fear of another 9/11, the vibration becomes strong, and tends to impact a large portion of the population.

The same holds true for self-esteem in women. If the collective vibration of women is fearful, beaten down, undeserving, weak, and unloving toward themselves, this vibration will silently penetrate the entire female population. Only those who already have high self-esteem, or who are working on gaining it and refuse to succumb to negative self-belief, are immune. And only they have the power to influence or raise the self-esteem and consciousness of the rest of the population.

For the collective self-esteem of women to rise to HIGH, we must ALL work on ourselves to become our strongest and best. Slowly, as more and more women do the work needed to regain healthy self-esteem, the vibration will rise. Soon women will love themselves and know of their value in the world. This vibration will influence men and women alike as it envelopes the planet. This will ultimately create a healthier and better world.

3

A RETURN TO SELF-ESTEEM

The Positive Energy Woman and Self-Esteem

A Positive Energy Woman is high self-esteem personified. She commands a life filled with successful relationships, financial stability, and an occupation she is passionate about. She laughs in the face of challenge, completely accepts her idiosyncrasies, and seems to attain her desires with the minimum of effort. Her energy and gifts are a valuable resource to the planet. The energy of a woman with high self-esteem is finely-tuned, and each aspect of her Energetic Triangle (spirit, sexuality, and inner strength) is thus balanced, healthy, and radiant.

Spiritually, she recognizes she is a divine being on earth. She is a gift to the world. She maintains a vigilant connection with a higher power and radiates love with an open heart as she expresses love and compassion for humanity. She honors her soul, to which she pays keen attention, and is open for inspiration and intuitive messages, for they are the guides of her life. She forgives others and forgives herself.

Sexually, she loves being a woman and reveres every aspect of her body, including its functions. She honors her hormones and her cycles and regards sexuality as a glorious mode of energetic connection and healing, rather than mere recreation. She honors her ability to bear children.

With her strength, the Positive Energy Woman knows her gifts and eagerly brings them forth to the world. She knows she is beneficial to the world. She appreciates her physical attributes and takes care of her body. She truly knows what she wants and who she was born to be, and she stands firmly in her beliefs and values. She understands her limits and sets her boundaries, enabling her to stay on track without overextending herself. She loves herself in spite of and because of her mistakes, and she learns from them. She also forgives others their mistakes.

In recent years in America, female self-esteem has begun to rise. College enrollments are increasingly female, more women are graduating as doctors and lawyers, and more women are owning and running their own Fortune 500 companies. At the same time, too many women still believe they are not as smart or strong as men or that they don't deserve to be paid as much as men. Many still feel that they need to depend on men for financial support. The belief that man is supreme still exists, and low self-esteem remains. Luckily, these negative attitudes are eroding, but they still exist, even in the 21st century.

Until a woman completely revitalizes every aspect of her Energetic Triangle—her spirit, her sexuality, and her strength—individual and collective low self-esteem will endure. We each have a responsibility to do whatever it takes to clear away the things that stand in the way of our greatness. The purpose of our lives is to grow into our highest potential and be the best we can be. Only when we are confident and clear can we give to the world the gifts that dwell inside of us. Only when we love ourselves can we fully love others and attract true love.

You CAN raise your self-esteem. It takes deep work to get to the wounds that make you feel "less than," but you CAN reprogram yourself into respecting your beauty, intelligence, and value. With numerous healing modalities, healers, and self-help books available for reading, there is no longer an excuse for low self-esteem to continue. Change may come quickly for you, or, as in my case, it may take years. Old negative messages are buried deeply in our cells, so we have to realize that it may take considerable work to clear out the old negativity. Each tiny affirmation of your goodness will plant itself inside you, but you must be conscious of it and appreciate it. You MUST embody each little success, no matter how insignificant you think it is.

Human beings are very flexible. We are capable of healing on every level. Low self-esteem is a very human characteristic. It's found in the personality level of our being. Our souls do not experience low self-esteem. Because we are souls, our true nature is to be confident in who we are, in what we are capable of, and how to bring it forth. Our damaged ego and beliefs reside on a personality level, which leads us to *believe* we are a certain way.

In reality, our soul is untouchable. It is an energetic field of love and wisdom, part of the cosmic web of the Universe with unlimited capabilities. Our soul dwells in our human body and merely witnesses the events of our lives; it is not affected by them. Our true nature is our soul's nature, and our soul is an extension of God/dess. Thus *we* are an extension of God/dess. Our potential from where we stand at this very moment is to be completely joyful, fulfilled, and satisfied with who we are and how we create our lives. Our personalities can become fulfilled and satisfied as we bring them to a more soulful level.

Changing negative beliefs about ourselves into positive ones is critical to loving and believing in ourselves; change is thus important to raising our self-esteem. We can change our old beliefs by healing our old wounds through a variety of healing modalities, from ancient practices to traditional psychotherapy to highly advanced, modern methods. Numerous healers offer treatments that effectively help you allow your self-esteem to grow. You can find these healers via the Internet or in your local metaphysical bookstores and publications. You can also heal on your own, and use books, journaling, praying, affirmations, etc., as your tools. The exercises in this book are a useful beginning to help you reconnect with your sexuality, spirit, and strength.

Loving ourselves is critical if we are to become effective on the planet. It can be challenging to change or release programming from early childhood. It's up to you to take the first step. In the meantime, there are ways you can shift your mind right now, right here, ways to feel better about yourself, especially in the areas of your feminine sexuality, spirit, and strength. Feeing good means feeling successful, and then creating more success.

Success + More Success = High Self-Esteem

Read and practice the following self-esteem boosters. If you truly believe and totally accept yourself, they will raise your self-esteem immediately.

Self-Esteem Boosters

Self-esteem is partly based on taking responsibility for ourselves. We are the rulers of our bodies and minds, and we have all the tools we need to love ourselves. Below are ways you can start to plant positive messages into your body and mind. One by one, these messages will help to build your self-esteem so that you are filled with self-love and exuberant joy about your life.

Appreciation of Your Female Body and Sexuality

o   Love yourself and your femininity. Acknowledge that it is an honor to be a woman in this lifetime. Know that our feminine energy is critical to the balance and healing of the planet.

o   Know that it is a cosmic gift to spend this lifetime in a woman's body, one of the most beautiful bodies of all creation. Honor your strengths and see the exquisiteness of your womanly form, your curves, dents, valleys, and mountains. Honor your body's functions and emotions, for they are what make our gender the mystical, magical being it is.

o   Be grateful for your sexuality and sensuality. Proudly exhibit your body in appropriate ways. Know that you have full control over the way your body looks and feels. Nurture it in a way that honors yourself.

o   Love, appreciate, and commune with other women. There is power in groups where feminine energy prevails. Self-esteem can be strengthened when women support each other, solve problems together, and love each other.

o   Learn women's history (or *herstory*). Discover the times when women were revered for their power. Learn of the contributions women have made to humanity. When you understand the creative, intellectual, and spiritual influences women have had on the planet through time, you can't help but be proud to be a woman. Let the glorious times of the past be a touchstone and an inspiration for the future.

Connection to Spirit

Life is meant to be an ever-expanding adventure. Life is a journey we take to hone our gifts, to live and express them. Your gift may enhance your life, a culture, or the world. When we love ourselves, we are special. When we harness the gifts within us that make us who we are, we can create a life that is as big, adventuresome, and rich as we would like it to be. When we love ourselves, we know who we are. Then we're big enough to share it. We know what we want, and we are confident to go after it.

o   Know that everyone, including you, is a divine emanation of a higher power. You were created exactly as you are by a potent power of love and light, a pure essence of the highest creativity. Whether you are agnostic or a believer in God/ dess, you must acknowledge the supreme miracle of your beingness. Your body and mind are marvels, impossible for any human being to create. You are beautiful, unique, and precious, and the world would not be the same were you not in it. Accept that you are valuable and you bring goodness into any number of people's lives. If you can truly understand that you are a walking representative of a Higher Power, a God/dess, you can only love yourself. How can you not love what a greater power created?

o   Know that you are a vessel of love, and that with your heart filled with love, you have the capacity to bring joy to the lives of others, as well as yourself.

o   Look at your current life on planet Earth as a gift for your soul as well as a gift to the planet. Yes, your life is a gift to the planet. Live life fully.

o   Discover the phenomenal feelings of connecting with the spirit within you and outside of you.

Acknowledgement of Strength

o   Appreciate your uniqueness, and know you have the capacity to make all of your dreams a reality, to become whoever you wish to be.

o   Discover and appreciate your talents. These talents are all gifts of a higher power. Your gifts began as seeds inside you before you were even born. I believe that it is the responsibility of each human being to bring forth her gifts from within and to use them to contribute to the goodness and wholeness of the planet. Honor your gifts, even if the only thing you think you can do is bake good brownies. There is a very important place in life for those brownies. Those brownies could contribute to the joy and happiness of many people. The joyful vibration created by those brownies will raise the vibration of the entire planet. So if you love to sing, sing. If you have a gift to write poetry, do so. This will not only make you feel wonderful, but it will also bring joy and happiness to others.

o   Know you have full control over your mind and can turn negative into positive merely by shifting your perspective and your attitude. Think positive thoughts. Even if you feel bad about something you did, or that someone else did, don't dwell on it. Replace negative thoughts with positive ones. If you feel like a loser, turn it around and think of those incredible, beautiful aspects of yourself. Say only good things about yourself and to yourself. And about others.

o   Serve others. Know that your contributions will make the world a better place. There is no better way to feel better about yourself than by giving to others. Help someone in need. Volunteer with community organizations.

o   Always appreciate the beauty of others, but never compare yourself to them. We will never be anyone other than ourselves, and we must acknowledge and remember our own unique beauty.

o   Negativity is a habit. It's easily addictive. *So is positivity.* Self-esteem starts with awareness of your thoughts and actions and a willingness to speak positive words and think positive thoughts about yourself. When you banish the negative and invoke the positive, your self-esteem is guaranteed to rise. "Thoughts become things . . . choose the good ones," spiritual philosopher Mike Dooley says.[52] We attract what we think about. The universe responds to our energy.

o   Enjoy the cleanup. Do your work to clean up old emotional and mental wounds. The concepts given above may help

36

raise your self-esteem a few levels, but if you have deeply-rooted issues that are a result of upbringing (including abuse or neglect), you may wish to consider the services of professionals who are trained to help with these issues.

o   Become physically strong and maintain good health. When you take care of your body, you'll feel better about yourself. The more you love yourself, the more you will want to take care of your body.

4

▼

IT'S ALL ABOUT ENERGY

Part of the mission of the Positive Energy Woman is to raise the energy of the planet. This can be done by *being* a positive person. Positive energy is contagious. One person's energy is absorbed by others, who, in turn, pass it along to many others. Positive energy also travels into the ethers and subtly influences the general vibration of the world. A person with positive energy—a woman who is joyful and filled with love and spirit—can make a huge impact on the planet.

Our positive energy is desperately needed on the planet today. We need the positive energy and actions of giving, caring, sharing, and loving to balance the negative energy of destruction, hatred, selfishness, and greed. One by one, as each of us raises our own energy into the highly positive zone, we will have a positive effect on others and on the planet.

What is energy? Energy is a vibration that exists in everything there is—living and inanimate. It is a cosmic substance that takes infinite forms, from etheric to solid. It is subtle yet palpable. I think of energy as a vapor that envelops and penetrates everything in our universe and beyond. Since the 1950s, quantum physicists have been studying energy and theorize that we are all united by a web of energy.

Webster's New World College Dictionary defines energy as follows:

1. Force of expression or utterance.
2. Potential force; inherent power, capacity for rigorous action.
3. Strength or power efficiently exerted.
4. Those resources, as coal, petroleum, gas, wind, etc. from which energy in the form of electricity, heat, etc. can be produced.
5. Physics: the capacity for doing work.[53]

In my studies of Tantra and Taoism, I have discovered the mystery of human energy. I have learned that humans are walking energy fields, that our energy system is as vital to human life as our circulatory system. In all living things, energy is *life*. The Taoists and Tantrics call it *life-force energy*. A living human has bones, organs, and a circulatory system as well as life-force energy. A corpse also has bones, organs, and a circulatory system, but it has no life-force energy. It has no life. Human beings are a*live*, not only because we have energy, but because *we are energy*.

But human energy is but a tiny fraction of all of the energy of the cosmos. Energy exists in *everything*—plants, animals, minerals, even manufactured objects, even our words and thoughts. It radiates from the earth and exists in the four alchemical (or magical) elements, earth, air, water, and fire. We receive it from the sun and the moon. Eastern healers call it *chi* or *prana*.

Perhaps the most subtle, yet highly influential, energy on planet earth is that of the human being. As human energetic transmitters, we can affect the energy on the entire planet with positive or negative energy. And as receivers, we are always affected by it.

Our energy rivals the weather. Perhaps only earthquakes and tornados are more effective at creating an energetic shift among a population. Human energy can inspire and raise the spirit of an entire population. Or it can instill the greatest fear and dread. Remember how the energy of the planet changed after the attacks on America on 9/11? Our normally positive spirit of hope and insouciance was instantly clouded by sadness and fear, which perpetuated as we mingled with other fearful souls.

The same concept applies in greatly uplifting ways, including the dawning of the Age of the Feminine. Over the past several years, feminine energy has grown in our country and around our planet. Women's groups and goddess groups have been formed and a feminine community has been established. An increasing number of women have taken leadership positions around the planet. Even men are shamelessly learning to access the feminine within themselves. Feminine energy is beginning to infiltrate society.

As more women raise their feminine energy, the energy of the planet will shift and eventually come into balance. The planet will be stewarded by an equal amount of feminine and masculine energy, which I believe will increase peace on the planet, honor its health and natural resources, and improve the quality of life in every country.

Human Energy

Humans are energy. We are our bodies, organs, cells, mind, and spirit. All these are energy. We generate energy in our bodies and spend energy as we act. We need energy to move, think, and for our organs to function. Energy levels are very easily felt, and so often we hear others say, or say ourselves, "I don't have enough energy to do that." Or, "I have SO much energy!" A healthy human body will have high levels of energy during the day, with less in the evenings, though some extremely healthy people maintain high levels of energy throughout the day and into the evening.

But energy is never stagnant. It never dies, dissipates, or disappears. It merely changes from one form to another. Energy moves, shifts, is received, given, spent, exchanged. It can be harnessed and multiplied. Here are a few ways human energy is generated, transmitted, and received:

1. *We absorb energy.* We get energy from food, and use it to fuel our body so that it can be healthy, which equals more physical energy. Energy from food is converted into energy to propel the human body and enable it to function. We also receive energy from the sun, plants, air, and water. The sun gives us heat and positive and negative ions and stimulates the brain chemical serotonin. The oxygen we absorb and breathe in gives us *chi*: the energy in the air gives us vitality and life.

2. *We spend energy.* The life energy we receive from food, water, and air is converted in our bodies into energy to fuel our actions. The energy we spend propels our bodies to move, think, and function in a healthy manner.

3. *We give energy to others.* We can consciously or unconsciously give our energy to other people. When we exude positive energy, we fill other people with love and to heal them. When we are filled with negative energy, we shower people with our anxiety and anger. Body contact is the most powerful method of giving energy to others. Hugging is a gesture many positive people share. Hands-on healers, such as massage therapists, Reiki masters and pranic (energy) healers powerfully harness their own energy or channel etheric energies. They project their energy through their hands onto the one they are healing.

4. *We receive energy from others.* When we allow someone to nurture us, we receive energy. When we are ill or in emotional stress and lacking energy, we unconsciously receive the energy that is directed to us by the nurturer or healer. This energy comforts and heals us. We receive the energy of those who love us. This loving energy uplifts us. Unfortunately, if we take in the energy of someone who abuses us, that energy will harm us.

5. *We simultaneously exchange energy with others.* We can give and receive energy with another person, especially during intimate conversations and love-making (positive energy), and also during fights and arguments (negative energy.)

6. *Our energy affects the collective consciousness.* Our energy is emitted into the air, on the streets, into the cosmos. It has an affect on all of life. Believe it. Your energy is *that* powerful. It is generated within you and flows outwardly into the energetic web of the Universe. Feelings of resentment and hate also resonate through the universe and put a negative vibration into the world. The world will respond to what it receives.

7. *We can raise our energy for energizing and healing ourselves.* With special breathing and visualization techniques, we can take our own energy, and "see" it moving up our spine and to our organs to where we can visualize the energy healing those places in our bodies. Various yoga practices, breathing exercises, and other exercises incorporate these techniques. Many energy practices for energizing and self-healing are explained later in this book.

8. *Energy generates more energy.* Oftentimes, we can generate energy by spending energy. Have you ever felt too tired to take a walk, but forced yourself, and after twenty minutes of walking had twice the energy as before the walk? Sometimes you can jump start your energy with a push of energy. For example, let's say you feel too tired to wash the dishes, but you force yourself to take the first step by rinsing the dishes. Once that step is taken, energetic forces kick in and you continue to wash the dishes. Then you wipe off the counter and sweep the floor, and before you know it, the entire kitchen is clean. Small energetic efforts initiate the generation of more energy.

The Positive Energy Woman is aware of the various forms of energy in life. She has an understanding of how to harness and change energy within herself and give it to others. She understands the energy of others and has the tools to receive energy from outside of herself.

Positive and Negative Energy

Energy is perceptible and palpable. How many times have you walked into a room and "felt a vibe" (and even identified the vibe as happy, sad, disturbed, or whatever) before anyone utters a word about what the vibe is about? Did you ever have a hunch about a stranger—her life, personality, and challenges—only to discover later that your hunch was correct? With awareness, we can tell much about a person by the energy they put out.

Energy is measured in wavelengths. In the human body, positive energy vibrates at a high frequency, and is experienced as love, joy, generosity, and compassion. Negative energy, which vibrates at a low frequency, is experienced as hate, anger, depression, and shame. Like a furnace, energy radiates from the body and is perceptible to others. Throughout our day and our life, our energy hovers between the highest high positive energy and lowest low negative energy, depending on a variety of factors. But with a conscious approach to life and certain practices, our energy can be controlled, and moved into Positive Energy realms, where it can remain.

The Positive Energy Woman has a high vibration that feels light. She is optimistic and has energetic qualities that are uplifting, joyful, loving, excited, aware, caring, open, filled with life. She has abundant vital life-force energy, and is healthy, invigorated, and enthused about life. The Positive Energy Woman is attractive. She is the giver and receiver of eye contact and smiles to and from strangers. It feels good to be around her. She appears safe and trustworthy. A positive person loves life, easily loves others, loves the world, and especially loves herself.

A woman with negative energy emits a heavy vibration. She is pessimistic and downbeat, often filled with sadness, anger, vengefulness, self-pity, hopelessness, and fear. She is shut down. A person in a negative space has a difficult time opening her heart. She often feels self-loathing and dislikes other people. This woman is less attractive and often has a sad, tired look on her face. She seldom smiles. We've all encountered a person who emits negative energy. We want to either help her or him or (more likely) run away. Negative energy is threatening. We can easily detect low energy in a person. A person can look great, and even move with fast movements, but if her energy is low or negative, we still feel it.

Energy can shift in a split second. It is easy for your vibration to shift from positive to negative, and vice versa. As normal human beings, we experience positive and negative energy, and all nuances in between, often in the same day or even in the same hour. It is important to be aware of our perceptions and how the events of life affect our vibration. The good news is that we can control our perception of what is happening, so something that we would normally consider negative or bad can become neutralized into "that's life." Something we would perceive as "normal," such as a call from a friend, can be boosted in importance to a fantastic, positive gift.

For example, have you ever felt upbeat and happy, and then you got bad news, like your checking account was overdrawn? Did you plunge from the heights of positive energy to the depths of negative energy? You may start thinking negative thoughts. "Crap! I never have enough money!" Your energy not only plummets, but it can go even deeper with more negative thoughts. "My job sucks, and if I just had it together enough to have finished college, I'd be making better money now. I'm such a loser!" Down, down, and further down you spiral until negativity fills your body and makes your vibration negative. You may stay in that space for hours or days, or (in some extreme cases) years. When you go out into the world, negative energy surrounds you. Often, should negative thinking become a habit, this kind of thinking will drive us into depression, where we can remain. (Clinical depression is triggered by deep emotional or chemical influences. Negative thinking is harmful to anyone suffering clinical depression, and professional assistance is often necessary to overcome the depression.)

But just as negative thinking will spiral you down, positive thoughts will raise you up. Let's say you got that overdraft notice from the bank and you dipped into a temporary negative space. Your inner voice wants to say, "I'm so lame. Why can't I ever do this right?" But you can direct your thoughts into a positive place, and say instead, "Well, this is a wakeup call. I'd better start paying more attention to my checkbook and figure out a way to make more money." This kind of thinking helps you feel that you have more control over your life. It may inspire and empower you to take action to make improvements in the way you handle your money. Your decision to take action will raise your mood and your self-esteem. Your vibration rises higher as you make constructive changes. You begin to positively affect every person you meet, and they will spread positive energy to others. The world becomes a *better* place, all because of your withdrawn checking account.

Energy Attracts Like Energy

Quantum physicists say that energy attracts like energy, so be aware of the kind of energy you emit. Positive energy attracts positive energy. Negative energy attracts negative energy. The Positive Energy Woman perceives everything as positive, emits positive energy, and thus attracts positive energy into her life.

You may know a wonderful woman who has the great job, a nice car, a husband or boyfriend who is passionately in love with her, and an abundance of money. Did she attract this with a positive vibration? Possibly. Her positive energy attracts good things from the universe. Likewise, you've heard of a hard luck Joe or Josephine who always has bad things happening to him or her. There is a good possibility that this person was struck down by an event perceived as negative, and he or she hadn't recovered before being struck by another negative event, then another and another, until this downfallen person remained perpetually sad, depressed, and negative. Remembering that negative vibes attract negative things, we must learn that the only way we can break out of a negative energy field is to shift our energetic vibration to a positive one.

People often respond to a vibration with a like vibration. A person with positive energy influences the energy and response of those around her. People will respond to her higher vibration and return a high vibration back to her. Energy is contagious, so your smile will raise the energy level of the person you smile at. When that person's energy is raised, they are inspired to share, and they will then smile to others, influencing and raising their energy.

The Positive Energy Woman knows that to attract goodness into her life, she needs to have a positive outlook and positive vibration. *Positive attracts positive.*

How is YOUR Energy?

You may not know it, but we have amazing control over our energy. We may be totally unconscious of our energy or believe it is out of our control. We may think our emotions and conditioning take the helm of our energetic output. But with conscious awareness and practice, we can be in a positive frame of mind most of the time, and thus be surrounded by positive people, events, and opportunities. Imagine being happy when the alarm goes off in the morning, feeling excited about going to your job, feeling loving toward the people you work with, fortunate to have a home and family to come home to and grateful at the end of the day. These positive thoughts will raise your vibration and will be carried by you throughout the day. People will be attracted to you, returning positive energy to you, and fill your days with more high vibrations.

Being a positive person is as simple as changing one thought. For those who may have lived in a state of negativity for a long period of time, it may take more thoughts, more work, and greater awareness, but they can do it. The purpose of the work and suggestions in this book is to raise your energy. To make lasting changes on your vibration, it will be helpful to learn a little science around the energy in our bodies.

What kind of energy do YOU exude? Positive and loving? Joyful and high spirited? Or negative and resentful? Angry and depressed? Imagine how you present yourself to the world. Understand that people perceive you based upon your energy. People are attracted to people with positive energy, and less attracted to people with negative energy. Charismatic people shine with radiant energy. They are the most influential people on the planet. They are the leaders and the entertainers. They have an energy that not only radiates from them but propels them to accomplish feats that would exhaust the rest of us. While this kind of charismatic energy is often a gift that a person is born with, charisma can also be cultivated by raising the energy in your body. Even people with low energy, low self-esteem, and a negative perspective of life (thus low energy) can raise their energy through a variety of practices.

I believe that knowing about energy and knowing how to maintain healthy energy in our bodies is critical to having a happy, fulfilled life. We Westerners pay no attention to our energetic bodies, yet practitioners in the Far East have made our energetic body their main focus for centuries. When I studied Tantra, I learned about energy. I have practiced many exercises over the years that have improved my life on a great many levels. Having a healthy energetic body is critical in being a Positive Energy Woman. But before we go there, let's learn about one of the main sources of human energy, the chakra system.

Energy Centers and Chakras

We learned in science class that the body is made up of a skeleton, muscles, organs, a circulatory system, a respiratory system, and a nervous system. What we didn't learn is that we also have a vast, invisible energetic network, consisting of *nadis, meridians,* and *chakras.* Our Western science teachers failed to share the valuable information that has been known in the Far East for centuries, but that is because only in recent years have Western cultures begun to acknowledge the existence of our invisible energy systems.

The spiritual adepts of ancient India identified an invisible energy system in the human body comprised of channels, called nadis. There are 72,000 nadis in our bodies that form a network similar to blood vessels and veins and carry our energy to every area of the body. This energy, called *chi, prana,* or life-force energy, comes from oxygen, food, spirit, and the earth. Traditional Chinese medicine practitioners refer to this network as meridians, which are the targets for acupuncture healing. Needles open low-energy meridians and encourage energy to flow to them.

Our chakras are the seven main invisible energy centers in our bodies. They are the source of all human energy. They are the located at various points along our spine and through our bodies and are associated with various organs. The word *chakra* comes from a Sanskrit word that means "wheel," and so the chakras are referred to as wheels of energy. They act as portals through which energy is emitted and received. The goal is to balance the energy in the chakras, enabling energy to flow freely through the body. Balanced chakras will help you feel emotionally controlled, physically healthy, and able to survive, thrive, love, express who you are, and accomplish your desires. If your purest, positive energy is blocked from flowing freely, imbalance in your chakras will reflect with imbalance in your life.

Chakra energy influences how you feel and the kind of energy you radiate. Each chakra is the source of a specific kind of human energy:

survival and trust, passion and sexuality, power, love, self-expression, inspiration and intuition, and union with Spirit. The quantity and quality of energy in your chakras influences the intensity of your energy. Balanced chakras enable you to fully feel and express the essential nature of the energy from each energy center. They are open to receive energy. Balanced chakra energy equates to feeling balanced in your life and having joy, inner peace, fulfillment, and power.

Unbalanced energy impedes our quality of life and inner happiness. When our chakras are either low in energy or overly energized—unbalanced in either direction—we are less effective in life, often unable to get along with others, unable to accomplish our goals, unable to attract the things in life that we desire. Unbalanced chakras can manifest negative feelings. Chakras that are closed or unbalanced are lacking in energy and less receptive to receiving energy from others.

Unbalanced chakras may be the result of childhood conditioning or other experiences perceived as negative. A young woman who is sexually abused may shut down her sexual energy center. The man who is told too often that he is stupid or useless may close down his power center. Until the blocked chakra is opened and balanced, the person will radiate energy that is less than exuberant, and live a life that is less than joyful. Chakra balancing exercises will also help to heal old wounds. Be aware that even thinking about past or current events may open or close a chakra.

If your goal is to become a positive energetic force on the planet, it is essential that you have abundant and balanced energy in all of the chakras. Your energy will touch the lives of people you come into contact with every day, and radiate into the cosmic energy field, where it enhances the cosmic energy. This energy, which as we know, is a gigantic web in which all exists, will touch the lives of everyone and everything. Remember, your energy will also attract like energy, so if you exude positive energy, good will come back to you.

Following is a short synopsis of our energy centers, with a description of the types of energy they generate. I give the Sanskrit name of each chakra along with the Western name.

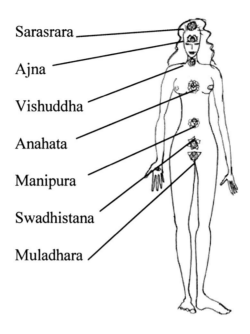

Sarasrara

Ajna

Vishuddha

Anahata

Manipura

Swadhistana

Muladhara

The First Chakra: Muladhara, or Root Chakra

The Muladhara chakra generates trust and survival energy. It is located, according to Tantric teachings, near the cervix in a woman and in the prostate in a man. Other energy practices locate the Muladhara at the base of the spine. This energy connects us with the earth and is concerned with physical survival.

When energy is strong in your root chakra, you will feel safe in the world, confident that you will not only survive but thrive. The energy from this chakra will help you succeed in your endeavors. People with strong first chakra energy are very grounded and very present in life. They take charge of their lives on earth.

If your chakra is out of balance, you may feel insecure and afraid. You may have a difficult time making a living and live in constant fear of everything from snakes to what is going to happen tomorrow.

The color red stimulates the root chakra. The sound that stimulates the chakra is *Uhh*.

Second Chakra: Swadhistana, or Sex or Pleasure Chakra

The Swadhistana chakra is the center for sexual, emotional, and creative energy. According to Tantric teachings, the energy center is in the woman's ovaries and in the man's testicles.

Just because it is referred to as the sex chakra, however, doesn't mean the second chakra is *only* about sexual activity, although this is the energy center that influences our sexual drive. The Swathistana chakra influences our level of gender energy. A sex chakra that is highly charged or even balanced will yield a woman who is feminine and feels good about herself as a woman. She has a healthy attitude about sex and is neither overly sexual nor closed off sexually. Highly emotional women may have unbalanced energy in this chakra.

If your sex chakra is out of balance, you may feel either unsexy or overly sexual. You may also feel uncreative and your emotions may be out of whack. You might become aware of your sex chakra when you are with someone to whom you are sexually attracted. You can feel yourself becoming more sexy and womanly. Conversely, if you are out of balance, you may feel shy and withdrawn. When you are in a creative state, bursting at the seams with creative ideas, and you feel like painting or drawing, dancing, cooking, writing poetry, or engaging in any other creative expression, your sex chakra is healthy and balanced.

The color orange invigorates the sex chakra. The sound that stimulates it is *Ooh*.

Third Chakra: Manipura, or Solar Plexus or Power Chakra

The energy generated in the Manipura chakra is personal power energy. According to Tantric tradition, our power center is located in the belly near the navel. It is associated with the pancreas and adrenal glands.

The Manipura chakra is our power chakra and is associated with our self-confidence and personal will. Having a balanced power chakra is very important as we make our way through the world. To have the confidence and initiative to get something done, you must have a healthy power chakra. Having confidence in yourself is imperative in today's world if you want to bring your gifts fully to fruition and be a positive influence in the world.

When your power chakra is in balance, you have a healthy perception of yourself. You feel comfortable walking into a room of strangers, and you aren't afraid to stand up for what is right for you. You take on new challenges and have a healthy curiosity in the world. You feel confident in yourself, empowered to be who you are and who you want to evolve into. You're fearless.

An overcharged power chakra, however, means "control freak," someone who is overpowering and wants to control everyone and everything. A person with an undercharged chakra is insecure, afraid to be who she really wants to be.

The color yellow stimulates the power chakra, as does the sound *Oh.*

Fourth Chakra: Anahata, or Heart Chakra

The heart chakra is where love energy resides; located at the heart, it generates love and devotional energy. With a strong heart chakra, you feel loving, devoted, and compassionate. The love you feel for your beloved, your parents, your children, your best friends, your pets, your favorite song—all these, and more, come from the heart. A person with a strong heart chakra is very loving at all times and to all people. A loving smile comes easily from someone whose heart is filled with love. Love is also associated with compassion, and if we want to be a positive influence in this world, compassion and love are essential. It is compassion that causes us to seek to understand the pain in others and reach out to help them.

Love helps us to connect and genuinely care for others. Love motivates us to think of others more than ourselves. Love will often drive us to perform feats that we think aren't possible. Love is the most positive of all energies our body emits. People motivated to help others and make the world a better place are driven by the heart. Love is the most positive vibration in the universe. Its vibration resonates powerfully through the ethers and raises the vibration of the surroundings. A person who is filled with love emits a very high vibration. A person with a heart full of love glows, smiles, hugs, compliments, cares, gives you a moment. A person "in love" feels beautiful.

If your heart chakra is out of balance, it is difficult to feel or express love. You experience low self-esteem and feel unworthy of love. You have a difficult time giving or receiving love. You feel neutral or hardened. You can feel when someone has a closed heart chakra. Their hugs are lifeless and cold. A person who can't love often doesn't love herself. To be a positive force in the world, you must have a balanced heart chakra.

The color green stimulates the heart chakra. The sound *Ah* also stimulates it.

Fifth Chakra: Vishuddha, or Throat Chakra

This chakra creates the energy associated with communication, spiritual communication, and self-expression. It is located in the neck at the cervical plexus and is associated with the thyroid and parathyroid glands.

A person with a balanced throat chakra can easily express herself verbally. She has no problem speaking the truth about who she is, even if it doesn't measure up to what her family or society expect. She is an excellent communicator of her thoughts and speaks well and listens with great interest. Our Vishuddha energy is the energy that expresses who we are—artistic, conservative, caring, serious, funny. We don't even need to say a word. Our energy will tell the world who we are.

A person with too much Vishuddah energy may talk too much and listen too little, may be arrogant or self-righteous, or may act in boisterous ways in order to get attention. A person with too little energy may feel uncomfortable speaking and be scared, timid, quiet, weak, unable to express his thoughts.

The fifth chakra is the portal through which your spirit expresses itself. Our prayers and other communications with spirit, whether silent or uttered aloud, flow from our throat chakra. Holy concepts and sacred texts are expressed here.

The color blue and the sound *Ay* stimulate the throat chakra.

Sixth Chakra: Ajna, or Third Eye

The Ajna chakra is the source of intuition, inspiration, psychic powers, and cosmic consciousness. Although some people simply point to the area between the eyebrows as the third eye, this energy center is actually located in the center of the brain, and its energy spreads both to the forehead between the brows and to the back of the head where the spine meets the bottom of the skull, called the medulla oblongata. It is associated with the pineal gland, an endocrine gland that secretes hormones

This chakra generates the energy of the Higher Self. It is the seat of our intuitive and psychic powers. It is helps us "read" a person or intuitively know the truth about a situation. It is where we receive divine guidance. A person with a balanced third eye is aware that there is more to life than what appears in three-dimensional form. She acknowledges and respects the feelings and messages she receives from within and is open to listening to positive influences from a Higher Power and other benevolent energies around her, such as angels.

The third eye is where inspiration is received or channeled. Those epiphanies and "aha!" moments that inspire us creatively, help us resolve a problem, and guide us to take a particular action are channeled through this chakra.

Spontaneous ideas, divine intervention, and the intuitive hunches that come under the umbrella of conscious awareness are channeled through the sixth chakra. The ego is released and a higher awareness of life is achieved. Great prophecies and divine direction are received through the third eye chakra.

A person with excessive third eye energy can be manipulative, an egomaniac, and/or religiously dogmatic. A person deficient in this energy can be undisciplined, afraid of success, and overly sensitive.

Indigo is the color associated with the third eye. The sound that stimulates this chakra is *Eee*.

Seventh Chakra: Sarasrara or Crown Chakra (the "Thousand-Petaled Lotus")

The Sarasrara energy center, our connection with the Infinite, is located at the crown of the head. It is associated with the pituitary gland, another endocrine gland that secretes hormones that influence metabolic and emotional reactions. The crown chakra is our connection to Spirit and opening to the Light. Through this chakra, we detach from the ego self and become an enlightened, fully realized being. You can let go of the material and dwell in a blissful state of spiritual beingness and live in moments of absolute peace and love. A clear crown chakra enables you to connect with the divine essence of God, Goddess, Universal Truth, or whatever you prefer to call this higher power, and you realize that you, too, are divine. Prayer and meditation will help to open the crown chakra. It is that connection to higher power or spirit that we feel. We feel expanded, moved, and grateful.

When there is an imbalance in the crown chakra, we will feel little joy. We do not experience the magic and mystery of a world beyond the three dimensions of our everyday lives.

Violet is the color associated with the crown chakra. There is no associated sound, although some people feel the mantra *Om* is the sound that connects us to the divine source.

Awareness of Energy

Like breathing, the function of each chakra is innate and automatic, yet we have the ability to take control. We breathe without thinking about breathing, yet we can consciously determine the amount of breath we take in, how long we hold it, and how slowly we exhale. Likewise, we can consciously open and close, or expand or contract our chakras to contain and exude more or less energy. We can control the amount of energy we emit to another person and control the amount of energy we receive from another person.

As you learn about energy and practice the exercises that help you energize and balance your chakras, you will learn that you can control the amount of energy you wish to project to the world. You can actually build up love, sexuality, power, and self-expression to make a positive contribution to a person and to the world. Learning how to read energy and being aware of the energy you exude can help you to connect more deeply with everyone you meet. When you learn how to open your chakras and radiate various types of energies, people will respond to you in kind. For example, if you open your heart and radiate love energy, people will feel your love and may respond to you with love. If you exude high doses of sexual energy, your sexual vibration will be noticed, and people will respond to your energy in any number of sexy ways

Similarly, you will respond to a person's energy. When someone exudes love energy to you, you will feel warm and safe with that person,

53

and you may open up to her or him. If someone radiates sexual energy, you will respond to that. You may feel turned on and stimulated or you may become guarded or repulsed. You will respond to that person in the way that feels most comfortable to you at that moment.

Energy awareness is a consciousness-raising exercise that allows you to identify your individual energy centers, feel the essential flavor of each energy, and experience how a thought can change the quality and amount of energy in each chakra. You will also become aware of the amount of energy you feel in each chakra, whether it is deficient or over-charged, so that you can consciously shift the energy and become balanced. If you discover that any of your chakras are shut down and in need of balancing, you can take action with the balancing and healing exercises described in this book.

The following energy awareness exercise can be practiced in two ways, alone or with a partner. When you practice it alone, you will learn about the chakras and your own energy and will experience conscious shifting of your energy. It is a great exercise and takes only a few minutes.

Practicing with a partner will take the exercise to a deeper level, as you will not only learn to radiate your own energy and experiment with its affect on others, but you will also have an opportunity to feel the fundamental nature of various energies as they are radiated by others.

Our chakras open up and shut down without our awareness, and yet we can have conscious control of how open and closed we want our chakras to be and how much energy we wish to radiate. Our sexual chakra is probably one of the easiest to recognize. Think about the last time you met an attractive person who turned you on and excited you sexually. Do you remember the energy in your sexual chakra? Did it radiate loads of sexual energy toward that person? Do you remember that feeling? Was there an energetic exchange? If that person was attracted to you, did you notice the sexual energy emitted by that person? Pretty powerful. Now think about someone whom you met recently whose sexual energy would be inappropriate, such as your grandmother or a child. Even better, think of someone who turns you off sexually and with whom you want to share ZERO sexual energy. Did your chakra close down? Did any sexual energy radiate from you?

In this exercise with a partner, you can actually feel the difference in the other person's energy when they open and close their chakras. You can feel it in yourself, too, and notice how you respond to your various levels of energy. You can perform this exercise solo, but it must be done in full awareness in order to truly feel and understand the power of the chakras.

Energy Awareness Exercise

This exercise can be practiced alone, but is more effective when practiced with a partner. Play soothing music. New Age instrumental music is perfect for this exercise. If practicing alone, stand in front of a full-length mirror if possible (but this is not necessary). When practicing with a partner, stand facing each other, looking into each other's eyes. (Perform this exercise with clothes on. Fabric doesn't block energy.)

Bring your attention to your first chakra, the survival chakra, located at the base of the spine and/or the cervix. Focus on the feelings of survival in your chakra. Feel your connection with the earth. Think about your job, your bills, and your ability to survive. Feel that energy, and put a positive spin on your survival and groundedness. Think about how successful you are in the world, how you are making your way, working and easily paying your bills. You've got survival down to a science. You barely need to worry. You make your way easily in the world. Feel that confidence and radiate that feeling toward your partner. Feel your own projection. Feel your partner's energy.

Now, just for the sake of this exercise, remember a time when you experienced financial challenges or imagine that your bills are overdue and you have no money. Or remember or imagine a disaster in which your home was destroyed. Notice how fear rose in your first chakra. How did that powerful survival energy disappear? Did you also notice a change in your partner?

Now forget those negative feelings and think about reality. Think about the home you have made, the fact that you have skills and can truly survive. Feel the strength of your first chakra return. Feel it in your partner, too.

Move to the second chakra, the chakra of sexuality and creativity, located in the vagina. Focus on how sexy you are. Think about someone who turns you on (it can be your husband, a movie star, even someone you saw at the grocery store) and put that person's face on your partner's face. Feel the chakra open up with sexual energy. Your body may subconsciously sway and move as the energy wells up. Allow it to happen. Feel it. Now consciously radiate that energy toward your partner, as if you are flirting with her/him, as if you want to turn her/him on. Shower her/him with your sexual energy. What does that feel like? Can you feel your energy grow and radiate? Now focus on her/his sexual energy. Can you feel it? How powerful is that? A lot of people call that sexual energy "juice." If someone has a lot of sexual energy, they are considered "juicy." Feel your juice!

Now imagine that the sexy person who turns you on morphs into your grandfather. Feel the sexual energy suddenly dissipate, feel your second chakra close down. Maintain that vision and notice the difference in your body. Notice the change in your partner's body. Funny, how suddenly the energy can shift.

Once again, think about that sexy person that turns you on, and allow your partner to morph back into that person. Can you feel your energy well up again? Once again, consciously project that energy toward your partner, as if you want to turn her/him on.

Move up to the third chakra, the power chakra, located in the belly. Now put a lot of energy into that chakra by thinking about something at which you are extremely proficient and confident in doing, such doing your job well, being a good friend or parent, playing a musical instrument or singing, or running marathons or playing tennis. Think about how great you are in those skills. Now imagine that you are a confident movie star or political figure, perhaps a queen, like Cleopatra, or an Amazon warrior. Feel the power of total self-assuredness and confidence expand in your chakra. (Wow, this is something many women don't often feel. Go for it! This is excellent practice.) Feel the power in your belly. Radiate that energy out toward your partner. What does that feel like? Can you feel the difference between power energy and sexual energy? Heck, yes! Feel your partner's power energy. Can you see the difference in her/him from before the exercise? Have you noticed a shift in the energy?

Now imagine that you are on stage giving a speech to a large audience. You stumble or forget what you're saying and the audience is visibly annoyed. Or imagine that you mess up at work. Wow, did you feel that energy shift? Did you feel your confidence just disappear? Hold that funky feeling for a moment. Feel how enormously different the energies are, and how not feeling confident will shift the way your body stands, how you hold yourself.

Now imagine that you still at the lectern but you have regained your composure. You give a captivating speech and the audience becomes attentive. They smile and nod. As you continue your grand speech, your confidence returns. The audience gives you a standing ovation. Imagine that you have done a great job on a project at work and you receive accolades from your boss. Feel your confidence and power continue to grow. Really feel that confidence. Embrace the power of your abilities inside of you. Feel the energy grow in your chakra. Allow it to radiate toward your partner. Feel the shift in yourself and from your partner.

Move your consciousness up to fourth chakra, the love chakra, located in the heart. (This is my personal favorite.) Focus on your heart and feel the love that dwells inside you. Imagine someone you love. Put her or his face on your partner. (Or perhaps you already love the person in front of you. Let this person be your focus.) Feel the love for that person, and see how your heart swells with the feelings of caring and warmth. Open your heart wide and allow that love to radiate toward your partner. Feel the love. Feel your partner's love. What an exquisite exchange of energy. Enjoy it for a few moments.

Now, for the sake of this exercise, think about someone who hurt you. Notice how quickly your heart shuts down. Imagine that this person is standing in front of you. Notice how reticent you are to give love, how your heart shuts down, even if you don't want it to. This is power of the chakras in action. Notice the difference in your feelings. Be conscious of the shift of energy in your partner, how the warmth of love reduced to a bit of a chill.

Now allow the image of the one who hurt you to slip away, and return to thoughts about one you love. Feel your heart open once again. Bask in the warmth. Or think compassionately about the one who hurt you. Feel love for him or her.

Now move your awareness to your fifth chakra, the chakra of communication and self-expression, which is located in the throat. Without saying a word, boldly communicate who you are or who you would like your partner to perceive you to be. Do this by allowing the energy flow out from your throat. Express who you are merely by looking at your partner and allowing the energy to flow. If you are a wild artist, allow that energy to flow through your throat chakra. Express yourself as who you are. Are you serious? Funny? Do you like to be the center of attention? Do you prefer to hang in the background?

Express who you are through your chakras. Do you wish to express something? Love? Joy? How silly you feel doing the exercise? Allow your energy to flow expressing this. Feel the energy.

Notice your partner's energy. How does her/his expression feel? Can you identify what this person wants you to understand about her/him? Can you feel his/her expression?

Now imagine you are in a sacred space where you can be very quiet and feel the peace. Notice your expressive energy withdraw. Notice the empty space between you and your partner, where only a moment ago there was active energy. Feel the absence of expression and the stillness of the energy in our expressive chakra. What is this like?

While your self-expression energy is still, move your focus to your sixth chakra, the third eye, the chakra of intuition, inspiration, and conscious consciousness, located between the eyebrows. This is where the ego self and the spirit self meet. Awareness of this chakra requires that you let go of ego and tap into spirit or the universal energy.

For this chakra, you must be still in your mind and body, without thoughts, judgments, or expression. Be at peace and become hyperaware of the universal energy around you, aware of your partner, or if alone, your own mind. If you can, allow your vision to go soft, almost into a blur, as you will not want to be distracted by anything or anyone. Remain in this peaceful state for a few moments, allowing messages, thoughts, and feelings to come through. See if you can pick up any images and thoughts from your partner. Do you pick up anything specific? A feeling of what she may have been thinking? If alone, what thoughts are coming through for you? Any inspirations? Any solutions to a problem you may be facing? Don't feel discouraged if you don't receive information, or if your mind swirls with chaotic thoughts. Just let it be. Third eye awareness is something we may have ignored our whole lives, so cultivating this chakra may be in order.

Now shift the energy. Release the quiet mind state and focus on the things that came to you when you were still. In a few words, tell your partner about the messages you received. Feel that incredible, expansive state dissipate as earthly thoughts flood your being. What a difference this is.

Now, once again release those thoughts and move your mind back into the place of quietude. Let go of the earthly thoughts and connect again with the universal energy. Allow the mind and eyes to go soft and again allow inspiration and intuition to come through, and remain here for a minute.

Finally, once you have returned to that soft and quiet space, move your consciousness up to the seventh chakra, the crown chakra, located at the top of your head. This is the energy center that most greatly connects with spiritual energy, where our spirit and Universal Spirit (God/dess) meet. Close your eyes and think of Universal Spirit, God/dess. Move into prayer, in which you communicate with the higher power. Let God/dess know you are present and wish to feel divine energy move into you. Feel the beauty of spirit move into you. Pray and focus until you feel yourself filling with spiritual energy. Allow yourself to fill up, and then open your eyes and look at your partner. Can you feel the spiritual energy flowing through her/him? Can you feel the spirit flowing through your own body? Savor these energetic feelings for a few moments. This inner peace and joyful place, this cosmic connection, is a place where we, as spiritual beings, can be—*and need to be*—as much as possible.

Now release your conscious awareness of the crown and spirit and come back into focus with the earthly world. Become present to everything around you. You may feel a shift in your being, but the spirit will remain inside you. Breathe, enjoy, love it. This concludes the exercise.

I hope that reading about the chakras and experiencing your energy through the Energy Awareness Exercise have helped you to distinguish your various energies. I also hope that you have recognized whether or not certain chakras are out of balance. The road to positive energy and a joyful, fulfilling life is balanced and energized chakras. The exercises that follow will help you attain balanced, healthy chakras.

Balancing the Chakras

As you now know, negative experiences push our chakras out of balance, blocking and clogging them, preventing positive energy from flowing through them. Feelings of well-being and joy are thwarted when an energy center is excessive or deficient in that energy. In order for positive energy to flow through our bodies, each chakra must be clear of negativity and open to radiate and receive healthy energy.

During your energy exercises, did you discover that you have a chakra that is low in energy? Are you fearful? Do you feel unsexy?

Powerless? Closed-hearted? Unable to communicate? Uninspired? Shut down to spirit?

Believe me, at some point in their lives everyone on the planet has experienced blockages in their chakras. It is part of being human. We can unblock our chakras and open them so that they may radiate an abundance of positive energy. We can allow the energy of the universe flow into and through us.

We don't hear much about chakra balancing in the West, but it has been a focus of Eastern philosophies and medicine for centuries. While this may seem esoteric and a bit woo-woo for our high-tech world, you should believe that you will feel better and happier when you incorporate a few simple energy exercises into your life. Our energy centers generally don't get balanced overnight, but dedication to certain practices will assure that your energy will be balanced.

Below are basic exercises to balance the chakras. These are simple and have an immediate affect, and if you practice them regularly your chakras will maintain their balance. As you will see in the chapters ahead, there are many, many methods to strengthen your energy centers. The exercises below are just the beginning. Enjoy.

Kriya Yoga: A Brief Introduction

Kriya yoga is a system of techniques used to generate, harness, and move energy through the body. The Western world is only beginning to discover and recognize the value of this ancient Eastern science, which was originally passed down only to initiates of certain mystical orders, to holistic health. The various techniques of Kriya yoga include breathing, mediation, mantra, yantra, energy visualization, and energy locks, all of which are highly effective in clearing, balancing, and energizing the chakras, meridians, and nadis.

I discovered the tremendous value of Kriya yoga during my studies of Ipsalu Tantra with Bodhi Avinasha. The effects of the practices are immediate. My experience was a profound awakening of physical, mental, and spiritual energy. I developed a radiant glow of loving energy that was perceived by others. I practice at least one of the techniques every day and regularly perform a routine incorporating all of the practices.

Here are some Kriya yoga techniques that can be used to harness energy and use it to energize and balance the chakras. These exercises are simple, but they illustrate your ability to harness and move energy through your body simply through conscious intention. The Kriya yoga techniques using yantra, mudra and meditation are presented in Chapter 9, *Tools to Connect Soul and Universal Spirit*, and further enhance generating and balancing energy.

You can learn more advanced Kriya Yoga techniques from a teacher or in books. The book I recommend most highly is *Jewel in the Lotus*, by Sunyata Saraswati and Bodhi Avinasha. Many of the techniques below were inspired by practices from this book.

Breathing

Few people know how to breathe correctly. Most of us breathe in shallow breaths, taking in only small amounts of air, only partially filling our lungs, and not completely exhaling the old, stale air. Breathing in full lungs of air infuses the body with chi, or life-force energy. Chi penetrates our blood cells, circulates around our bodies, and streams through the thousands of meridians, or energy channels, of the body. Just breathing deeply seven times is tremendously beneficial. For those of you who don't normally focus on your lungs and wish to learn how to breathe properly, here we go.

Chi exists in all of us. It is found in great abundance in the air we breathe. It not only keeps us alive, but it also keeps us healthy and vibrant. In Taoist and Tantric exercises, breathing is used to circulate chi from the air and through the body. Breathing energizes us, physically, mentally, and even spiritually. Ever notice the glow of someone who has just taken a walk or worked out? Much of the glow comes from the infusion of air through our bloodstream and into all of our cells. Breathing exercises can also bring a dose of chi into the body and give you the same radiant, healthy glow.

While we breathe automatically and unconsciously to stay alive, the benefits of conscious breathing far surpass mere survival. Breathing exercises are a practice of focused inhalation and exhalation, lung expansion and visualization. The few minutes that it takes to perform a breath exercise yield wonderful results. You'll feel calmer, more confident in yourself (from time spent with your body so intimately), and closer to a higher power or cosmic plane. Deep breathing exercises also energize the brain, enabling us to become more focused and clearer in our thinking.

Learning to Breathe

First, let's get to know our lungs. Our lungs are the long organs in our chest. They are divided into three lobes: the lower lobe, the middle lobe, and the upper lobe. In normal, shallow breathing we fill only the middle lobe. To experience the benefits of breath work, you also need to consciously fill your lower and upper lobes. To become familiar with your own lungs, focus for a moment on each lobe.

Lower Lobe Breathing

Focus only on your lower lungs as you inhale through your nose. Allow your belly to extend as your lower lungs fill with air. Feel your sides and back expand as the lower lobes fill to capacity. Hold for a count of 3. Now exhale through your mouth, pushing all of the air out with the assistance of your stomach muscles. Perform this three times.

As normal Americans, we rarely allow ourselves the luxury of breathing into our lower lobes. We try to keep our waists looking slender. In a perfect world, an extended belly, free to take in lots of air, would be beautiful.

Middle Lobe Breathing

We are most familiar with the middle part of our lungs, but rarely do we consciously fill this lobe completely. To do so, inhale deeply through the nose, and direct the air only to the middle lobes. The rib cage will expand. Feel the muscles in your ribs and back stretch, too. Hold for a count of 3. Exhale through your mouth and push the air out of the middle lobes with your ribs. Perform this three times.

Upper Lobe Breathing

We breathe into our upper lobes in times of distress and fear with shallow, rapid breaths. Our lungs extend as high as our sternum, but rarely do these lobes receive the luxury of buckets of air. Focus now on breathing into the upper lobe by inhaling through your nose and directing the air only into the part of your lungs just beneath your shoulders. To fill this lobe completely, lift your shoulders and bring them forward on the inhale. Notice the stretch in your muscles in your shoulders. Notice how lifting and stretching your shoulders increases your capacity for air. Hold for a count of 3.

Exhale through your mouth while dropping your shoulders and pushing all of the air out with the help of your upper rib muscles. Perform this three times.

Now that you are familiar with the structure of the lungs, it is time to *really breathe.*

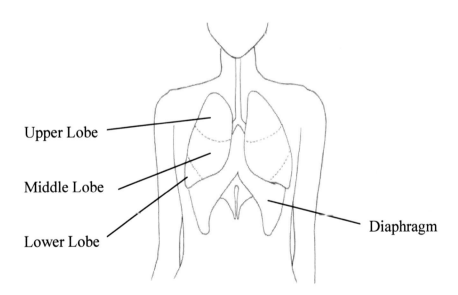

Upper Lobe

Middle Lobe

Lower Lobe

Diaphragm

Complete Breath

1. Sit in a chair, spine straight, head erect, hands on knees, and eyes closed, or on the floor in lotus position.
2. Inhale slowly through your nose, directing the air into the lower lobes until they are full, your stomach is completely distended, and your back and sides are expanded.
3. Continue to inhale as you fill the middle lobes until your ribs are fully expanded.
4. Continue to inhale and direct the air into the upper lobes, lifting your shoulders, filling the lobes until your lungs can contain no more air. (The inhale will be slow and smooth, gracefully moving from the lower lobe to the middle lobe to the upper.)
5. Tense all of the muscles in the body while holding your breath for as long as is comfortable.
6. Take a quick sniff of air through your nose to relieve the tension in your lungs. Exhale slowly through your mouth, releasing all tension from your body and emptying the upper lobe completely, then the middle lobe, and finally the lower lobe. Push all of the air out of each lobe with your shoulders, ribs, and stomach as you go. Push until all of the muscles of your torso are tense and all of the air has been pushed out of your lungs. Relax for a beat.

Repeat the process six more times, for a total of seven times. A beneficial practice is to inhale to a count of 20, hold the breath for a count of 20, then exhale to a count of 20.

NOTE: Sometimes we don't have time for a focused Complete Breath workout. You can replace it by merely consciously inhaling deeply, holding the breath for as long as possible (without straining), and exhaling slowly. Perform this any time during the day, as many times a day as you think about it. The infusion of air to the brain and body is invaluable to the body and the mind.

CAUTION: If you have high blood pressure, heart problems, or have had a stroke, please consult your physician before performing this exercise.

Energy Locks

In Tantric and other Eastern practices, breathing exercises are performed with the assistance of Energy Locks, including the Chin and Root Locks. These locks help our bodies hold our chi and keep it circulating through our bodies. The combined Root Lock and Chin Lock create a vacuum, which is very important for containing the energy in your body. Without these Energy Locks, energy can leak out through our noses and other bodily orifices as we do our Breathing Exercises.

Following is a description of the Chin Lock and the Root Lock, which are incorporated in many Kriya yoga and Tantric breathing and energy exercises.

Chin Lock

This pose blocks the airway at the upper palate and nostrils to keep the air from exiting our noses and mouths during breathing exercises.

1. Sit in a chair, spine straight, head erect, hands on knees, and eyes closed, or on the floor in lotus position.
2. Inhale deeply through your nose. Hold your breath.
3. While you're holding your breath, move the back of your tongue up against the back of your throat, as if cutting off your nasal breathing passage.
4. With neck straight, tilt your head downward slightly.
5. Hold your breath as long as is comfortable.
6. Raise your head to its normal position and move your tongue from the upper palate into its normal, relaxed position.
7. Sniff and exhale slowly through your mouth.

Root Lock

In Tantric and other yogic practices, much focus is placed on the anal orifice and the muscles surrounding it. This orifice can be a portal for energy drain. Holding the anus tightly while performing breathing and other exercises not only causes the energy to remain in the body, but also actually assists in pulling energy from the lower chakras to the upper chakras.

1. Sit as described above.
2. Inhale deeply through your nose. Hold your breath.
3. Perform the chin lock.
4. Contract your anus and vagina tightly.
5. Hold for as long as is comfortable.
6. Release chin and root locks.
7. Sniff and exhale through your mouth.

Now that you know how to breathe and contain energy with the locks, incorporate them into a daily breathing practice. Seven rounds of breaths and lock will energize you.

CAUTION: Do not perform this exercise if you have high blood pressure, heart problems, or have had a stroke.

Energy Movement Meditation

The most important exercises of Kriya yoga is the movement of energy through the body to the various chakras. With the Energy Movement Meditation, you'll incorporate breathing and energy locks, as well as a visualization meditation, to create this energy movement. The following exercise will familiarize you with the power of consciously harnessing chi and moving it to heal and energize your body. This technique is used in more advanced exercises presented later in this book.

1. Sit in a chair, spine straight, head erect, hands on knees, and eyes closed, or on the floor in lotus position.

2. Begin to perform a Complete Breath, inhaling through your nose.
3. As you inhale, visualize a ball of silver energy rising from the earth to your root chakra. As your lungs continue to fill, the silver ball rises through the trunk of your body and up to your heart.
4. Once at the heart, hold your breath, perform the chin and root locks while seeing and *feeling* the ball of energy at your heart.
5. Hold for a few seconds, then sniff and exhale gently through your mouth, visualizing the ball of energy moving down through your body and out through your root chakra.
6. Perform three times.
7. Next, perform the Complete Breath. This time, visualize a golden ball of light entering your crown chakra, moving through your head and down your neck and to your heart as you breathe in.
8. Once the golden ball is at your heart, apply the chin and root locks and hold your breath for a few seconds. See and *feel* the ball of energy at your heart.
9. Sniff and exhale, visualizing the ball of energy moving up through your neck and face and back out of the top of your head.
10. Repeat three times.
11. Sit quietly and feel the energy in your body.

Mantras

Mantras are sacred sounds, words, or strings of words, most often in Sanskrit, an ancient Indo-European language, though sometimes we create mantras in our modern vernaculars, too. These sounds and words have highly energetic vibrations that correspond to our chakras and travel into the universe, influencing the energy of the cosmos and attracting positive energy toward you. Practiced by Buddhists and Hindus for centuries, mantra is finally beginning to be recognized as a healing or empowerment tool in the Western world, even though its power and effectiveness in improving our lives has been documented through the centuries. Little by little, the mantra is being recognized as a simple, powerful tool that can help us achieve inner peace, clarity, love, and balance in our energetic body. When practiced with intention, mantra is powerfully healing and has noticeable results in short sessions.

The word or tone of a mantra carries a specific frequency, an energetic vibration, which affects a specific chakra. These sounds and related chakras are as follows:

Mantra	Chakra
Uhh	Root
Ooh	Sex
Oh	Power
Ah	Heart
Eh	Throat
Ee	Third Eye
None or *Om*	Crown

The lower vibrational sounds increase and balance the energy of the lower chakras, and the higher vibrational sounds affect the upper chakras. A sluggish, low-energy power chakra will increase in energy when its corresponding tone stimulates it.

You may naturally utter these sacred sounds without even realizing it. For example, when engaging sexually, and your sexual chakra is stimulated, you may go *Oooooooh!* When hugging someone you love, heart to heart, you may say, "*Ahhhhhhhh.*"

Easy Mantra Exercise: Toning Meditation

The Toning Meditation will help you balance your chakras by sending energy into each chakra with its corresponding sound. If you have been feeling out of sorts or emotional, this exercise will help you feel calmer, more clear-minded, and more joyful. If one of your chakras is out of balance, either low in energy or overly energized, chant the sound that corresponds to that chakra, and the energy will balance itself. The effects are immediate, and if practiced regularly, the benefit is long-lasting. This is a meditation unto itself, and it is also pre-meditation if you wish to meditate longer. Here's how you do it.

1. Sit comfortably on a chair, with eyes closed.
2. Focus on your root chakra. Once you are able to identify and focus on that survival center, inhale deeply, and while exhaling, chant *Uhhhhhhh* deep in your throat. Feel the vibration in your body and see if you can send this vibration to your cervix, at the top of inside of the vagina. Once you get to that point, chant the mantra for one to two minutes (or as

long as you would like.) After you feel complete, be still for a minute or so and feel the peace in your body.

3. Move your attention to your second chakra, in your ovaries. Once you focus on your second chakra, inhale deeply, and while exhaling chant *Oooooh*, feeling the deep vibration in your body. Move the vibration to your ovaries. For this chakra, I like to say *Ooooh* as if I am making love. Once you begin to vibrate your ovary chakra, chant for one to two minutes (or as long as you would like.) After you feel complete, be still for a minute and feel the peace in your body.

4. Move the attention up to your third chakra, your power center. Get in touch with that energy center, inhale, then chant *Oh*. Send the sound of *Oh* out from your mouth. Notice the difference in the vibration. It is higher and feels more "outward" than *Ooooh*. Chant *Oh* until you really feel it in your belly. It helps to imagine yourself radiating power from your belly as you chant. Once you feel the vibration in your power center, continue to chant for one to two minutes. Then be still for a minute.

5. Now move to your heart chakra. Feel your heart, and chant *Ahhhhhhh*. Chant as if you are happy and in love. Feel the vibration of this sound move in your heart. Chant *Ahhhh* for one to two minutes, and if it helps, move your arms as if you are giving someone a hug. After a few minutes, release the mantra and be still.

6. Focus your mind on your throat chakra, and chant *Ehhhhh*. (This sounds like the English letter A.) Feel the vibration in your throat as you chant for one to two minutes. Your voice may go up an octave. Chant as if you are speaking to the world. Then release the mantra and be still.

7. Moving up to the third eye, chant *Eeeeeee* with your voice in a high register. Feel the vibration resonate throughout your head, especially in your forehead. Continue the chant for one to two minutes, then release it and be still.

8. Finally, at the crown chakra, focus on the top of your head, the portal for spirit, and just sit in silence. Imagine the positive vibrations of the universe entering into your head. Receive the peace and love that flow into you. Allow love to flow out of your head. Continue for one to two minutes, then release and be still. At this point, you may enter into a deeper meditation, dance, or resume your daily activities.

Sacred Mantra

The tones of mantras exist in words of every language. Ancient Buddhist and Hindu spiritual adepts recognized the power of mantra, which included various tones that affect specific chakras. They wrote hundreds, if not thousands, of mantras to invoke the Universe, the Goddess, and other deities to express gratitude, bless an event, or solve a problem. In a sense, these mantras were, and are, prayers. Vibrations of these prayers travel into the Universe, sending positive energy along the way. The chakras are opened and balanced and receive the positive energy of the Universe. These mantras are tools for spiritual growth. They positively affect each practitioner's daily life, instilling a sense of calmness, clarity, strength, and joy.

The mantra below is a classic mantra. You will hear many of the basic sounds (*oooh*, *oh*, *ah*, etc.) articulated in it. While the mantra sends out positive vibrations into the cosmos, it is also positively charging your chakras.

Om Mani Padme Hum.

(Pronounced *Om Mah-nee Puhd-may Hoom.*)

The translation of this beautiful mantra is "the All is a precious jewel in the lotus flower, which blooms in my heart." (The *All* in this mantra means the Universe, God/dess, etc.) This mantra energizes and balances the *shakti,* or feminine energy, represented as the lotus flower, and the *shiva*, or masculine energy, represented as the precious jewel.

Sit with your legs crossed, eyes closed, and repeat this mantra for several minutes. If you have mala beads, use them to count as your chant 108 times. Notice the shift in your energy after you have completed a round.

You will find more mantras in Chapter 9, *Tools to Connect Soul and Universal Spirit.*

Other Chakra Balancing Modalities

Essential oils

In the olden days, people made fun of aromatherapy. Today, however, many people see and feel the positive effects essential oils have on the health of the body and human spirit. High-grade essential oils are basically the "blood" of a plant, flower, or root, and they contain antioxidants and other biological substances that have been found to be healing to the body and soul. Like a mantra, every oil carries a frequency that corresponds to a particular chakra. Merely smelling a particular oil will create an immediate balance in the chakra, as the frequency of the smell effects the vibration of the chakra. When the oil is applied to the front or back of the body in the area of a chakra, long-lasting healing and balancing of the chakra occurs, as the healing properties of the plant blood is absorbed into the physical and energetic systems.

Essential oils are serious healing tinctures to be used only topically *and never to be consumed internally*. Some have strong potencies that can be very irritating to the skin. Bergamot, lemon, mandarin orange, and angelica, for example, can cause a rash and may permanently discolor the skin when it is exposed to sunlight. Extreme caution should likewise be used with fennel, clary sage, and sage during pregnancy, as they have some affect on hormones. Pure essential oils are not used full-strength, but are diluted in a carrier oil, such as almond oil, peanut oil, or lanolin. Because of the penetration action of oils, it is important to use high-grade oils, such as Young Living or Oshadhi. These oils can be purchased from health food stores, metaphysical shops, and representatives who sell high-grade oils.

NOTE: Please consult a professional aromatherapist or essential oil vendor before experimenting with essential oils.

Essential oils promote healing on all levels, spiritual, physical, and emotional. Because they're easily accessible and can be applied as needed, they are a wonderful emergency-balancing tool. If you feel out of balance in any way—angry, sad, weepy, hyperactive, stressed out—apply the oil prescribed for that emotion and feel the affect almost immediately. Most massage therapists who specialize in calming massages and chakra balancing have a vast range of oils they use in their work.

The following oils correspond to the energy of each chakra. Be sure to use caution when using an essential oil on your own. Be safe and dilute the oil before using it. Remember, it is best to consult an aromatherapy expert before you start experimenting with essential oils.

First chakra: Will help you feel more grounded, able to cope through stressful times. Try patchouli, vetiver, oakmoss, rosewood, angelica, frankincense, myrrh

Second chakra: Will stimulate creativity and sexuality. Try ylang-ylang, vanilla, cardamom, jasmine, rose, sandalwood.

Third chakra: Will help you feel stronger, more self-assured. Try ginger, bay laurel, black pepper, orange, eucalyptus, juniper, vetiver.

Fourth chakra: Will open your heart to love. Try rose, jasmine, melissa, neroli, clary sage, lemon verbena, geranium, benzoin.

Fifth chakra: Will help you to feel more communicative or will subdue overcommunication if you're out of balance. Try blue chamomile, roman chamomile, bergamot, eucalyptus, benzoin.

Sixth Chakra: Will enhance your psychic and intuitive capabilities. Try cedar, cistus, rosemary, peppermint, fir, frankincense, sandalwood, spruce.

Seventh chakra: Assists in connecting with the Cosmic Forces/higher power, etc. Try rose, jasmine, sandalwood, rosewood, lavender, frankincense, myrrh, benzoin, fir, spruce. [54]

For detailed information about essential oils and their use for healing, I highly recommend two books: *Reference Guide for Essential Oils*, by Connie and Alan Higley, and *Aromatherapy for Lovers*, by Tara Fellner.

Crystals and Gems

As I said at the beginning of this chapter, *everything has energy*. This includes rocks and stones. Crystals and semi-precious stones are conduits of energy and hold and radiate energy at a variety of frequencies. For example, quartz crystal was used in our old transistor radios to attract a radio frequency. While crystals seem to be very popular with the New Agers, women of ancient cultures, such as Hindu and Arabian women, wore gems and jewels around their necks, not only for their beauty, but for their energetic powers. Huge clusters of crystals and amethyst are placed on altars and sacred sanctuaries to draw in the benevolent energies of the universe.

Like a mantra, every color carries a frequency, and every type of mineral carries its own frequency. Scientists of gemstone healing have determined the frequencies of each stone and the chakra it corresponds with.

The fascinating book, *Color and Crystals: A Journey Through the Chakras*, by Joy Gardner, brings light to the energies of various stones and their effects on the chakras and organs. She explains how a chakra that is low in energy can be stimulated when a stone associated with that chakra is placed on the chakra. If the chakra has excessive energy, an antidote color, usually the color of the opposite chakra will calm the energy down. (According to *Color and Crystals*, the three lower chakras are "opposite" the three upper chakras, and stones that correspond with the three lower chakras serve as antidotes to the upper three chakras. The heart, located between the upper and lower, is considered a neutral chakra, so needs no antidote.)

Practitioners who specialize in chakra balancing place stones on the patient's body and allow the patient to lie still while the minerals' frequencies penetrate into the body. Many people buy stones or crystals and carry them in their pocket or wear them on a necklace. Stones can be purchased in a New Age store, a mineral shop, or via the Internet. They are not expensive, and you can carry around as many stones as you wish. I love crystals and stones and have small pieces on altars throughout my home. Below is a list of stones that correspond to the chakras.

First chakra
Associated color: red
Stones: red garnet, black obsidian, smoky quartz

Second chakra
Associated color: orange
Stones: tiger's eye, carnelian

Third chakra
Associated color: yellow
Stones: citrine, turquoise, malachite

Fourth chakra
Associated color: green or pink
Stones: green jade, green aventurine, rose quartz, watermelon tourmaline, malachite

Fifth chakra
Associated color: blue
Stones: sodalite, azurite, lapis lazuli, clear crystal quartz

Sixth chakra
Associated color: indigo
Stones: lapis lazuli, sodalite, amethyst, clear quartz crystal, and purple, blue, white, or gold fluorite

Seventh chakra
Associated color: violet
Stones: lapis lazuli, sodalite, amethyst, clear quartz crystal, purple, blue, white, or gold fluorite [55]

Energetic Chakra Massage

Having tried oils or gems, we may find that we need to take more aggressive measures to balance our chakras. Our awareness may come after we've experienced a trauma, such as a break-up, problems at work, or ill will within our family. If we feel unhappy and unbalanced and we're unable to shift the energy on our own, we can visit a specialist in chakra balancing and massaging. These specialists have the gifts and skills to read your energy, diagnose the problem areas, and treat them in any number of ways, including massage, energetic hand-work (including hands on the body and hands on the energy field), placement of stones and/or essential oils on the chakras, and in some cases, sound energy from the voice or instruments, such as Tibetan singing bowls, to balance and heal the chakras.

A session with a healer may bring up emotions. Sometimes an energy center is shut down because of emotions that have not been dealt with and are stored in the center. When negative energy is drawn out, feelings may come up along with it, bringing up tears, anger, etc. It is important to feel, express, and release these emotions. The healer can assist you with this. Once you have expelled the negative energy, your chakras will be clear and you will feel calmer and able to move on with your life. Your vibration will rise and people will notice a difference in your energy.

You may be lucky enough to have a practitioner of this nature in your area. They usually advertise in the holistic health and New Age publications. However, you can treat yourself fairly effectively if you apply the techniques you have learned above. Practice complete breathing, visualize the light running through your body, tone, use essential oils, and/or place stones on your body.

Smile. Connect with Other People

It is important to remember to emanate love toward every person and in every situation. People can feel your vibration, and that is the vibration they will remember YOU as being. Be an emanation of love and light. Make it a habit to emanate a vibration of love and joy. What we do and the actions we take can be expressions of God/dess. There is nothing more attractive than a bright smile and a loving connection. Give your smiles away abundantly. You are a divine Giver and the other is a divine Recipient. Let it be your mission to raise the mood and vibration of others, to inspire love around the planet. Smile in joy and in love. See how many people respond in kind. Love the world and watch the world fall in love with you. *Smile!*

Part Two:

SEXY

5

FEMALE SEXUAL ENERGY

Clothing and jewelry don't make a woman. Her energy does. And female sexual energy is what makes a woman beautiful, sensual, feminine, and sexy. She has the "juice" that keeps her youthful and exciting. She has an attractive, approachable vibration and a healthy attitude about relationships and intimacy. She is neither a vixen nor a wallflower, but is balanced with obvious sexual charm that is appropriate and under control. She is confident in her demeanor, she possesses a healthy attitude about her body, and she is comfortable in her own skin.

The first aspect of becoming a Positive Energy Woman relates to sexual energy. The second, or Swadhistana, chakra is the center of creativity. Its energy drives the juice that drives us. A woman with balanced sexual energy is loving and filled with self-love. She feels confident with herself as a woman. She is fearless in expressing herself. She recognizes her own beauty and sees the beauty in others. A woman with balanced sexual energy is beautiful, no matter what her age, body type, or fashion preference. She seems youthful and healthy, she's filled with passion and verve for living.

The sexual chakra is the source of creative life-force energy, one of the most powerful, most beneficial energies in our body. The Taoists call this energy *jing*, which they consider even more potent than chi, the essential life-force energy that circulates the body.[56] Tantric belief is that the sexual energy is the essence of kundalini.[57] The sexual chakra is source of life-force energy, which enables our physical bodies to function and can mend our psychic wounds and improve our general health. Sexual energy is the only energy in our body that can be increased to double or even triple the amount.[58] With certain practices, we can keep our sexual organs youthful and our sexual energy alive and charged up, keeping us juicy and youthful, whether we are in our 20s or 80s.

Maintaining balanced sexual life-force energy is critical to being a vibrant, balanced, joyful woman. In fact, the amount of sexual energy we possess is commensurate with our zest for life. Here are a few of the benefits of maintaining healthy sexual energy:

1. You will become healthier, more vital and radiant.
2. You will be filled with a sense of spiritual and physical wholeness, increasing appreciation and love for yourself.
3. You will feel sexier, more sensual, more feminine.
4. You will provide feminine energy to the universal energetic web, which will assist in healing and balancing the energy of the planet.

Practicing a few easy exercises will help you become the sexy, exuberant woman you've always wanted to be.

The Power of Sexual Energy

I once attended a focus group of women who reviewed a women's fitness product that was based on strip dancing and designed to help women move their bodies in sensual ways. A tasteful video demonstrated the beautiful and sensual moves that would help women shape up their bodies and feel more feminine. The moves were not at all crude or lewd, but slow and yoga-like, with accentuated stretching moves on the hips, thighs, abdomen, and chest muscles.

But feedback from the focus group was surprising. Many of the women felt offended by the concepts and the moves of the dance. One woman said that she felt shamed watching the video. Several women were turned off by the sexiness of the moves. In our discussion, women expressed their distaste for the words "sexy" and "sexual." Only a few woman expressed enthusiasm for the product. Mind you, this focus group was held in a major California city in the 21st century.

I believe many women fear sexual energy, both their own and others'. Many of us have completely shut our sexual power down. We have forgotten how to feel sexy and be sexy. Few of us are conscious of the sexual energy we emit, and still fewer of us know how to deal with excess sexual energy in a way that is healthy and beneficial.

Sexuality is as much a force of the human psyche as power, love, creative expression, and drive for success, yet those other energies do not elicit in us the complicated and confused feelings we have around sex. We are simultaneously attracted to and afraid of sex. As one of the most powerful forces of human existence, sexual energy fuels our biological drive to attract a partner with whom to form a sexual union and, ultimately, to perpetuate our species. However, as humans evolved and became more multidimensional beings, our applications and definitions of sex multiplied, and through the ages we have accepted in our psyches and souls that the sexual act might be an act of worship of the Goddess and women's innate link to life and regeneration. Sex is many things—a vehicle for enlightenment, a demonstration of commitment and sanctity of marital union, a form of life-force energy capable of healing, an indulgence of physical ecstasy, a mode of entertainment, and a symbol of sin and impurity. With all of these views and philosophies around sex, not to mention our own physical drives, it is no wonder sex is such a controversial subject.

Primal and pleasurable, sexual energy is a complicated human force tightly entwined with our physical body and our emotions, as well as our spiritual, cosmic energies. In order to gain a little understand of this powerful energy, let's look at the various facets of sexual energy and human sexuality.

The Science of Sexuality

The source of a woman's sexual energy is her reproductive organs, specifically her ovaries, which produce the hormones estrogen, progesterone, and estrodial. These hormones, and others produced in the endocrine glands, regulate our menstrual cycle (including the release of the egg from the ovary) and influence our libido. During a woman's lifetime, she will experience the highest sexual drive during the years that she menstruates, although for many women, their libido remains strong long after menopause.

On a strictly primal level, humans can be considered nature's sexiest species. The human woman is the only mammal that experiences prolonged and multiple orgasms. She's also the only mammal that will engage sexually at any point in her cycle, unlike most other mammals, which will copulate at only certain points of the fertility cycle. She is also the only one who can refuse to engage sexually.[59] Foreplay demonstrated by humans far exceeds that of other primate species.[60]

Our first assumption around our primal, sexual drive is that it assures population growth for the survival of our species. But Desmond Morris, a zoologist who studied the behavior of Homo sapiens and our fundamental, biological nature and is the author of *The Naked Ape*, has a different theory. He breaks sexual behavior down into three characteristic phases: pair-formation, or courtship; pre-copulatory activity, or kissing, hugging, usually in a horizontal position to stimulate each other sexually; and the copulatory phase. Morris says, "The vast bulk of copulation in our species is obviously concerned, not with producing offspring, but with cementing the pair-bond by providing mutual rewards for the sexual partners."[61] Pair bonding should assure that the woman remains faithful while the man goes hunting. It also contributes to the development of parental duties shared by both parents. Morris surmises that "the repeated attainment of sexual consummation for a mated pair is clearly, then, not some kind of sophisticated, decadent outgrowth of modern civilization, but a deep-rooted, biologically based, and evolutionarily sound tendency of our species."[62] Anthropologists and sexologists agree that great sex is a natural bonding activity, and because of its intense pleasure, women are often motivated to engage in sexual intimacy. Orgasm makes us feel sexier and more open to attracting a partner. Men are attracted to women who show signs of sexual interest.[63]

Modern science proves that during pleasurable sexual interactions, high levels of neurochemicals and hormones, such as estrogen, oxytocin, dopamine, and testosterone, are released, often causing the woman to feel high, and desirous of forming a romantic bond with her lover.[64]

When we think of sex, we think of the animal instinct to mate and procreate. Sexual energy in this context is demonstrated by the flaunting of one's charms to attract a partner. According to Luann Brizendine, author of *The Female Brain*, in situations of short-term coupling, usually men are chasers and women are choosers. A woman's primitive instincts are to find the healthiest mate who will give her children, plus the resources and commitment to raise them.[65] Darwin theorized that males of all species strive to woo the females, while the females choose among the suitors.[66] But with the heightened sexuality of the human being, constant expression and outlet are demanded.[67] A woman will often wear lipstick, high heels, and a pushup bra to accentuate her feminine attributes. And once she has won the attention of a potential suitor, she has the power to say "no," or "I'm unavailable."

Sigmund Freud (1856–1939), who is known as the Father of Psychoanalysis, was among the first to study human sexuality on a psychological level. His interest began with his study of a woman suffering from a nervous breakdown, which he discovered was caused by sexual abuse. From that case, he theorized that all hysteria was derived from unconscious memories of sexual abuse in infancy, a theory that caused great controversy in his later years. Freud also theorized that the libido developed in various stages from infancy through adulthood. If sexuality is repressed through any of these stages, mental health is jeopardized. He also developed the Electra complex, which is a daughter's love of her father and jealousy of her mother, and its male counterpart, the Oedipus complex.

By the way, hysteria was not a condition discovered by Freud. The word comes from a medical term, *hysterikos*, which refers to a female medical condition caused by disturbances of the uterus (*hystera* in Greek.) Until the early 20th century, the term was almost always a female condition. Earlier, during the 19th century, hysteria was used to describe what we think of today as sexual dissatisfaction, and was treated by genital massage or vibrator treatments by the physician to bring the patient to orgasm.[68]

Wilhelm Reich (1897–1957), a student of Freud and another noted 20th century psychiatrist and psychoanalyst, linked sexuality and neurosis. He emphasized "orgiastic potency" as the main criterion for psycho-physical health. Reich's theory of orgiastic potency states that the ability to feel sexual love depends on a physical ability to make love. He further theorized that unreleased psychosexual energy can produce energetic blocks in the muscles and organs that act as "body armor" and prevent the release of energy. Orgasm, he said, is one way to break through that armor. He blamed moral and social structures for sexual repression and said that living an active, guilt-free life is the cure. He also developed a therapy we now call Bioenergetic Healing, in which psychoanalysis is coupled with physical movement and touch.

Perhaps the most in-depth study of human sexuality was performed by Alfred C. Kinsey (1894–1956) during the 1940s and 50s. His best-known books are *Sexual Behavior in the Human Male* (1948) and *Sexual Behavior in the Human Female* (1953), both of which focus on the physical act of sex, including orgasm, masturbation, petting, heterosexual coitus, homosexual behaviors, and bestiality. Only after reading Kinsey's groundbreaking research did Americans learn that women are as capable of sexual response as men. Kinsey's work helped lead to the sexual revolution of the 1960s.

In the 1960s, with the advent of the birth control pill, sexual freedom exploded. Liberated from the dangers of accidental pregnancy and religious doctrine, and yielding to the natural urge to connect and experience sexual pleasure without restraint, society's mores began to relax, and women could make choices about their sexuality. We might think this is the happy ending of the story of sex, but for forty years or more, our society has seen conflict between the forces of sexual drive and religious and social mores. Many women latched on to the freedom to expand themselves sexually, but then they found themselves experiencing emotional, physical, and energetic repercussions that they didn't expect. With sexual freedom comes responsibility. We can make personal choices and decide whether we will refrain from sex until marriage, become intimate with multiple partners, remain celibate, or all of the above.

Today, sexual energy is still in many ways a mystery. It is misunderstood, misused, misdirected. Many of us are mystified as to how to deal with sexual energy. It exists in all of us, yet some of us want to ignore it and pretend it isn't there, while others flaunt it to extremes. Many women consider sex a subject too taboo to discuss except with their closest girlfriends. We're often highly judgmental of women with exuberant sexual energy and call them sluts or whores. And even though we are reticent to educate our children about sexuality, pornography is one of the most profitable industries in the world, and rapists and sexual violators run amok. The bottom line is that because of our social conditioning, we are afraid of sexual energy. We're afraid to feel it, express it, or share it.

Once we learn that sexual energy is more than attracting a mate for sexual intercourse, we will give our sexual energy greater respect. I believe that the planet will be a healthier place when we accept sexual energy as a precious gift. It is our source of womanhood. It is spiritual energy. It is healing energy. It is to be honored in ourselves and in others.

In my studies and exploration of feminine sexual energy, I have found two philosophical practices to be extremely valuable in understanding and using sexual energy: Tantra and Taoism. Both practices contain physical and spiritual components as well as transformational possibilities. Because I believe the energetic union of body and spirit is critical to our wholeness, most of the exercises in this chapter originate from Tantric and Taoist traditions. First, here is a brief history of Tantra and Taoism. Because my focus over the years has been Tantra, I delight in giving you a history of its development and philosophy.

The Spirit of Sexuality: Tantra

Several millennia ago, spiritual adepts in the East, recognizing the dynamic energies of the universe and human body, identified sexual energy as a vehicle for enlightenment. Those of us raised in the puritanical Western churches probably see any kind of sexual ritual as the antithesis of religious enlightenment, but practitioners of the cult called Tantra that arose in Asia around 1,400 years ago discovered, refined, and disseminated practices with sexual energy as a path of spirituality through ecstasy.

The word Tantra comes from two Sanskrit words, *tanoti*, meaning "to expand," and *trayati*, or "liberation."[69] Through the practices of Tantra, one's awareness of the soul would expand, causing liberation from the confines of physical limitations. A path based on energy, Tantra is a practice in which sexual energy is generated and harnessed for purification of the energetic body. By merging feminine and masculine energies, either within one's own body or by merging soulfully with a beloved, oppositely energetic partner (such as masculine and feminine), a pathway can be created through which energetic communion with the Higher Power could occur. Enlightenment and bliss are the rewards.

Only in the early 20th century, in the work of Arthur Avalon (the pen name of Sir John Woodroffe, 1865–1936), did Tantra find its way to the Western world and into consciousness of spiritual seekers. When I became interested in Tantra in the mid 1990s as a part of my spiritual exploration, I was quick to learn that this path is not one of rote prayer or static meditations. It is a rich, active practice of sensual stimulation with music, art, movement, breath work, visualization, and the worship of the divine in others and the self. Tantra inspires a rich lifestyle that goes beyond a spiritual practice, and integrates fully into our entire being and daily experiences.

In the Western world today, Tantra has the reputation as being the "sex yoga," but its value is not based on becoming a better sexual partner (although that can become a delicious side affect). Its value is using sexual energy to purify the energy body to become a conduit for higher, spiritual energy to attain enlightenment and supreme bliss.

Tantra arose as a religious path around 600 CE as an offshoot of both Hindu and Buddhist paths, but scholars believe Tantric practices are much older, probably a secret, sacred art passed along orally from teacher to disciple.

Following ancient Hindu traditions, especially those recorded in the original Vedic texts, in which both goddesses and gods were revered for their mystical powers and influences over every aspect of life, Tantra practices reverence for both the feminine, Shakti, and the masculine, Shiva. Evidence from Neolithic India (5,000 BCE to 2,500 BCE) indicates that a creator goddess was worshipped, echoing goddess cultures from other parts of the world. However, also parallel with other cultures, new philosophies of religion and women emerged.

Hindu texts called the Upanishads, written around 500 BCE, reveal energy to be the essence of both human life and of spirit. The Hindu discovery of subtle energy and its attributes as a vehicle to enlightenment, indeed, expanded humankind's perceptions of energy and humans as spiritual beings. They created a system in which masculine and feminine energies were identified with philosophies and practices to use them for spiritual growth. The Upanishads brought the concept of chakras and human energy into human consciousness.

The Upanishads also present Brahman as the Self and the All, the cosmic universal energy that exists in everything. Brahman created Rayi, the feminine giver of form symbolized by the moon, and Prana, the masculine primal energy represented by the sun. Together, Rayi and Prana create all of the beings of the planet. Rayi, "one with all things that take form in the universe," is also considered food. Prana is "the soul of the universe, the light that animates and illuminates all." The texts advise that it is devotion to Prana that will allow us to attain immortality. "The sun, the light, is indeed the source of all energy. The sun ends birth and death." Those who follow the "path of the moon," in which offspring is desired, but who worship Brahman, are destined to return to earth after death. So revered is Prana in the texts that it is called the primal, life-force energy, and soul of the universe and is identified as the primary element of spiritual purification. The wisdom of the sages asserts that Prana is the necessary element to transcend the wheel of birth, death and rebirth.[70]

The Upanishads aggrandize masculine energy with associations to the sun, illumination, immortality, and even the giver of life, whereas feminine energy is minimized and considered an obstacle to enlightenment. In the texts, the union of Prana and Rayi creates a month, which is divided into two fortnights. The dark fortnight is Rayi, the bright fortnight, Prana. "Sages perform their devotional rites in the light, with knowledge; fools, in the dark, in ignorance." Together Prana and Rayi create life, but the "seed" (translated in some versions of the text as "semen") is considered the giver of life.[71]

At another time and place in Asia, during the eighth through twelfth centuries CE, another spiritual philosophy emerged. Mahayana Buddhists developed philosophies of spirituality and enlightenment that included very little about energy, or even a god, instead proclaiming the route to enlightenment to be through individual meditation practices. Monasteries welcomed both women and men, and for the most part the path considered women and men equals in nearly every aspect, except in one regard. It was believed that women were incapable of attaining Buddhahood, the highest goal of Buddhism.

Over the centuries, as people crisscrossed Asia and shared their religious concepts, ideas about energy, masculine, feminine, God, and enlightenment merged. Tantra was an energetic response to these two highly masculine paths. It wasn't contained and taught only in monasteries, but was carried into villages and throughout the countryside by lay people and teachers, including women. Eventually Tantra established a foothold in the Indian subcontinent, in the Himalayas, and in East Asia and Southeast Asia.[72]

The Tantrics believed spirituality was attainable through family. Rather than shunning desire, passion, and ecstasy, as the Buddhist monks and nuns did, they embraced these things and asserted that enlightenment could be attained from Tantra.[73] Unlike Buddhism, in which a male is iconic and in which it was impossible for females to attain Buddhahood, Tantra embraced both female and male as Buddha and placed an emphasis on the worship of female deities and the embodiment of female divinity.[74] Tantric teachers and texts emphasized a reverence for women and taught that worshipping women was a form of devotion to the female deities. Goddesses were represented as powerful and spiritually independent, and great works of art depicted them as wrathful yet beautiful, demonstrating that there is "pure energy even at the heart of aggression."[75]

Hindu Goddess Parvati, Consort of Shiva

Because it forced one to confront every aspect of the self, including anger, desire, and fear, while a spiritual guide assisted in the self-transformation process, Tantra was considered a "quick path" to enlightenment. Miranda Shaw, author of *Passionate Enlightenment: Women in Tantric Buddhism*, states that the goal of Tantra is "to maintain a clear realization of emptiness in the midst of passion, for this makes it possible to turn passion into supreme bliss."[76] She concurs that the self is more than body and soul, but a multi-layered mind-body continuum whose energetic layers are interwoven and interactive, which can bring about transformations and provide a bridge between humanity and divinity.[77]

Unlike the Hindu holy texts, Tantric texts never demeaned women or made them inferior to men, but rather held them in the highest esteem. In Tantric literature, men are portrayed as the supplicants and lovers of women. "A woman didn't need approval to participate or advance in Tantric circles," Shaw writes, "but a man's progress was marked by his relationships with women."[78] In ritual, it is the woman who is adored as the goddess; she can propel the male partner to bliss and illumination.

Tantric masters refined Hindu concepts of masculine energy, Shiva, and feminine energy, Shakti, perceiving them to be equally powerful, and recognizing that all beings contain both energies within them. Only through entwining feminine and masculine energy—bringing heaven and earth together—can oneness of body and spirit be attained. The goal is to create a balance between the polarities of masculine and feminine energy and reach a place of androgyny. Tantric master Bodhi Avinasha, co-author of *Jewel in the Lotus*, writes, "To balance the male and female energies, you have to be on the earth and in heaven simultaneously." She continues, "Shiva energy is static principle, pure consciousness, beyond qualities. Shakti is the dynamic aspect of reality, the world face, cosmic energy in motion. Shakti propels from static consciousness to dynamic manifestation."[79]

Tantric methods are used to create the union of Shakti and Shiva, with the most important component being kundalini energy, which Tantrics believe is the most powerful energy in the body and the propeller of spiritual enlightenment. Originating in the *kunda* gland, located behind the sacral bone at the bottom of the spine, activated kundalini energy circulates up and down the channels of the spine and through each chakra.

In Tantric tradition, kundalini energy is depicted as a snake, traditionally considered Shakti, or feminine energy, coiled at the base of the spine and in the sex organs. When kundalini is activated by sexual or Shakti energy, it uncoils and moves up the spine toward Shiva, the divine energy of the seventh chakra in the crown. Here, Shakti and Shiva unite. Kundalini then travels back down the spine, bringing Shiva down with Shakti. The joyous union of masculine and feminine energies inspires bliss and liberation. It is important to have clear chakras to allow an open pathway for kundalini to move up and down the spine. Unless we raise our own feminine energy, enlightenment is not achieved.

CAUTION: Please note that kundalini is high voltage energy, and until the chakras and nadis have been conditioned to receive it, a premature kundalini rising can cause tremendous physical and emotional discomfort. Experimentation on one's own is not advised. *Please work with an experienced teacher.*

Tantric ritual has always been an essential component of the spiritual experience. As Avinasha states, "To expand consciousness, to liberate us from the physical level of our being, we use the five senses to their limit and go beyond that limit."[80] The various practices and rituals practiced by Tantrics awaken all of the senses, sparking joy and transporting us into states of bliss as we strive to attain a connection with the divine. Mantras, mudras, prayers, meditation, and energy exercises purify the soul and encourage the rise of kundalini. In advanced circles, sexual ritual is performed by Tantrics who are proficient in energy exchange and transmutation. However, in many rituals sexual energy is engaged and exchanged with barely any physical contact.

Several qualified teachers offer introductory Tantra workshops. My teacher, Bodhi Avinasha, has groomed several protégés who teach around the world. You can find more information at www.IpsaluTantra. com.

The Healing of Sexual Energy: Taoism

The spiritual path of Taoism emerged in China around 500 BCE, and like Tantra, has found its way to the West in recent decades. Taoists recognized the duality of the universe, the polar opposite energies of

Yin (female and dark) and Yang (male and light), and their intrinsic nature in all of life. Everything in life is made up of complementary energies of Yin and Yang, and Taoist principles guide the dance to maintain the balance between the two.

The Taoists identified Chi (with the uppercase C) as the ever-present energy that exists in all of the universe, and chi (lowercase C) as the life-force energy present in the human body. The Chinese also discovered the meridian system, a series of energy channels associated with the organs and glands, and learned of the importance of maintaining clear channels for the sake of good health. They recognized that the cause of disease is a blocked meridian; when this block is cleared, the disease is healed. They also recognized that clear energy channels contribute to a deeper spiritual connection.

Taoist adepts learned the benefits of life-force energy and its potency for vitality, and developed systems to harness energy and move it through the meridians to maintain youth and good health. With their emphasis on virtuous living, the Taoists believe that the energy of love, joy, kindness, gentleness, respect, and honesty will deliver life-force energy to the organs to strengthen them.[81] Recognizing the especially potent and positive life-force energy, or *jing*, generated in the sexual organs, and its potential for health and spiritual growth, the Taoists learned methods to maintain and control the energy.

So valued is sexual energy that the Taoists warn against wasting it. Man's sperm contains life force called *ching*, which is more potent than chi. Ejaculation carries between 200 and 500 million sperm and uses up a third of a man's daily energy.[82] When sperm is ejaculated, a man is thus drained of energy and vitality. Taoist adepts believe that the use of ching for anything other than producing a child is a waste. However, sexual activity is not avoided, but rather encouraged, for if harnessed and used correctly, this valuable energy can greatly increase a man's health and vitality. The practice requires that a man retain his ejaculate during orgasm and circulate the life-force energy that dwells in the ejaculate into the body and through the organs.

Most of a woman's sexual energy originates in her ovaries, where eggs are produced and which hold the potential for human life. Like a man, but to a much lesser extent, a woman can lose vital energy during orgasm, but her greatest depletion occurs during menstruation. When the egg is released from the ovary and is unfertilized, it is expelled from the body in a flow of the blood that was held in reserve to nurture a potentially new life. The life-force energy held within the egg and blood drains from the woman's body, depleting her of life-force energy and vitality.

With Taoist exercises, women can build up the sexual energy in their sexual organs and channel it through the meridians to the other organs and glands, energizing them for optimal health. Hormones are regulated and the body remains youthful, sexually balanced, and healthy. In addition, symptoms of uncomfortable periods are often alleviated. The tone of the vagina and surrounding muscles increases, discouraging energy leakage. If a woman disregards the importance of stimulation of her sexual energy, her yoni will deteriorate, her organs will lose their vitality, and her energy will dissipate.

The greatest authority I have found regarding Taoism and sexuality is Mantak Chia, who is a prolific writer on the subject of energy and sexuality. He co-authored *Healing Love Through the Tao: Cultivating Female Sexual Energy* with his wife, Maneewan Chia, and teaches energy workshops around the globe. For more information, log onto www.universal-tao.com.

Yin Yang

Balanced Sexual Energy

Sexual energy is located in the second chakra. In a woman, this is the area around her cervix. The Sanskrit word for a woman's sexual organs, particularly the vagina, is *yoni*. The yoni is the source of our feminine essence and radiance. The hormones estrogen, estradiol, and progesterone are regulated by the ovaries and influence our true nature, which is to be nurturing and giving, emotional and sensitive. It is this energy that lights the fire of a woman's sensuality and passion. A woman with a balanced second chakra is thus confident, has a healthy sexual drive, and radiates feminine energy that is appropriate for the moment. She is eager and willing with her partner, and if she is single, maintains sexual pleasuring on her own. The practices that bring the sexual chakra into balance reduce stress and contribute to better regulated emotional responses.

A woman with an *unbalanced* sexual chakra is fairly easy to identify. She often exhibits an urgency to find a sexual partner and packs her calendar with events at which she can hunt for sexual prey. She may act inappropriately and dress in clothing that screams, "Look at me, I'm a hot woman!" She may act flirty and seductively with the opposite sex and too quickly go to bed with a love interest. She may take on several lovers in a short period of time. If her hunger is not satisfied, she becomes frustrated and possibly aggressive and angry.

Such an excess of sexual energy may create a cycle of low self-esteem in a woman. She may attract lovers who she thinks are interested in her and engage intimately with them before finding out their true intentions. When a man doesn't call afterwards, and she realizes he was cashing in on her generous offer for sex, she will disrespect herself and possibly put herself down as "not good enough." As she repeats the cycle, giving more sex to get less love, the cycle repeats, and her self-esteem plummets.

It is also easy to recognize a woman who has a deficiency of sexual energy and feels neutral and asexual. Lacking confidence and preferring to hide from attention, she becomes the proverbial wallflower. She may not date, and she resists parties and other social occasions. She may dress to camouflage or downplay her feminine figure and expresses very little of her femininity to the world. She is often uninterested in or "uptight" about sexual topics. Her sexual drive is low, as is her overall vitality. She lacks radiance and often goes unnoticed in a group. She may be fearful of male energy.

In both of these cases, it is possible that unbalanced sexual energy is the result of childhood conditioning, psychological issues, hormonal imbalances, and health challenges for which more advanced healing methods are necessary. But for general energy imbalances, Swatistana exercises are greatly beneficial. A woman with overcharged sexual energy will feel less urgency for satisfaction as she learns to convert her sexual energy into whole-body healing. She will think more clearly when in the presence of masculine energy. She will attract lovers who are of higher integrity, and her self respect and self-esteem will increase dramatically. A woman with a low-energy second chakra will feel more feminine and sexy and more confident in herself as a woman. She will charge up her libido, which stimulates a healthy sex drive. Overall, she will become a healthier, more radiant woman.

Menopause and Hysterectomy

The Swatistana chakra is a nonphysical energy center, and while it is associated with the ovaries, the energy center will always be present, even if the cervix and ovaries have been surgically removed or if the body has moved through menopause. Sexual energy can be stimulated and maintained through various exercises.

Second Chakra Energy

Sex Energy and Creativity

Why are we so attracted to musicians, artists, movie stars, and other creative types? *Because they are sexy.* They are high in second chakra energy, which translates into creative energy. Women with balanced sexual energy are highly creative and easily express their creative ideas through a variety of channels, including art, business, family and other human relations, and even personal appearance. They create beauty and sensual pleasures, cleverly overcome challenges with inspired ideas, and follow their hunches on beneficial opportunities.

Creativity is an expression of the soul, and when we bear forth our inspiration, we grow in confidence and self esteem. Confidence is very sexy. Keep the following formula in mind:

Balanced Sexual Energy = Creativity = Confidence = Sexiness

I cannot say enough about the importance of expressing ourselves creatively. Creating something can bring joy to our soul. It is our soul's language. When we allow our inner expression to come forth, we feel balanced, healthy, alive, and filled with love and appreciation of ourselves. Studies show that people who allow their inner voices to emerge have a strong sense of self, and higher self-esteem. Gloria Steinem writes that creative people have higher-than-average self-esteem and (interestingly) higher than average degrees of androgyny. Creativity comes from intrinsic interest to express the self, not from external reward. The ability to express creatively requires confidence.[83]

Many people have discovered that when they channel their sexual energy into creative pursuits, great works can be born. Napoleon Hill, author of the classic *Think and Grow Rich*, writes that "Sex energy is the creative energy of all geniuses. There never has been, and never will be a great leader, builder, or artist lacking in this driving force of sex." He explains that genius comes from mind stimulation by opening it to "available forces," which he defines as "inspired ideas," hunches, Infinite Intelligence and intuition. And the stimulus that empowers one to tap into these forces is sex energy that has been "transmuted from desire for physical contact, into some other form of desire and action, before it will lift one into a state of genius."[84] From an analysis of 25,000 men, Hill discovered that men over the age of forty make their greatest accomplishments, and more often beyond the age of fifty, because of they are less over-indulgent in the "physical expression of the emotion of sex."[85]

Hill's studies (conducted in the 1930s) did not include women, but I believe that there is a connection between the scientific fact that women focus on (think about) sex several times *less* than men[86] and their inherently strong intuition and connection to Infinite Intelligence. Perhaps it is our transmuted sexual energy that inspires us creatively throughout our lives, rather than only after the age of fifty.

We can increase our creative energy and all of its manifestations by stimulating and balancing the second chakra. Following are several useful exercises.

Sex Chakra Balancing Exercises

By now, you must be super ready to charge up and balance your sex chakras. Most of the exercises covered in this chapter, which come from Tantric and Taoist practices, are very basic and will help you generate and circulate chi in your body and "juice you up" as a woman. They are all useful in stimulating and energizing the sexual chakra, which will help you feel sexier, healthier, and more alive!

Shake Those Hips

The sex chakra is seated in the bowl of our pelvic area. Our hips are the most powerful part of our womanly body, and it is from our hips that the powerful, feminine energy exudes. In symbolic representations of a woman's body, breasts and hips are the most prominent features. A woman's hips are wider than a man's so that she can accommodate a baby. A woman's hips sway when she walks, they move sensually when she is making love.

We need to keep our hip area loose and fluid to maintain our health, beauty, and vital sexual energy. A few easy movements will keep our hips flexible and strong, charge up our sexual energy, and help it circulate around our body. Once mastered, which could take as little as a few minutes, the exercises given below can be incorporated into dance movements. Practice the following exercises to percussive, rhythmic music.

Hip Thrusts

1. Stand with your feet shoulder-width apart, hands on hips.
2. While keeping your upper body straight, thrust your hips forward, then tilt them back so your back arches at the hip area. Move the hips forward and backward to the beat of the music, really feeling the full extent of your hips in motion. Continue for a two or three minutes.
3. Focus your breath to the movement of your hips. Inhale while your hips are tilted back. Exhale as you thrust your hips forward. It is best to inhale through your nose and exhale through pursed lips. Perform this for two or three minutes.
4. Now it's time to add a yoni squeeze. When your hips are thrust forward, squeeze your yoni, exhale through your

mouth, and say the mantra *Ooh*. (Remember, this is the mantra to stimulate your sex chakra.) As your hips tilt back, release, squeeze, and inhale through the nose. Then thrust your hips forward again, squeezing the yoni, exhaling, and saying *Ooh!* Perform this for three or four minutes.

5. Performing this same action of thrusting and tilting back with the yoni squeeze, breath, and mantra, bend your knees and lower your body as if you are sitting in a chair. Continue this movement for one or two minutes.

6. Go lower still. Squat all the way to the floor, maintaining the same rhythm and movement. Imagine you are sitting on top of a lover and stimulating him (or her) with your hip movement. You may place your hands on the floor to help maintain your balance. Continue for another minute or two.

7. Finally, when you are exhausted, release the movement. Come all the way down to the floor. Sit on your knees and bend your body forward to the floor, arms extended, as if you are prostrating yourself before someone. This position allows the energy to flow up the spine from the pelvis to the rest of the body. Stay in this position for one minute and release. Imagine what wonderful things this exercise is preparing you for!

Hip Circles

Hip circles loosen the pelvic girdle. If you are a beginner, it is best to start this exercise slowly and then build up speed as you feel more comfortable with the movements. Essentially, with this exercise you will move your hips around in a big circle while your upper body remains in place.

1. Stand with your hips shoulder-width apart.

2. Slowly move your hips in a big clockwise circle by thrusting them forward, then to the right, tilting them back, then thrusting to the left. Feel the stretching of your hips, upper thighs, and buttocks as you move. All your focus is on your hips, so your upper body should remain somewhat still. Repeat the circle six more times.

3. Change directions and move your hips counterclockwise in a big circle. Repeat six more times.
4. Now it's time to speed it up a bit. Return your hips to a clockwise rotation and move the hips a little faster. Speed up the movement, the hips moving in big circles, while the upper body remains as still as possible. Repeat six more times.
5. Rotate in the opposite direction at the higher speed, seven times total.
6. Continue the movements, rotating the hips in opposite directions at various speeds, for three to five minutes, or as long as you can do this comfortably.

Sexy Moves: Dancing

Now let's incorporate the hip movements into dance. Dancing, especially with powerful hip movement, is one of the most potent methods of generating and balancing our female sexual energy. Dancing stimulates, clears, and energizes our feminine energy centers and opens the energetic doors to pulsations of love, creative expression, spirituality, and sexuality. Dancing charges up our feminine essence and makes it flow outwards. It helps us feel and become more feminine. It conditions our bodies to move in more flowing, feminine ways. Dancing conditions our bodies to become stronger and improves our posture.

To be vital, healthy, and vibrant women, we need the stamina to sustain exuberant, active lovemaking for a healthy, satisfying period of time. Dancing helps us to raise our endurance, and loosens up our body so that we can be dynamic, creative, beautiful love goddesses.

The act of dancing is an ancient, primal form of expression. There is a general consensus among historians and anthropologists that all other forms of dance were derived from the original sacred dances.[87] Andrew Lang, author of *Myth, Ritual and Religion* writes that we "cannot find a single ancient (religious) mystery in which there is no dancing."[88]

Dance is a universal expression that has been performed in the most primitive to the most sophisticated of cultures. Cave paintings dating back 40,000 years show people dancing. It is believed that shamans originally facilitated trance dancing in their tribes so that the participants could reclaim their "soul parts" and channel spirits. Dance enabled them to live in the spiritual world and the physical world simultaneously and transcend the physical into ecstasy.[89] Paintings of Sumerian priestesses show them as dancing women, twirling, hair flying, snakes in their hands.[90] Egyptian royal tomb art shows dance performances at celebrations, feasts, funerals, and religious services. In India, before the advent of Buddhism, princesses and cultured women studied dance.

Dancing helps us dissolve and release negativity. It contributes to our emotional, mental, physical, and spiritual healing. It brings us into a state of full presence, helping us get out of our heads. It disconnects from worry and burdensome thoughts and leads us to feel true spiritual freedom. We can also fully "feel" our body and its miraculous structure of muscles and bones. We can appreciate the sensuality of our arms, breasts, hips, and legs as we move in beautiful positions.

By giving yourself a minimum of twenty minutes of dancing two or three times a week—really moving and stretching the body in a creative way—you can greatly enhance your feminine sexual energy and tone your muscles. Toned muscles are not only attractive, but they're extremely important in order to be healthy. And healthy is SEXY.

Dance Exercise

Dance to your favorite songs. Dancing to songs you love will make this a fun exercise rather than a chore. Dance and feel just how sexy you are. Allow yourself to be carried away by the music. Let your body be moved and driven by the music. Feel the swaying of your hips. If you can, dance in front of a full-length mirror so that you can see your body as it moves. Watching yourself dance will not only help you learn how to move and position your body, but will also give you the opportunity to see just how incredibly beautiful your body looks as you dance. Find songs with different rhythms. Begin with a slow song. This is your warm-up. With this song, focus on stretching the muscles in the body. Move very, very slowly, as if in slow motion, as if you are dancing in honey. Stretch your arms and reach out as far as you can. Bend forward at the waist to stretch even further. Now bend to the side at the waist, slowly bend to the other side, spread your legs wide open and slowly move your weight from one leg to the other, back and forth. Move your legs, slowly and feel the music in your body. Incorporate slow hip movements, like circles or a cat stretch. Experiment with your body, moving and stretching. You're not a ballerina. This is not about form, but feeling your muscles stretch and move. Stretch. Be creative. No one is watching.

The next couple of songs should have a moderate beat. Continue to move your body in a stretchy way. Watch yourself as your limbs move away from the body, your arms making circles, undulating and moving like a snake. Incorporate hip thrusts and circles. Move to the beat.

Your next song can be the same rhythm or faster. Continue the movement, really focusing on hip movements. Remember, you can move your hips while moving your arms, feet, etc. Belly dancers do it all the time.

Finally, move to faster, more rhythmic songs like techno or house music, or even good old disco. Really let your body move to the beat. At this point, your movements will become aerobic. Your limbs will still be stretching and moving, your head will be moving, and you can even leap into the air. Experiment and have fun.

Continue dancing your heart out for at least twenty minutes or up to an hour. With regular dancing, you will feel healthier, your body will become toned, and you will also become a great dancer.

If you feel that you want to take dance lessons, I highly encourage it. There are several dance forms, such as ballet and modern dance, that can train your body. African dance and belly dancing can also help you connect with the primal essence of your feminine being.

I highly recommend a form of movement that is currently taking the country by storm. This is the S Factor developed by Sheila Kelley. Based on moves performed by exotic dancers, S Factor teaches women to move their entire bodies in slow, circular movements. An added bonus is learning to pole dance, which requires tremendous strength and skill. This workout is reputed to help women feel sexier, stronger, and better about themselves as women. Log onto www.sfactor.com to see if there is a class near you. The workout is also available on DVD.

Breast Energy

So much emphasis is placed on a woman's breasts in our culture. Models, movie stars, and television celebrities possess glorious bosoms, and if they weren't born with them, they enhance what they have with push-up bras and implants. But our breasts are so much more than adornments. They are the glands that feed life. They not only give milk to babies, but also contain and emit strong doses of feminine energy.

Until I began to study Tantra, I felt insecure about my size 36AA breasts. I felt unattractive compared to women with larger breasts. I had a very difficult time even finding a bra that fit. I did bust exercises, lifted weights, used various creams, and even indulged in an electrical current therapy to stimulate growth and firmness. These all seemed to work to a certain extent, but never did I bulge out of a full A-cup. I even investigated breast augmentation, but decided it wasn't for me.

The greatest exercise, I discovered, was full and utter acceptance of my little breasts. I am an emanation of the Goddess, and I have a divine body. I finally learned self-love and began to love my body for what it is. Our bodies, after all, are the carriers of our soul and spirit. I began to love the breasts I was given and began to be very grateful for their health and cuteness.

Breast Health: Massaging the Breasts - The Deer Exercise

Years ago, I heard about a Taoist exercise that claimed to make the breasts grow. By merely rubbing the fingers in circles around the breasts, I heard, the breasts would grow up to two inches. Wow! Ms. Small Breast here latched right onto that exercise. Two inches would take me up to an A cup, if not a B. Every day, after showering, I would rub circles around my breasts. Even now, several years later, I continue to perform this exercise.

My breasts still aren't B cups, but the benefits of this simple action are so beneficial that I will do it every day, forever. I feel energetic, sexy, and in touch with my body. And while my breasts are still hovering in the A-cup range, they are toned, firm for my age, and healthy. Best of all, I am proactively keeping my breasts healthy. Rubbing the breasts aids in the elimination of toxins, and it increases the flow of chi in them, which greatly contributes to breast health.

The Taoists discovered an energetic connection between the breasts and the organs and glands in the body. They learned that by stimulating the breasts, the life-force energy in the ovaries is activated, and by circulating it throughout the body, the organs and glands are filled with chi, which charges them with revitalizing, healing energy. Negative emotions are replaced with positive feelings of peace, harmony, and joy.

The breasts are especially associated with the pineal, pituitary, and thymus glands. The pineal gland, located at the top of the head and associated with the crown chakra, controls the body's time clock. The pituitary gland, located behind the third eye, controls growth, metabolism, and other bodily functions. The Taoists consider the pituitary gland to be the master gland that activates all other glands. The thymus, located near the heart center, is considered the gland of rejuvenation. It is believe that when this gland is properly stimulated, the aging process can be reversed.

The Taoists developed a breast stimulating exercise called the Deer. In this practice, the hands rub around the breasts in circles in many repetitions to initialize energy stimulation in the ovaries. It can be practiced while standing or sitting. Taoist masters Mantak and Maneewan Chia explain the ancient practice in their book, *Cultivating Female Sexual Energy*, which describes the science of sexual power and health. A basic overview of the exercise is given below.

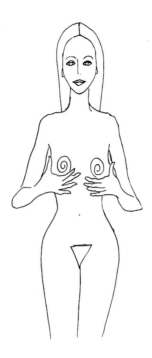

The Deer

This exercise is to be performed on naked skin, and is most convenient to do after a shower. Using massage oil or an all-natural body lotion is optional.

1. Rub your hands together vigorously to warm them and bring energy into them.
2. Place your tongue at the roof of your mouth. The tongue in this position acts as a bridge as the energy flows from the back of the body to the front, completing the energy circuit of the body.
3. Place the index fingers, middle fingers, and ring fingers of both hands on your breasts, about an inch from the nipples. Rub very slowly and gently, pressing lightly into the breasts, just enough to push them into your rib cage. Move in inward circles, with your hands moving up your sternum, around the top of your breasts, and down the sides of your breasts. Very

103

quickly, you will feel the energy in your clitoris and vagina activate. Enjoy it as you breathe steadily.

4. After a moment, imagine the energy moving to your crown chakra to stimulate your pineal gland. Focus on the energy for a minute. Continuing to rub and breathe, and allow the delicious energy to hover for a minute at your third eye to stimulate your pituitary gland, and then at your heart to energize your thymus gland. Feel your mind open and your heart fill with love and compassion as you continue to rub and stimulate the energy.

5. Continue rubbing, your tongue still at the roof of your mouth, breath still steady and strong, and now visualize the energy of the glands merging and flowing systematically to your organs. Start with your lungs, and focus on the energy and allow it to increase. Systematically, with focus and intention, move your attention to your heart, and feel the energy bloom inside it. Concentrate and experience love energy. With the same concentrated focus, see the energy move, grow and move from one organ to the next, including your stomach, kidneys, liver, and intestines. The entire process of breathing, massaging, and moving energy takes about ten minutes. Performing this exercise daily will contribute to overall health and vitality.

Modified Deer with Hip Thrusts

In its purest form, the Taoist Deer exercise provides full-body health benefits by providing chi energy to all of the organs. However, in a modified form, it can be performed in less time and deliver much of its health and vitality benefits directly to the breasts. The modified Deer is described here.

1. As with the original Deer, rub your hands together vigorously to warm them and bring energy into them. Place your tongue at the roof of your mouth. Place your index fingers, middle fingers, and ring fingers on your breasts, about an inch from the nipples. Rub gently at a moderate speed, lightly pressing

into your breasts, but just enough to push them into your rib cage. Move your hands up your sternum, around the tops of your breasts, and down the sides of your breasts. Up and in is the motion.

2. While massaging, bring the rhythm of your breath in with the movement of your hands. Inhaling while your hands move up your sternum, exhaling as your hands move down the sides of your breasts. Be conscious of your breasts and any energy that may be aroused in your ovaries, uterus, or vagina.

3. Now add hip motion. By pumping your hips during the breast-rubbing movement, you stimulate more chi and oxygenate your body even more. Your hip motion also stimulates the energy in your sacrum and sexual organs, which is extremely beneficial for women.

4. As your hands move over the tops of your breasts, thrust your hips forward and exhale. As your hips are in the forward position, focus on your anal and lower vaginal muscles and squeeze them tightly. (If you chant *ooooooh* while squeezing your yoni, it will activate your organs even more. Do as you do during the hip exercises described above.)

5. As your hands move back down the sides of your breasts, release the squeeze and tilt your hips back, inhaling. Do the exercise slowly enough to allow you to really squeeze and release your yoni muscles as you move your hips. Perform twenty-one times. Rubbing your breasts with inward circles detoxifies them, as the lymph glands are drained by the rubbing action. Detoxified breasts mean a lowered risk of breast cancer.

6. Now move your hands in the opposite direction and repeat the same actions twenty-one times. By changing the direction of the motion of your hands around your breast, moving down your sternum instead of up, you assist in the toning of your breasts and help prevent sagging and possibly help lift any sagging that has already occurred.

7. Rubbing in outward circles (down your sternum, and around the bottom and to the sides) tones the breasts. Legend has it that inward circles increase the size of the breasts and outward circles decrease the size.

A lot goes on in the body with this little exercise. In only a few minutes, you will give your body an energetic shower that will set you off right on your day. The Deer is an opportunity to be fully present in your body and to appreciate your breasts.

Self-Pleasuring

Ever noticed how blissful you feel after good sex with someone you care about? Sexual energy gives us that famous glow. We feel positively beautiful and confident. We think we can only achieve this kind of experience from lovemaking, but with this next technique, you can create the glow on your own.

There is actually a link between sexual expression and self-esteem. In her book, *A Revolution From Within*, Gloria Steinem cites an article that reports that orgasms and other forms of sexual expression are so important to self-esteem that a majority of psychiatrists believe that people who are deprived of orgasms and regular sexual outlets experience loss of self-esteem.[91]

While chakra-balancing exercises are highly important for sexual health and well-being, I believe it is equally vital to give your body an occasional nuclear-powered blast of sexual energy. Your sexual energy is at its highest when you are sexually stimulated and at the precipice of an orgasm. An orgasm is an energetic explosion in which megatons of beneficial life-force energy are released and drench your cells and organs. Your entire body is positively charged, your cells heal, and your energy field radiates energy.

Sex with a partner is the most common way we raise our sexual energy to its greatest heights. However, you don't need a partner to get the benefits of a sexual energy shower. Self-pleasuring is the next best thing. Even if you have a sexual partner, self-pleasuring is extremely therapeutic. It is one of the most powerful ways to stimulate a burst of sexual energy on your own. Most people think of self-pleasuring, or masturbation, as merely a way to "get off" sexually, but masturbation in itself has many positive benefits. It releases stress and built-up sexual energy and feels pleasurable. When performed consciously, it increases your femininity and keeps you juicy and youthful. Self-pleasuring is thus extremely important for women who don't regularly engage sexually with a partner. Many women without partners are abundant in sexual energy and feel frustrated without release. Fortunately, self-pleasuring in the proper way will satisfy their sexual urges and benefit them body and soul.

Women with partners will also greatly benefit from self-pleasuring. If a woman's sex drive is low, it will raise her overall sexual energy and help her feel sexier and more apt to want to create an energetic connection with her partner. Empowering our sexual energy raises our confidence, which may help us feel more secure about communicating with our partner. Discovering the moves and sensations that bring us the greatest pleasure will help us to better communicate to our partner those things that turn us on, perhaps bringing new life to a wilting sexual relationship.

With or without a partner, denying your sexual energy is doing a disservice to your body and soul. Not only do you miss out on great pleasure and opportunities to give your body an energetic gift, but you may become sexually frustrated and direct your energy in ways that may not be most beneficial, such as moody outbursts or burying yourself in work to redirect and burn off the energy. You may have difficulty concentrating. If you ignore it long enough, eventually your sexual energy will dry up altogether.

For women who are unable to achieve orgasm, self-pleasuring is not only energizing, but also therapeutic. There are a number of reasons a woman doesn't climax, including psychological remnants of sexual abuse and other trauma, religious programming, poor health and/or unbalanced hormones, or even having a partner who doesn't turn her on. When self-pleasuring is practiced, the furnace of the second chakra fire is stoked, and the abundant energy is available for use in the body. Self-pleasuring in the safety of a private, comfortable space, in full control of the stimulation, may actually help a woman reach orgasmic pleasure. Climaxing is extremely liberating and may eventually help a woman to climax sexually with a man. In the case of sexual trauma, please know that self-pleasuring is no replacement for psychological, therapeutic healing. Emotional wounding needs much deeper healing than self-pleasuring alone can give, but it can be a tremendous first step.

Whether you are a woman with no sexual wounds or one with deep scars, take heed that the energy stimulated and released in an orgasm may stir up emotional memories of all kinds and cause you to go into emotional process upon orgasm. You may release grief or mourn an old situation or relationship that you may not have completely dealt with in your mind and heart. Crying is not uncommon in self-pleasuring, and the good news is that by releasing the sadness, you are purifying your body, especially your sexual chakra, and releasing wounds and healing scars that stand in the way of your complete inner joy.

Perhaps the topic of masturbation makes you feel uncomfortable. It is not something we normally talk about, even with girlfriends. Or maybe you think it is a wrongful act. Perhaps you were told through your religious upbringing that masturbation is a sin. The patriarchal religions decided self-pleasuring was a sin when they declared that sexual feelings were meant ONLY for marriage and procreation and not to be wasted on recreation. This suppression of human sexuality is relatively recent (starting only four or five thousand years ago); prior to that, the earth- and Goddess-based religions celebrated sexuality and self-pleasuring was no doubt a part of the festivities. Other paths, such as Tantra and Taoism, venerate the vital energy present in our bodies and see it as a key to life.

Like all our sexual activities, self-pleasuring is a natural gift, especially when performed with reverence for our body. Our body, with all of its mystical feelings and functions, is a miraculous gift, and self-pleasuring is our birthright.

Self-Pleasuring Exercise

The Taoists and Tantrics, those world-renowned experts on sexual energy, have given us methods that best harness our sexual energy for overall healing. The exercises you are about to learn are techniques used by both of these masters of energy. The exercise includes two basic steps:

1. Stimulating the genitals to raise sexual energy
2. Harnessing the energy with breath and circulating the energy throughout the body.

With this exercise, your sexual energy is stimulated and raised to the point of orgasm. But rather than orgasmically releasing the energy through our sexual organs and into the air, the energy is pulled up into the body and transmuted, or changed, into healing life-force energy, which disperses through the body and cells.

Self-Pleasuring Preparation, Part One: Yoni Stimulation

The yoni is a pleasure zone, with folds and caves that feel good when touched in certain ways. When you touch yourself to make your yoni feel good, your yoni will make your body and soul feel good. The yoni has three very sensitive areas, which when stimulated manually or during sexual intercourse, will bring a woman to heights of pleasure and send her into a climactic state of bliss during orgasm. These three orgasm-making areas are listed here:

1. The clitoris is the tiny organ hooded by flesh at the top of the outer lips of the vagina. This little organ is home to a giant-size ganglion of nerve endings that raise sexual energy when stimulated. Stimulation feels really good.
2. The cervix is located deep in the vagina at the mouth of the uterus. This area is stimulated by the deep thrusting of sexual intercourse or when a dildo is inserted deep into the vagina.
3. The G-spot is the rough-feeling tissue located an inch or two inside the vagina at the front wall (the side facing the belly). This area is stimulated by a penis during intercourse. It can also be stimulated with a finger or toy designed specifically for the G-spot.

When any area of the yoni is stroked with the intention of stimulating it, warmth occurs as blood engorges the area and nerve endings come to attention. During self-pleasuring, a woman may wish to touch herself with her hands or use a vibrator to arouse sexual energy. Do what feels comfortable to you.

Vibrators

Vibrators may be new territory for you, so let's talk about them. Vibrators, sex toys, and dildos may carry a certain stigma. While some women may associate them with pornography or nasty sex, vibrators are actually fantastic health aids for women. Originally created specifically to stimulate sexual pleasure, vibrators raise the sexual energy that maintains the health of the sexual organs.

For single women (and married women, too), a vibrator is the next best thing to a boyfriend. With a variety of shapes, from a realistic-looking penis to long, smooth, colorful tubes to flat, buzzy things you lay directly on the clitoris, these toys stimulate a woman's sexual energy, help her feel good, and assist her in achieving orgasm. Since the woman is in control of the pressure and movement of the vibrator, she can stimulate herself in ways that feel best to her and either extend the feelings of pleasure by playing with herself for a long time, bringing herself close to the brink of climax and then stopping and starting back up again, or giving herself focused stimulation for a quick orgasm. Women who have a difficult time climaxing may benefit from the use of a vibrator or sex toy, as they can experiment alone and receive stimulation that is more powerful than manual stimulation.

Sex toys are easier to acquire than you think. You can go into an adult store, which by the way, is no longer just a seedy back-alley shop geared to men buying porno. Nowadays, it's more likely to be a mainstream retail outlet for women and men who enjoy sensual pleasure. Taking a trip to an adult store is not only fun, though; it's educational, too. You will be amazed at the variety of toys available and at the people who patronize these stores. They aren't just men looking for pictures of T and A, but also businesswomen, moms, bride's maids looking for gag gifts, couples, respectable gentlemen—you name it. Sex toys are gaining respect, and people who honor their bodies no longer avoid the places that offer the products that bring them pleasure.

Of course, if you wish to acquire a toy in top secrecy, there are mail order and the Internet. The selection is wide, and you will have fun just looking at the infinite options for sexual pleasure. Also, some adult toy companies offer parties for the home that are like Tupperware parties where the hostess offers a selection of different toys for purchase.

Rumor control—vibrators have been given a bad rap, as some say they are addictive and spoil women, making them less orgasmic with a man. Not true. Studies have shown that women who use vibrators on their own are *more* orgasmic with men, as they are more aware of their bodies and what turns them on. Women who use vibrators can feel more sexually free, and if a woman brings a vibrator into a love-making session, it can increase the couple's fun and intimacy.

Self-Pleasuring Preparation, Part Two: Transmutation Breath

In Tantric practices, the breath is extremely important, not only to introduce oxygen into the body, but for controlling energy. The Transmutation Breath will pull the highly energized sexual energy up from the sexual chakra, and transmute, or change, it from sexual energy into healing, life-force energy, which we then breathe into all other chakras and organs.

You will actually feel the energy sweep though your torso and ripple out through your limbs as you perform the Transmutation Breath. Afterwards, you will feel sexually satisfied and energized, your auric field will be glowing, and a magnetic radiance will surround you. (Please refer to the breathing and Energy Lock exercises in Chapter 4 to prepare for this part of the self-pleasuring exercise.)

It is important to get a feel for the Transmutation Breath technique before applying it to the self-pleasuring exercise, so practice it first.

Transmutation Breath Technique

1. With your mouth closed, touch the tip of your tongue to the roof of your mouth, about an inch from the back of your teeth.
2. Inhale slowly through your nose. As you inhale, visualize the sexual energy from your genitals moving through your torso to your third eye.
3. Once your lungs are full, apply a root lock by squeezing your anal and outer vaginal muscles. Squeeze tightly and hold.
4. Simultaneously, apply a chin lock by closing off your sinus cavities with the back of your tongue and tilting your chin down toward your chest. The combined root lock and chin

lock create a vacuum, which is very important for containing the energy in your body.

5. Hold the breath for a count of 7.
6. Take an extra sniff of air and then exhale slowly through your lips, releasing the root lock and chin lock.
7. Feel the energy spread through your body and infusing every cell with healing energy.
8. Repeat this six more times, for a total of seven breaths.

NOTE: Because the Transmutation Breath will help a man delay ejaculating, this is an especially effective exercise for men who ejaculate prematurely. Share this technique with your man.

Self-Pleasuring Exercise: Bringing It All Together

Now it's time to bring the practices of yoni stimulation and Transmutation Breath together for an energetically stimulating and healing time. Be present in your body as you feel the delicious sensations, knowing you are benefiting the body in many ways.

1. Lie down on your bed in a comfortable position.
2. Stimulate your yoni. If you are familiar with manual stimulation and self-pleasuring, you may have a favorite method for achieving orgasm, which may be touching your clitoris, inserting a vibrator into your vagina, etc. Do what feels best for you. For those of you who are new to self-pleasuring, you may wish to experiment. My recommendation for this exercise is clitoral stimulation. The clitoris is extremely pleasure-inducing and the most accessible of sexual organs. Use your fingers or a vibrator to stimulate it to arouse energy. Sometimes just the tactile stimulation will get you going, but other times, fantasy may help. Imagine making love to your husband, boyfriend, or fantasy lover.
3. As you stimulate your yoni, feel the energy rising and the warmth spreading through your pelvic area. Maintain the stimulation for at least five minutes. (The Tantrics say that it is most beneficial to maintain sexual stimulation for

twenty minutes, but even five minutes of stimulation is very therapeutic.) The longer the sexual energy is stimulated and present in the second chakra, the better. If you come close to climaxing in a short time, pause and touch another part of the body, such as your thighs or breasts, so that the energy will subside. Once the sensation of climaxing has subsided, return to stimulating yourself. After five to twenty minutes, bring yourself to the edge of an orgasm.

4. Perform the Transmutation Breath by inhaling deeply, and imagining the energy flowing from your yoni up through your torso into your third eye.

5. Clench your yoni muscles in a root lock and go into a chin lock to keep the energy inside your body. Feel the warm wave of energy wash over your body. Hold the breath for a count of 20.

6. Release the root lock and the chin lock, exhale slowly, and imagine the energy leaving your third eye and moving through your body.

7. Continue to tease yourself to the brink of orgasm three or four times, performing three or four Transmutation Breaths with each near-climax.

8. Finally, let yourself go with a full, head-on orgasm. Perform several Transmutation Breaths so that you will have taken seven breaths in total during the exercise.

9. Now is a good time to relax, pray, think positive thoughts. Allow your body to be still so that the energy fully penetrates it. You may naturally flow into meditation.

This exercise can be performed two or three times, if you would like, but be sure to continue the Transmutation Breaths, as you want to contain all of the healing energy. Perform self-pleasuring as many times during the week as you can. For women who don't have much sexual energy, this is especially important. I recommend that you perform this exercise a minimum of once a week. You can also learn various Tantric versions of the Transmutation Breath in *Jewel in the Lotus* by Sunyata Saraswati and Bodhi Avinasha.

As you become familiar with this exercise, you may want to experiment with the visualization of the energy as it travels through the body. Using sexual energy to heal all organs, the Taoists visualize the breath traveling up the spine, up and around the brain, and down the front of the body, washing over the organs, and returning to the yoni.

This circulation of energy is called the Microcosmic Orbit, and is fully explained in *Healing Love Through the Tao: Cultivating Female Sexual Energy* by Mantak and Maneewan Chia.

NOTE: In Tantric union with a partner, breathing is extremely important. It creates an energy circuit between the male energetic body (traditionally a man) and the female energetic body (traditionally a woman). Conscious breathing with a partner during sexual union increases intimacy and brings more depth to the sexual experience.

Healing Sexual Trauma

Over the years in workshops and professional situations, I have interacted with women who at some point reveal that they had been sexually abused. Years after the abuse, many of these women were struggling to heal the wounds of violation. I always thought sexual abuse was a rarity that happened to only the poorest and least sophisticated people, but hearing these stories, I was shocked to discover that women of all walks of life, even wealthy women living in the best of situations, have been victimized.

In a sexual union, the energies of men and women mingle. In healthy relationships where each partner is a healthy and positive human being, this energy is healing and beneficial. But when a woman is raped or violently abused, she takes in the negative energy of the violent man. This energy will often remain in the woman's body and psyche for the rest of her life, creating a scar in her energy field. We all know that it takes scars a long, long time to fade away. Sometimes they never do.

However, a woman who has been sexually abused can be healed to a certain point. The exercises in this chapter and other chapters in this book can help in the healing process by inviting her to reconnect with and love her body, maybe for the first time since her trauma. The exercises will help her realize that her physical body is a vehicle for divine energy and that she is much greater than the wound. The healing energy charged by the exercises will help to ease negativity from the chakras and infuse them with positive energy.

CAUTION: Please note that I am not a medical physician or psychiatrist, and *these exercises are by no means a replacement for professional assistance.* They can, however, aid in the healing experience. Be warned that if trauma has been harboring dormant, these exercises may actually stir up old feelings and cause you to plunge back into trauma. If you have been victimized by sexual abuse, please consult your medical professional before you begin performing these exercises.

I recommend the book *Aphrodite's Daughters* by Jalaja Bonheim, which offers an outstanding collection of stories of the sexual experiences of women, from the most joyful and delicious to those telling of horrendous abuse. If you have experienced sexual abuse, reading this book may help you find a virtual sisterhood of women who have also endured your pain. Perhaps some healing comes from knowing you're not the only one facing this challenge.

6

YONI MAGIC

As a woman, you are the owner and shepherd of one of the most mystical and mysterious masterpieces of all creation. A vagina. Your vagina, along with her sister organs, the uterus and ovaries, are what define you as a female human, and empower you as a feminine energetic force. As you know by now, I refer to the vagina as the *yoni*. Translated from the Sanskrit language as "womb," "origin," and "source," and more literally as "vulva," the yoni is associated with divine female energy and is the sacred symbol of the Great Goddess.[92] Your vagina or yoni may be the source of your greatest pleasure, your deepest agony, or your utmost confusion. It may be the garden for the joy of your life or your cemetery of bad memories. You may share it widely and willingly. Or hide and protect it. It may be healthy and juicy, or it may experience disease and cause frustration and sadness. It may have given birth, or it may remain barren. It may have been violently abused. It may be your place of celebration or your source of shame and guilt. Our vaginas carry a lot of history, not only our own personal story, but the chronicles of many millennia of women's history. Appreciating and treasuring your yoni, and honoring it for all that it does and is, is essential to loving yourself as a woman.

While every woman possesses a vagina, most of us are not quite sure how to treat it or care for it. We don't understand its power. We know very little of our own vaginal history. Most of us were raised in a culture in which we never uttered the word *vagina*, our mothers always modestly referring to it as "the privates" or "down there" or using some other vague language. In our religious upbringing, we may have been taught that touching our vagina is bad, that we must save our virginity until marriage, and that women who engage in sex outside of marriage are seductresses and sinners. The sex education we received in school was clinical and consisted of medical drawings of the organs and a brief explanation of menstruation. We learned about sex and the sexual functions by talking with our girlfriends or through fumbling experimentation, sometimes with boys, sometimes alone. For many women, therefore, even in their adult years, the yoni is a very mysterious place.

The power of the vagina has long been hidden and barely thought of except as a sexual organ and a place for a baby to be made. But believe me, the vagina has more than a biological function. It is a multi-dimensional gift to humanity. Physically and sexually, it can be the source of great pleasure for a woman and a man, with its bundles of nerves and muscles and flowering flesh that feel exquisite when touched. Energetically, it is a life-force generator, the source of human sexuality and creativity. It helps us remain youthful. Spiritually, it is the woman's connection to her inner goddess, and for men it is considered the portal of enlightenment. Historically, it has been worshipped for its life-generating powers and its representation of the Great Goddess. Culturally, it has been the target of laws, mores, and values. As an object or commodity, it has been sold and photographed for the sake of money or fame.

As a woman, I think it is imperative for you to understand the glory of your yoni and the significant role it has played in our spiritual and cultural development.

You may never consider your vagina, other than when you menstruate or feel an abundance of sexual energy. But please know that your yoni is one of the most precious and powerful things on earth, for it has the potential to create raw, powerful, and positive energy that will have a profound affect on you and others, both men and women. Your yoni is not merely your feminine genitalia. It is the source of powerful, feminine energy that can be used to connect with spirit, others, and, most of all, your feminine self.

Yoni as a Symbol of the Goddess

There is no denying that goddess and yoni worship prevailed in ancient times. Archaeologists have discovered representations of yonis and the goddesses in Europe, Asia, Australia, and Africa. Figurines, paintings, and relief sculptures dating back as far as 40,000 BCE prove that since humans first developed a consciousness of the divine they worshipped a goddess. Scholars suggest that this reverence for the female stemmed from a woman's mystical abilities to create new life. Creation stories were spun, and the Goddess was celebrated as the Creatrix of life.

Rufus C. Camphausen states, "That the Yoni was the first to be recognized as having immense magical powers and importance can easily be understood by looking at certain aspects of life known to our earliest ancestors. One of these is the simple fact that, as now, only women were able to bring new life into the world."[93] Birth is an awesome sight, even today, and was no doubt a holy, magical experience to early human.

Equally mystifying was a woman's blood. Of the approximately 270 different primates, thirty-one menstruate, and only one, the human, loses a significant amount of blood.[94] Unlike a normal wound in which bleeding is associated with pain, or even death, a menstruating woman can bleed for days for no seeming reason and with no consequence. Who but a divine being could live while bleeding for days? Leonard Shlain, author of *Sex, Time, and Power*, surmises that this phenomenon was perceived as a supernatural power that might induce a fear of women.[95] Many cultures celebrated menarche, or the first period, with ritual to impress upon the girls their new power and responsibility.[96]

The richest prehistoric cliff art in the world is found in sub-Saharan Africa, where modern humans emerged. A primary symbol of our oldest mother, the pubic V, often painted ochre red to symbolize the blood of childbirth and menstruation, was painted in African caves as long as 40,000 years ago. Rock paintings in the shape of spirals, straight or wavy lines, petals, and concentric circles in series, symbolizing woman and the Great Mother, have been found in central and south Africa. Lucia Chiavola Birnbaum, author of *dark mother*, writes that "after 50,000 BCE, migrating africans [*sic*] took these signs to all continents, where they are seen today in the caves and cliffs around the world."[97] Italian archaeologist Emmanuel Anati confirmed that "the oldest divinity we know is centered on a woman." He calls ochre red "the most ancient evidence of artistic creation in the world."[98]

Archaeologists have discovered artifacts representing the Goddess and Her (our) yoni in sites throughout Europe. Drawings of pubic triangles and vulva shapes dating from 30,000 BCE to 14,000 BCE have been found on rocks and the walls of caves.[99] Renderings of women were also found, one of the more famous of which is the so-called Venus of Laussel, a 26,000 year-old relief carving found in a cave in France. This is a woman holding a horn in one hand resting her other hand on her belly. In a cave of Austria, a rendering of a group of three dancing women was carved in a cave wall about 32,000 years ago.[100]

Drawing of Venus of Laussel

When French archaeologist Andre Leroi-Gourhan studied the Paleolithic art of sixty-two sacred caves in southwestern Europe, he discovered that eighty percent of the female symbology, including vulvas and the female figure, was found in a central location in the cave, whereas eighty percent of male symbology, including animals and hunting scenes, was found in peripheral areas, such as the entry of the cave and tunnels. He also discovered several smaller caverns decorated solely with vulvas, which Leroi-Gourhan surmises were "sanctuaries" that may have been used for sacred worship, including fertility rites and sexual initiations.[101] Tiny sculptures of women with pendulous breasts, bulbous thighs and buttocks, and well-defined pubes, carved in rock and ivory, have also been found in many locations. The so-called Venus of Willendorf, a tiny sculpture dating to about 27,800 BCE, is probably one of the best known artifacts. Standing with her arms over her large breasts, a round belly and large hips, this ochre-covered figurine was found near the Danube River in Austria.[102]

Venus of Willendorf

In her digs in Turkey, Greece, and Italy in the 1970s and 80s, archaeologist Marija Gimbutas discovered artifacts that gave more evidence of Goddess worship. Hundreds of stone, bone, and ceramic figurines dating from 7,000 BCE to 3,000 BCE feature breasts, buttocks and thighs, pubic triangles and vulvas, and various linear designs incised in the clay. Spirals, circles, V's, and triangles representing the yoni and feminine energy appear on these figurines and on vases and ritual objects. Gimbutas' study of these and many other symbols derived from nature, such as wavy lines, zigzags and vertical lines, helped her see the emergence of a symbolic "language" of the Goddess. With the prevalence of female figurines, with their beautiful, symbolic designs, a notable absence of weapons and warfare, Gimbutas surmised that in Neolithic Europe (7,000 - 3,000 BCE), woman, the Goddess, and the giver of life, were venerated, and that egalitarian societies in which men and women were equal existed. Men were represented as partners or consort of the goddess. Gimbutas found symbols of the male, such as phalluses, but female symbols and sculptures were predominant.[103]

Neolithic Goddess Figurine

Around 700 CE, when Tantric Buddhism fully emerged in Tibet, India, and Southeast Asia, worship of the feminine power, or Shakti, the energetic catapult toward enlightenment, continued. The yoni, often symbolized by the downward-pointing triangle, became an emblem of the divine feminine and continues to be a focus of worship today. The yoni triangle appears in several yantras, which, when meditated upon, invoke the nurturing energy of the goddess. The Sri Yantra is perhaps the most powerful and revered of all sacred yantras. Illustrating the union of Shakti and Shiva energy, this yantra pattern is composed of several downward-pointing Shakti, triangles uniting with the upward-pointing, Shiva, triangles, rendering a harmonious balance between the polar energies.

Sri Yantra

Sculptural and painted representations of the yoni are also found in temples and sacred sites throughout India. They are often ritual objects. Sculptures, paintings and artifacts of the vulva, and of goddesses exposing their yonis with thighs spread open, are present in the settings of Tantric ritual,[104] to which offerings of flower, honey and butter are made. The elaborately decorated facades of the Devi Jagadamba temple in Khajuraho and other temples feature sculptures of naked women and men engaging in sexual activity, many of which show men adoring the yoni.

Art and artifacts of the yoni and females exposing their vulvas have been found in Asia, Africa, South America, and Europe. In the British Isles and Western Europe, for example, sculptures such as these are carved into the walls and above the doorways of cathedrals and monasteries. The Sheila-na-Gig, or Sheela, shows a woman with her legs agape to fully expose her large-lipped yoni. One of the most famous Sheelas is carved into the stone wall of the church at Kilpeck, Hereforshire, in the British Isles. This wide-eyed being appears to be androgynous, except for her yoni, which she holds wide open, inviting us to look or enter.[105] In some instances, the doorway below the Sheela represents the yoni, perhaps showing the entry through a gateway to the safety of the womb of the Mother Goddess.[106] Many of these sculptures are, indeed, well worn from hundreds of years of people touching the sacred yoni as they enter the church. Some believe that the Sheelas served as protectors, their yonis warding off evil, reflecting the ancient beliefs of the great philosophers and historians Pliny (23-79 CE) and Plutarch (46-126 CE), who reported that even great heroes and gods ran from the sight of the naked yoni.[107]

Rendering of the Sheila-na-Gig at the church at Kilpeck, Hereforshire

The Sexual Ritual

In the eyes of some of our ancient brothers and sisters, sexuality and spirituality were one, and mortal women were considered the closest link to the Goddess. In these cultures, sexual ritual was a holy act. There was no shame or anxiety, only a reverence for her feminine nature.[108]

Innana, Queen of Heaven and Earth and goddess of civilization and culture, music, and love making, was revered around 4,000 BCE, in the ancient Mesopotamian city of Sumer. Great temples were built in her name, such as the Temple of Eanna, established in Sumer's first city, Uruk. There the great goddess presided over civil and religious activities. Sacred records indicate that sexual priestesses, called *hierodules*, performed sacred rites to Inanna.[109] Some scholars speculate that high priestesses took the role of the goddess, with the king of the land becoming her bridegroom, and together they joined in sacred marriage, as a symbolic rite to assure fertile land and abundant crops.[110]

In nearby Babylon, Inanna was called Ishtar. Ancient records indicate that the customs of Ishtar included sexual rites performed by special temple priestesses, who were often known as Charites, or Graces, since they were skilled with a unique combination of beauty and kindness, called *charis*, which later translated into the English word, charity. Merging mother-love, comfort, and mystical enlightenment, the Charites transformed animal instincts of sex into spiritual love.[111] It was also customary for a virgin to prepare for marriage by sacrificing her maidenhood and experiencing her first sexual deed under the auspices of the temple. The Greek historian Herodotus reported that it was customary for every woman, at least once in her life, to sit in the temple and engage sexually with the first man to throw a coin at her, which she gave to the temple.[112] While today we can only speculate as to the actual traditions of the temples, evidence from art and artifacts points to the probability that sexual rituals were performed as sacred acts of worship to the goddess. Centuries later, these sacred, sexual practices of priestesses and lay women were interpreted as acts of wickedness, and goddess Ishtar was branded the Mother of Harlots.

Aphrodite, goddess of love and beauty, was worshipped at a temple established in the eighth century, BCE, at the highest summit of the Acrocorinth temple complex in Greece. Ancient reports indicate that more than a thousand women lived at and served in the temple, until it was destroyed by the Romans in 146 BCE. We can speculate that the women served the temple with all of the reverence of the priestesses of Sumer and Babylon. But in the first century, when Christian apostle Paul arrived in Corinth to convert the townspeople, the city was considered corrupt, and he perceived the union of a man with a sexual temple priestess as sinful.[113] All that remains of the temple today is rubble. The concept of the sacred sexual priestess appears to have disappeared along with it.

A Yoni Ownership Guide

I once overheard a man say, "Women *think* men have all of the power, but really *women* do in their sexuality. Men would do anything for sex. Women have leverage. But women, wanting acceptance or fearing they will be alone, will just give it away for no reason."

Wow. That stopped me in my tracks. It's true. Today, so many women feel they have little power and give little regard to the precious treasure they possess. We fail to see the multidimensional significance of our yoni. We practically ignore it. We hardly ever worship it. I believe it is imperative for women to recognize the spiritual, emotional, and physical aspects over which our yonis preside. It is only when we gain respect for our own sexual mystique that perhaps a wave of respect and reverence for the yoni by everyone will crest.

It appears that even in our earliest cultures, women understood the power of the yoni. It was the female who decided how, when, and with whom they would engage sexually. In *Sex, Time, and Power*, Leonard Shlain theorizes that 150,000 years ago, the earliest Homo sapiens female made the connection between sex and pregnancy. At that time, mortality during childbirth was extremely high, and women were very cautious about becoming pregnant. It was the female of the species who consciously overrode her drive to mate, particularly when she was ovulating, and decided to say no to a male's sexual advances, a phenomenon Shlain calls free will.[114] Shlain surmises that the development of free will inspired the male to hunt for gifts in the form of meat to impress the female and so gain her sexual favors.[115] Likewise, in ancient, matrifocal cultures, women engaged sexually with a variety of men, and often not knowing or caring who the fathers of their children were. Later, with the rise of certain religious and legal customs (like the laws of inheritance), women were forced to withhold sexually until they married.

Women have sometimes recognized the value of the yoni and withheld sexual favors until suitors charmed them enough, and in some cases, used it as leverage to get what they wanted. *Lysistrata*, written in the fourth century BCE, by the Greek playwright Aristophanes, illustrates this power. Lysistrata, a female leader opposed to the Peloponnesian War, rallies the women of Sparta, Corinth, and Boeotia to withhold sex from the men until they cease fighting. The warriors, unable to go for long without the "feminine touch," eventually capitulate. This same tactic was used more recently in 2006 as the women of a small town in

Colombia being destroyed by gang violence and murders engaged in a "cross-legged strike," withholding sex until the men withdrew from violent activities and disbanded the gangs.[116]

Probably the most influential force on our current Western perception of sex has been the Judeo-Christian religion. Patriarchs and Church fathers established guidelines to control lineage and inheritance and provided a framework within which individuals could operate sexually. As religion took over cultures and the religious laws were adopted by the people, sexual energy came to be seen as a threat to one's entrance into heaven. For all of their good intentions to separate order from chaos, our religious forefathers established laws and guidelines that instilled in women conflicting feelings of their sexual power. Women were conditioned to repress their sexuality and hide their bodies. Proverbs warned men to beware of "the loose woman, the seductress, the adventuress . . . for her house sinks down to death."[117]

In our puritanical culture in the United States, a woman who exhibits her innately sexual nature is often called seductress, sinner, whore, tease, easy. All of this name-calling reinforces a woman's fear of her innate sexual self as her reputation is created by those who judge her sexual expression. "She slept her way to the top." "She'll sleep with anybody." "She's a good lay." The diminished reverence of women's sexuality sends our gender into the lower realms of self-esteem.

But our perceptions of sexuality began to shift during the 1960s with the creation of the Pill and the rise of women's liberation. Dismissing the traditional, passive womanly roles and concepts of sexuality, women began to express themselves more freely. Sex became acceptable. Society began to accept the new standards of behavior. In general, women have taken greater control over many aspects of their lives and have gained some respect and equality.

Today, women are re-learning the multidimensional power of the yoni and enforcing practices that heighten the health and energy of our own bodies. We're gaining an understanding of feminine energy and exercising wisdom in our sexual behavior and choices. Our first step to understanding our sexual nature is to know that our body, including our yoni and our sexual energy, is a divine creation with dynamic capabilities for healing, connecting, and energizing. We must honor the sex act and understand that it delights both men and women. It is a sacred gift to the one we share it with. We must reinstate sacredness of our bodies and our sexual energy and re-establish our position in the world as powerful beings. We must take responsibility of our bodies and sexual energy and do what we can to protect them. We are in charge of our vaginas, the decision-makers of our lives. We must be wise with our vagina and use it discerningly, and grant its power and pleasure only to those we love and trust and who love, deeply honor, and respect us.

I believe it is vital for a woman to understand her sexual self if she wants to make the right decisions concerning her yoni. Sex can be a vehicle for spiritual growth and a sacred way to connect with a man. It can be a physical, earthy pleasure. Or it can be a commodity. All of these are fine, but it is important for a woman to know herself and decide what is most honorable for her body and soul. What makes her truly happy? She needs to know what generates positive energy in her, what drains her or creates negative energy in her. She needs to participate in the sexual actions that are most suited for her. It's fine if she wants to pose for pornography, as long as she understands what she is doing is more than merely earning money. What is happening to her soul, to her energy? If posing for pornography creates a positive vibration in her, it is good. If it makes her feel demeaned, she might want to consider a new career. It is fine to have sex with someone you don't know very well, as long as you use your best judgment (and condoms) and understand the results of the sexual exchange. But does the experience leave you feeling beautiful and empowered? Or used and horrible?

If a woman has sex with someone because she is too weak or fearful to say no, or because she wants love or approval, she will feel drained afterwards. She may feel dishonored by the man and have negative feelings about herself. It might benefit these women to refrain from having sex, examine their fears and reasons for engaging sexually, then take measures to improve their perception of themselves and their need of approval from others, and raise their overall self-esteem. It would benefit them to avoid certain men at all costs, as many men unconsciously drain women of their energy and make them feel used. Transmuting their sexual energy through self-pleasuring could be greatly helpful for these women. Their energy will rise, their sexual chakras will heal, and their self-esteem will improve.

Women need to honor themselves enough to commit to doing only what makes them feel good. Even the slightest doubt, the tiniest nagging fear, is an indication that something is not right, and a woman must be honest with herself (and her partner). If she is pushed or tempted, she must stand firm. And if she makes a mistake, she must forgive herself and understand that everything is a learning experience.

If a woman has a lot of sex with one or several lovers because she likes sex, has an abundance of sexual energy, and a desire to satisfy it, she needs to be aware of the effects of all this sex; is it draining her or revitalizing her? I feel that sexual experimentation is a positive activity, as long as the woman consciously uses her energy and engages with men who sincerely honor and respect her. But if the sex is energetically draining her and lowering her self-esteem, it would benefit her to reconsider her lifestyle. If she feels energized, happy, and empowered from her experience, she is most likely consciously and energetically connecting with the appropriate people, and generating positive energy.

Sexual expression is a vital part of the soul of many women whose love and appreciation of masculine energy is demonstrated by sharing and releasing her sexual beauty with a variety of people. She may feel a past life as an ancient sexual priestess and be unconsciously sharing her feminine energy to heal and generate a positive influence in her partner, which ultimately uplifts the energetic web of life. For her, sex is fulfilling, empowering, and generates positive energy. She intuitively identifies men who honor women. She has a positive radiance that enhances her feminine energy.

In all sexual encounters, I recommend that women engage sexually only with men (or women) who honor them, who have positive energy, and who are partners for potentially positive sexual experiences in which both partners feel empowered. Engaging sexually with someone is a grand experience in which tremendous energy between two people can be exchanged. If your partner has positive energy, you will receive his or her positive energy. If it is negative, you will receive that, too. Once you receive someone else's energy, it will stay with you for several days. Be very discerning, therefore, in your sexual encounters. Use your wisdom and intuition to judge the intentions of a person and the goodness of a situation, and don't hesitate to stop if something doesn't feel right. Do not worry about hurting his feelings or receiving disapproval. I agree with author and sexual philosopher Camille Paglia, who says that date rape is partly a woman's responsibility.[118] Make wise choices about the company you keep and the situations you put yourself in. Be sure you send out clear energy. You can be sexy and still have strong boundaries. You can be sexy and maintain clear communication. You can bestow positive energy on the world and command respect.

Whether you are having sex for money, having lots of sex because you love it, or having no sex at all, beware of one danger—self-judgment. Our puritanical society is quick to judge women who are sexually active. People may call her a slut, a whore, or a tart. If she is not sexually active, they may say she's uptight, frigid, or dried up. Please know that your sex life is your business. BUT, this being said, it is critical that you know how it feels to YOU. Do YOU feel OK about yourself after a sexual extravaganza? Do YOU feel energized and happy? YOU are the priestess of your body temple and the gardener of your own flower bed. How you feel about your experiences can guide you to do what is best for YOU. You must be honest with yourself. Once you determine who you are and what sex is for you, and once you establish and enforce your boundaries, then you will feel good about yourself and create positive energy within. If you have made mistakes that have caused you anguish, then you must forgive yourself and commit to doing only the things that are good for you.

If you feel you have deep negative feelings about your sexuality, whether you feel your energy is out of control or have no energy at all, take time for yourself and take stock. Are you engaging with a lot of men because you feel empty and desperate for love? Were you drunk and are you now regretful? Are you afraid of men and sex? Do you suffer from sexual trauma from past experiences? Take time for yourself and write down what is on your mind. Practice the sexual exercises in this book. You may also want to seek out a counselor or attend a workshop that will help you heal and take charge of your body and energy. Tantra workshops are excellent. You can find many Tantra teachers and web sites on the Internet. My teacher, Bodhi Avinasha's, website is http://ipsalutantra.org. The Body Electric (www.thebodyelectricschool.com) and the Human Awareness Institute (www.hai.com) are also fantastic places where you can learn about your sexual energy and heal any wounds that stand in the way of your happiness.

When women begin to understand the magnificence of yoni energy and learn to use it wisely, we may not only influence positive changes in our selves and self-esteem, but may also subtly influence a rise in general consciousness regarding the yoni. Perhaps women will gain more respect, and men will be more honoring of women. Female self-esteem as a whole will rise and will, hopefully, spread around the world. If all women use their sexuality in empowering ways, it will raise and strengthen the feminine vibration around the planet.

Yoni Power

The physical design of the yoni is divine. The vagina is the tubular organ that receives a man and his seed. It enables a woman and a man to unite physically, energetically, and spiritually. At the entryway of the vagina is the clitoris, which gives a woman great pleasure during the act of intercourse. At the other end lies the uterus, the incubator for growing life. It regularly sheds its lining and bleeds until it supports a baby. The hormones generated in this part of the body can rule a woman's emotions and sex drive. Sexual energy gives life force energy to a sexual partner and to the self. It is a mysterious, multi-dimensional, and miraculous part of the woman's body. No wonder woman and her yoni was worshipped and revered in ancient times!

Indeed, the yoni is a sacred entryway to the cave of wonder and power, the portal to ecstasy, enlightenment, and healing. To honor yourself, you must honor your own yoni and all of its dynamic powers, functions, and capabilities. It is important to maintain your vital, feminine health by keeping the yoni healthy and strong. To enjoy sexual pleasure, you must learn what feels good and what doesn't feel good, and maintain good vaginal health.

In honoring our yoni power, one of the first things we can do is love our menstrual cycles. Unlike ancient times, when blood was considered the sign of the Goddess, today women barely think about menstruation until they have to buy tampons or pads. Or if their period is late. Some women disdain their monthly flow, especially if they experience severe cramps or heavy periods. Some women call it "the curse" and hate every aspect of it. We need to remember the life-giving significance of our blood. Menstrual blood is the symbol of our femininity, life, and fertility. When you bleed, therefore, relish it as part of your womanhood. Celebrate it every time you change a pad or a tampon. If you have cramps, treat yourself gently, and tune into the workings of your body. The average woman menstruates from the age of twelve until around the age of fifty. These thirty-eight years are our fertile years, during which we are filled with the most vital life force energy. We need to honor our bodies during this time. We need to teach our daughters about the glory of menstruation and perhaps revive the traditional initiations when a young woman steps into womanhood with the onset of her menses. And, for heaven's sake, let's please discourage any woman from supporting the pharmaceutical companies who push pills that cause them to bleed only once every three months! This is not only horribly dishonoring of the nature of a woman's body, but it is probably unhealthy and dangerous.

We must acknowledge the power we have as women who can create new human life. This is a divine power. Incubating and growing life in her body is a function that only a woman can know. Many women and men consider motherhood to be a woman's purpose for living. Some religions still encourage women to bring forth as many babies as possible. But other women have no desire to have children, preferring to express their creativity in other ways, and/or avoid childbearing altogether as a way to not contribute to overpopulation and the strain on the planet's resources. Some women change their minds. A career woman in her mid-forties may finally acknowledge the biological clock ticking inside her.

While it is a blessing that women can take charge of their bodies and decide whether or not they want to have a baby, I think our methods of birth control leave much to be desired. The most convenient ones, such as the Pill, the birth control rods that are implanted under the skin, and now the birth control patch, work for many young women, but they often wreak havoc on our hormones and give us headaches and vaginal yeast infections as well as emotional disturbances like depression and aggression. Old-fashioned rubber barrier methods, such as the diaphragm and cervical cap, can be inconvenient and uncomfortable, not to mention nearly impossible to get out! The rhythm method, in which the woman tracks the days of her cycle and has sex only on the days she is infertile, can be effective if her cycle is extremely regular and she is very cautious on the days that are anywhere close to her fertile days. The good old condom is a good choice, but many men and women don't like the barrier.

As the owners of yonis, it is up to us to protect and maintain our general health. We must protect our yoni from disease and practice safe sex by using a condom. It only takes one messy encounter to contract a sexually transmitted disease that can range from being a nuisance to being life-threatening—chlamydia, herpes, gonorrhea, syphilis, hepatitis, genital warts, and HIV. Make it a practice to use a condom until you know and trust your partner.

Our general health is reflected in our yoni, and its smell is one indicator of that health. When a woman is completely healthy and devoid of toxins, her yoni will smell mild. For example, a male friend of mine dated a woman who was a strict raw vegetarian and ate no meat or dairy and drank no coffee or tea. He told me her yoni smelled like a garden. Wow! What woman wouldn't want such a sweet smelling yoni? With some discipline, we *can* have it. A body plagued with food allergies and bombarded with low-quality foods might be the home of a yoni that smells foul, that grows the smelly, cottage cheese discharge of candida (yeast), and incubates the bacteria that cause odor and itching. Eating a healthy diet will help you to maintain a healthy yoni. If you have candida, you can cure it with proper nutrition and a few remedies. There are several books on the market on the subject. One I recommend is *The Complete Candida Yeast Guidebook*, second edition, by Jeanne Marie Martin and Zoltan P. Rona., M.D.

A healthy woman has a toned yoni with strong muscles. To maintain your sexual health, it is vitally important that you keep your vaginal muscles strong. Not only will they help to pump up vital life force energy, but strong muscles will also contribute to enjoyable sex and assure that you remain continent. As we have children and grow older, our muscles lose tone and become flaccid. Unless we take proper care of our yoni and perform exercises that strengthen the muscles, we may accidentally pee in our pants when we sneeze or run.

In the exercises in this chapter, you will learn methods that will increase yoni strength and energy. But first, let's do a brief review of the basic anatomy of the yoni.

Yoni Anatomy

I once saw a comic in which a man was standing behind an x-ray machine. The image of his "inner plumbing" was a simple pipe. In the next frame, a woman stood behind the x-ray machine. The image revealed her insides to be a complicated network of pipes, faucets, drains, and valves going every which way. There's truth to this. A man's sexual system is fairly simple compared to the complexity of a woman's, which is composed of an intricate network of organs, glands, muscles, chemicals, and hormones that interact with each other and influence every phase of a woman's life. A woman's body is designed primarily for reproductive purposes; she can conceive, incubate, give birth to, and feed a child, and there's also a nice side component: receiving and giving pleasure through sexual intercourse. The interplay of a woman's inner workings influences her entire being, physically, mentally, and emotionally. Throughout a woman's life and during the waxing, fullness and waning of her reproductive years, sexual chemistry and energy remain in flux, causing a multiplicity of feelings, sensations, drives, and impulses that change from day to day. Part of the mystical power of the yoni is its influence over its owner's moods, physique, sex drive, and more.

But Americans are fairly clueless. They often use words such as "pussy," "beaver," and "poon," or derogatory names like "slit," "hole," and "cunt." These words diminish the sacred beauty and power of the yoni. If we used words that honor or beautifully describe the yoni, such as those used in Eastern cultures, we could not only begin to honor our own yoni, but perhaps inspire more reverence and appreciation of the yoni among men. Consider using names that illustrate the physical and mystical beauty of our vaginas: Lotus, Venus Mound, Gateway of Love, Mystical Valley, Pillow of Musk, Golden Gate, Mystic Rose, or Jade Gate. Be creative and give your yoni a sacred name. Or simply call it yoni.

Knowing your yoni and its power and capabilities will help you to appreciate yourself as a woman. Let's take a look at the various parts of our female anatomy.

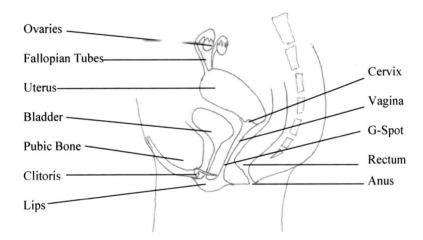

Mons pubis: This is the hair-covered upside-down triangle shaped-area at the front of the female body between the abdomen and the legs. Fatty tissue covers the pubic bone, with the lower portion of the tissue forming the outer lips. This area was the inspiration for the ancient symbol of woman, the downward triangle, an emblem of the sacred feminine. Taoists and some others refer to this area as the Mound of Venus.

Vulva, outer and inner lips: This fleshy area is the gateway to the vagina, referred to as the labia. The outer lips, labia majora, are the two

133

pillowy pouches covered with pubic hair and holding sweat glands. The inner lips, labia minora, are the smooth and slender lips that hold glands that generate moisture when stimulated. When sexually aroused, the lips engorge with blood and swell up to three times their normal size. The Sanskrit term for the vulva is *yonipuspa*, which translates as "vulva flower."[119]

Clitoris: The hooded button at the head of the opening of your love canal is a bundle of nerve endings that, when stimulated correctly, build great pleasure in the body and mind. The clitoris functions very much like the male penis, in that it engorges with blood when stimulated. Touch, rubbing, or vibrating the clitoris sends sensations deep into the yoni and triggers the stimulation of sexual energy, at which point lubrication begins to ooze from the vaginal walls.

Vagina: This is the tubular organ into which a man thrusts his penis and through which menstrual blood flows and a child is born. The vagina consists of tissue and highly flexible muscle which a woman can consciously control. Two glands at the opening of the vagina secrete a thick, lubricating liquid that increases as a woman is stimulated sexually. The Tantrics refer to this as "flower water," "musk of desire," or "musk of intoxication," and it is perceived as a valuable, healing fluid. The muscles at the opening and surrounding the vagina can be strengthened and toned through exercise, contributing to a woman's overall health.

Ovaries: Two of the most important components of female sexual energy are our ovaries, which are located at the ends of the two fallopian tubes attached to the left and right sides of the uterus. The Taoists believe that ovaries are the primary source of feminine sexual energy, called *jing*, which is even more potent than the life force energy of chi.[120] It is the energy from the ovaries that contributes to the development of higher consciousness, vitality, youth, and sexual health.[121] According to the Taoists, thirty to forty percent of a woman's energy goes into the production of sexual energy, which regulates our menstrual cycles and the production and process of the egg during the cycle.[122] So potent is the jing generated by the ovaries that the goal of many Taoist and Tantric practices is to harness its power and use it to heal all other organs in the body.

During a woman's fertile years, the ovaries produce eggs that travel through the fallopian tubes to the uterus to be fertilized or discharged through menstruation. During an average woman's lifetime, she will have as many as 300 to 500 menstrual periods. While the popular belief is that a female human is born with her lifetime supply of eggs, new scientific evidence indicates that new eggs are produced throughout her reproductive lifetime.

The ovaries produce estrogen, progesterone, and testosterone, which induce puberty, signal the hypothalamus and pituitary glands during the menstrual cycle, and maintain bone strength and brain function. Estrogen and progesterone affect several parts of the female brain, including the amygdala, the center of emotions; the hypothalamus, which controls the body's organs; and the hippocampus, the area of learning and memory.[123]

From the time a girl is eighteen months old and continuing for two years, her ovaries begin producing estrogen in amounts that compare to an adult. Some scientists believe this surge of hormones primes the brain and ovaries for reproduction.[124]

Uterus: This pear-shaped organ is the incubator for the embryo and fetus after an egg has been fertilized by sperm. When a woman is not pregnant, its thick lining of blood, which is generated to nourish the implanted fertilized egg, is shed every month. This is the menstrual flow.

Cervix: Located at the very top of the vagina, the cervix is the entryway into the uterus. In Tantric theory, the first chakra is located here. (But please note that a chakra is a non-physical energy center, so even if the uterus, and thus the cervix, are removed, the energy still remains.) For some women, the cervix is sensitive in a very pleasurable way, and it can be very enjoyable for a woman to have her cervix massaged manually. Deep penetration in which the head of the penis moves against the cervix may also be pleasurable.

G-spot: This is a spot of spongy, sensitive tissue located on the frontal wall of the vagina, about a finger's length inside, between the public bone and cervix. Containing a cluster of nerve endings, blood vessels, glands and ducts, the G-spot engorges with blood when stimulated. For some women, stimulation produces great pleasure, often bringing them to orgasm. At the point of climax, it is not unusual for many of these women to ejaculate, squirting fluid from her urethra. Women who are unaware of this kind of occurrence may believe they have leaked urine. This fluid has properties that are very similar to a man's ejaculate (but without the sperm). Tantrics call it *amrita*, a Sanskrit term meaning "divine nectar," and it is believed to have great healing powers.

It is interesting to note that the G-spot wasn't discovered by Westerners until around the turn of the 20th century and was not made public until 1982 in a book titled *The G-Spot*. It is likely, however, that women who participated in the art of love making, particularly Tantra and Taoism, have always known about their G-spots.

Pelvic floor: The vagina, lips, and anus are surrounded by groups of small muscles referred to as the pelvic floor. This web of muscles forms a hammock-like structure that supports the reproductive organs and controls every little part of the exterior of the lower body. The muscle groups that create this web include the pubococcygeus muscle, which contracts the vagina and is often called the love muscle; the urogenital diaphragm, which surrounds the urethra and controls the urinary stream; the anal muscles, which control the anal sphincter muscle; and the pelvic diaphragm, located just outside of the anal sphincter muscles.

You can identify the various muscles of your own pelvic floor by focusing on each group, one at a time, and squeezing it tightly. Many exercises given in this book require you contract (squeeze) the muscle groups of the entire pelvic floor, including those at the vagina, urethra, and anus. Squeezing all of them once, often called the Root Lock, both pumps up sexual energy, and tones the muscles. The perineum, the little area located between the vaginal opening and the anus, is an important area of the Root Lock and the source of energy generation, and the focal point for many Taoist and Tantric exercises.

Good overall health, vitality, and sexual radiance are the result of a toned pelvic floor and strong muscle groups. By maintaining healthy muscles, vital energy is generated and maintained. A nice side effect is that toned muscles feel tighter, and bring more pleasure to you and the man during sexual intercourse.

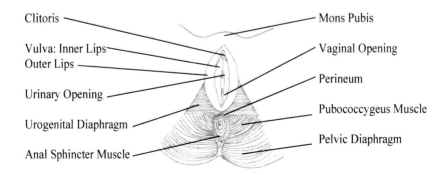

Yoni Toning Exercises

You can have great control over your vagina. I remember one of the first erotic movies I ever saw. It was set in a bar, where a beautiful, nude Asian woman performed on stage. Her first trick was to place a cigarette at the mouth of her vagina and puff smoke from the cigarette. She blew smoke rings with her vagina! Her second feat was squatting on the stage, picking up a ping pong ball with her vagina, and sucking it into herself, then bending over backwards, pointing her vagina at the audience, and spitting the ball out at them!

A Korean War veteran once described to me the talents of Korean prostitutes he had known. They would serve up a treat called King Chakabobo, in which the woman would sit on a man's lap, with him penetrating her. While she barely moved her hips, her vaginal muscles grabbed his shaft, held it tight, and undulated up and down, massaging it into ecstasy. The man described it as one of the most incredible sensations he had ever felt during intercourse.

These two stories illustrate the incredible muscle control a woman can have. No doubt it would take plenty of practice to strengthen our vaginal muscles so finely, but building our other muscles also takes practice. Asian women are legendary for their yoni control. They are taught from an early age various exercises that help them to move their vaginal muscles. All women have the same potential to move their yoni muscles. All it takes are a few simple exercises that you can do anytime, anywhere, and your yoni will become tighter, more flexible, and healthier. Yoni exercises also help you gain control of the various muscles in the vagina. They help you generate and move your feminine energy throughout your body. This will contribute to a youthful, sexy glow.

Easy Vagina Exercise

The easiest and most fundamental exercise you can perform to strengthen your pelvic floor is "squeeze and release." Gynecologist Dr. Arnold Kegel identified and recommended this simple movement (now called the Kegel exercise) to his patients, especially women who had given birth and were experiencing incontinence, to encourage strength and elasticity in their pelvic floor.

This simple exercise, performed a few minutes a day, can help to strengthen the muscles very quickly. It can be performed at home, in the car, or while watching TV or talking on the telephone. It engages all of the muscles of the pelvic floor and is easiest to perform while seated.

1. Concentrate on your vaginal and anal muscles and squeeze them as tight as you can, taking care not to engage the abdominal or gluteus muscles. The sensation is the same as if you stop the stream while urinating.
2. Hold the squeeze for ten seconds and release it slowly.
3. Relax for five seconds, then squeeze the muscles for ten seconds.
4. Continue this action for at least ten rounds. Repeat several times a day. It's fun to squeeze to the beat of music, so turn it up and go to town!

The Vajroli Mudra

The Vajroli Mudra is a Tantric exercise that takes yoni muscle building a step further by adding breathing, energy visualization, and energy locks. This not only strengthens our vaginal muscles, but it also moves our feminine energy through our body. This exercise is equally beneficial to a man, as it will increase his masculine energy and "staying power" when he engages the muscles around his penis, or lingam.

1. Sit with your legs crossed, palms on thighs.
2. Place the tip of your tongue at the roof of your mouth.
3. Focus on your yoni.
4. Inhale slowly through your nose, visualizing the energy flowing from your yoni up your spine and to your third eye.
5. As you inhale, contract all of the muscles in your pelvic floor (see previous exercise). If you can, tighten the muscles high in your vagina, around your cervix. It's almost as if you are sucking your vagina up higher into yourself.

6. Once your lungs are full and your sexual energy is in your third eye, hold your breath and apply and chin energy lock.
7. Now, quickly relax and contract all of your yoni muscles ten times while holding your breath.
8. On tenth breath, take a quick sniff through your nose, then release your breath through your nose and relax your muscles. Perform this exercise seven times.

Lower, Mid, and Upper Vagina

Now it's time to learn how to move the different areas in your vagina. Making these muscles stronger and creating a mind connection to your vagina by willing the various areas of the vagina to contract will allow you to undulate your vaginal muscles as Korean women do. But first, let's learn about the various sections of the vagina.

The lower vagina is the muscles around the opening of the vagina. These are the muscles you have already been exercising in the previous exercises. The mid vagina is the mid-section of the vagina. The upper vagina surrounds the cervix.

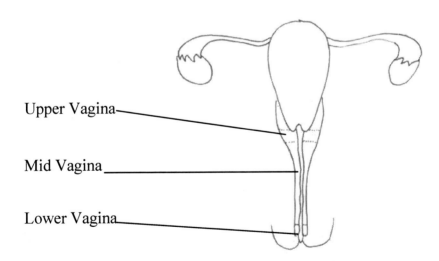

Upper Vagina

Mid Vagina

Lower Vagina

Lower, Mid, and Upper Vagina Exercise

This exercise will help you become familiar with the muscles and learn how to move them.

1. Picture the lower vaginal muscles around the opening of your vagina. Inhale. As you inhale, squeeze as tight as possible at the opening of your vagina, your anal sphincter muscles, and your urethra muscles. Hold for a count of 10. Breathe normally as you hold. Release. Perform three times.
2. Visualize the muscles at the mid-section of your vagina. Inhale and squeeze, once again using the assistance of your anal muscles to create a strong squeeze. You can feel the energy in the colon area as you use it to squeeze your central vagina. Breathe naturally, hold for a count of 10, and release. Perform three times.
3. Finally, visualize the muscles at the top of your vagina, by the cervix. Breathe in. As you inhale, focus on the muscles and squeeze the upper vagina tight. Be sure to employ the anal sphincter muscles to help with the squeeze. You may inadvertently use your stomach muscles as you squeeze, but your ultimate goal is to learn to squeeze without the influence of your stomach muscles. Focus on your upper yoni as you count to 10. Release. Perform three times.

To help you begin to learn to control your muscles, squeeze your vaginal muscles in this manner:

1. Squeeze your lower vagina and hold for three seconds. Release.
2. Squeeze the mid-section muscles and hold three seconds. Release.
3. Squeeze the upper section muscles and hold three seconds. Release.
4. Squeeze the mid-section, hold three seconds. Release.
5. Squeeze the lower section, hold three seconds. Release.
6. Repeat so that you are squeezing the muscles up and down your vagina.
7. Perform for three to five minutes. Repeat several times a day.

A toned, elastic yoni is your gateway to youth. Yoni exercise is considered physical exercise, and all exercise increases the flow of vital life-force energy throughout your body and your heart rate. This in turn stimulates a vital, magnetic glow in your face and around your body.

In a sexual situation, the movement of the yoni muscles undulating up and down over the man's erect shaft can create a sensation in him that will intensify his enjoyment. The ability to control the vaginal muscles in this way offers a magnificent enhancement in sexual play.

Yoni Breathing

In this next simple exercise, you control the muscles as if your vagina were a lung, tightening the muscles as you inhale and deflating and pushing the muscles outward as you exhale.

1. Sitting or standing, inhale deeply. As you breathe in, draw in and squeeze in unison all of the yoni muscles and grip tight. Clenching your vaginal muscles like a fist and holding your breath, maintain the clench tightly for a count of 10.
2. Exhale slowly, and slowly relax the muscles in unison. As your lungs deflate, allow your yoni muscles to open wider and wider.
3. Continue to exhale. As you push out the air of your lungs, relax the muscles completely, then bear down on the muscles and push, opening your anal muscles, as if you were having a bowel movement. Perform as many times as you feel comfortable, up to fifty times.

Yoni Eggs and Benwa Balls

In China, the queen and concubines of the royal palace used stone eggs in their exercises to strengthen their vaginas. Those who mastered the techniques with the egg remained youthful and healthy and maintained the muscular strength of younger women. Today, women are rediscovering yoni eggs and incorporating them in their exercises. Yoni eggs are made of smoothly polished stone. Obsidian, a volcanic rock, is ideal for its weight and energy, but any mineral will do. The size of the eggs ranges from quail egg to large chicken egg. The egg is used in advanced exercises. It is not recommended that it be used until you are familiar with vaginal anatomy and have practiced the more fundamental pelvic floor strengthening exercises.

Insert the egg into your yoni. Engage your vaginal muscles to move the egg up and down inside of your vagina. Some women keep the egg in their yoni as they move around the house. The muscles are exercised merely by holding in the egg. More talented women will insert two eggs, and by using their vaginal muscles, will move the eggs apart, moving one egg in one direction and the other egg in the opposite direction, and then moving them back together. When a certain level of vaginal strength is attained, a weight suspended by a string can be added to the egg (which is specially designed for weight attachments.) The extra weight will cause the muscles to increase in strength. At first, the exercises take extreme concentration and the eggs hardly move at all, but as with working your other muscles, with practice, your yoni muscles become stronger and moving the eggs is easier.

You can buy yoni eggs at some gem and mineral shops or on the Internet. If you are interested in more details and want a variety of egg exercises, read *Healing Love Through the Tao: Cultivating Female Sexual Energy* by Mantak Chia.

Benwa balls work on the same principle. Two balls made of metal or stone and ranging from the size of a marble to about the size of a ping pong ball are inserted into the vagina. You can use your muscles to move the balls up and down your vaginal canal.

Pelvic Floor Exerciser

Inspired by the Kegel exercises, an Australian medical equipment company, Cardio Design, created a wonderful device that a woman can use to measure the strength of her yoni and help "coach" her during her vaginal workouts. The Pelvic Floor Exerciser, or PFX, has a sensitive tube that is placed in the vagina and a meter that reads the strength of the muscles (on a scale of 1 to 10) when they are contracted. The user contracts her muscles as strongly as possible, with a goal of hitting the 10 mark, and holds for ten seconds, then releases. Performing this exercise ten times per session, ten times a day, quickly strengthens and revitalizes any vagina, whether it has been stretched from childbirth or atrophied from lack of use. Visual evidence of your improving vaginal strength is very motivating. You can order the PFX on the Internet at www.cardiodesign.com.au/.

Yoni Healing Massage

Many women may have negative energy or psychic scars stored in their vaginas. This negative energy may be left over from sexual violence or less hurtful sexual experiences. Though these women may not be aware of their wounds, the psychological scars may be obstacles to enjoyable sex, orgasm, or even overall happiness and radiance. The vagina can be cleared of much negative energy through the use of many of the exercises described in the Energy and Strong chapters. However, some scars are so deep that the intervention of a healer may be necessary. Yoni massage is one such healing practice.

With yoni massage, the vagina is rubbed and stroked by the healer's fingers. In this slow, relaxing process, scars (both psychic and energetic) are sought. When a scar is touched, the woman being healed may feel sensitivity and a memory may be triggered. She may go into emotional process and cry or scream. The healer holds the space and encourages the woman to feel the old hurt, continuing to gently massage and project healing energy into the area. Usually, once the process has ended and the wound released, the scar will be healed. Some yoni healers may stroke the yoni until orgasm is reached or the woman being healed may spontaneously go into orgasm. Orgasm is extremely healing and energizing.

It may be difficult to find a yoni healer in your area, as there are very few. The Internet is the best resource for finding one.

Books to read:

Rufus C. Camphausen, *The Yoni: Sacred Symbol of Female Creative Power.*
Nancy Qualls-Corbett, *The Sacred Prostitute.* Gives historic details about the sexual priestesses of ancient times.
Jalaja Bonheim, *Aphrodite's Daughter.* A collection of stories of women's sexual experiences.

Bodhi Avinasha and Sunyata Saraswati, *Jewel in the Lotus.*
Mantak Chia and Maneewan Chia, *Healing Love through the Tao: Cultivating Female Sexual Energy.*

The Vagina Monologues by Eve Ensler is an award-winning play that celebrates the vagina. Consisting of monologues describing the tales of the vaginas of various women, ranging from humorous to tragic, the play touches every women who can potentially relate to many of the themes. Ensler also initiated V-Day, a global movement to stop violence against women. Learn more about Ensler, *The Vagina Monologues* and V-Day by visiting www.vday.org.

7

CONNECTING WITH A BELOVED

Intimacy is a deep, energetic way of relating in which two people explore each other and venture into physical and spiritual experiences together. The connection occurs when their hearts are wide open to each other, when trust and respect are present, and when appreciation is expressed. Chakra energies reach out from one person to the other.

A sexy woman has abundant, yet balanced, sexual energy. She has the ability to connect on a deeply energetic level. When she is with someone to whom she is attracted, she connects deeply, and her energy is delicious and palpable. A sexy woman creates an intimacy that is exciting and satisfying, whether it leads to sex or not. The intimate, energetic connection is the key to her charm. The sexiest women can engage intimately and deeply without intercourse, and sometimes without even touching, as she reaches out with her heart and sexual energy.

Sexual Energy and Attraction

As you know, the most joyful, healthy, and attractive people on earth have clear and balanced chakras. These people are attractive and have positive vibes, or charisma; their self-love is evident. A sexy woman has balanced sexual energy, a vibration that is welcoming, approachable, loving, and gracious. A woman with a sexual chakra that is deficient sexual energy may not appear inviting, much less sexy, whereas a woman with excessive sexual energy may seem "easy," be said to "come on strong," and seem threatening to some people. Be sure to practice the exercises in the Energy, Sexual Energy, and Yoni chapters to strengthen and balance your sexual energy.

We have control over our chakras and can determine how little or how much energy we radiate from each chakra. This is equally true for the sexual chakra. A sexy woman is judicious with the amount of energy she radiates. If she is with someone new, she may hold back her energy, but if she is with someone she loves, she may radiate nuclear reactor's worth of energy to him. If she is really interested in someone and wants to get his attention without seeming *too* interested, she can control that level of radiant energy. Your ability to control your energy will help you create a connection that is as superficial or deep as you want.

Energetic Connection

Can you remember the feelings you had when you were with someone for whom you had a deep attraction and affection? Did you feel alive and "buzzed" with excitement and anticipation? Did your heart open with love? Did your genital area twinge with excitement? Did you feel alive and open? Did colors seem brighter and jokes funnier? Did you feel more attentive to your friends? More concerned with how you looked? Did you feel closer to God? Did you feel like a Goddess embodied? You were experiencing a positive energy connection.

Energetic connecting happens to everyone in every kind of relationship. But with someone for whom you have loving, sexual feelings, this connection can be transformational. Intimate, sexually-energetic connecting is more than just a superficial feeling of excitement and lust. It is a deep movement in the core of our various energy centers that causes the soul to grow. It is the vehicle through which we may transcend the human dimension and move into the realms of spirit.

Most times, when you are with someone with whom you share a strong attraction, energetic connecting is at work on a very subconscious level. Your chakras are activated and sending out powerful energy. At the same time, they are reading and responding to the energy radiating from the other person. With intense attraction that results in a lasting friendship or relationship, all of the chakras are fairly open. One of the most exciting feelings in the human body is experiencing the dynamics of radiating high energy while receiving high energy from a partner.

When we form a total-body energetic connection with another person, all of our chakras are in sync. Your root chakra vibrates because you feel safe with the person. Your sexual chakra pulses with the primal desire to mate. Your power chakra opens and closes as it projects power and then yields to the other as he or she comes forth with his or her power. Your heart is open as love for the other person flows forth. Your fifth chakra allows you to express who you are, ask for what you want, and share your thoughts. Your third eye energy is engaged as you intuit things about the other person. When the connection is at a "soul mate" level, your crown chakra is open and spiritual energy (spirit from the cosmos) moves in and out of the chakra, sending forth essence of your spirit. In a deep, loving relationship, this spiritual energy is greatly present. The spiritual rituals of marriage are inspired by this energy field, where commitment becomes a connection of the soul overseen by god/dess him/herself.

As relationships form and couples remain in them for a long time, their individual energies seem to merge and create a new, distinct energy field. The couple moves into a more comfortable energetic place, where the excitement of the newness and exploration is replaced with comfort and ease. It's like driving a new car. At first you are hyper-aware of the unique qualities of the way the car handles, the new-car smell, the location of the radio, the sensitivity of the brakes. But after a few weeks, you find yourself very comfortable in the car. You don't think so much about the new-car things any more. Driving your car has become second nature.

Intimate, energetic connection can occur just as easily with a new friend as with an old lover. In addition to an energetic connection, there are more physical expressions for a sexy connection.

Physical Expression

When a sexy woman decides it is time to connect physically with her beloved, she does so in ways that are subtle yet powerful and multi-dimensional. Moving into the third level of sexiness, she engages her various energies into physical demonstrations. Performing these actions indicates a great attraction toward the person and deepens the intimate connection. Just as some of the actions and gestures we use to indicate our interest in a person are unconscious, if we imitate the Tantrics and engage consciously, we can raise ordinary gestures to higher degrees of connection and intimacy.

Energetic Touch

Sexy women are aware of their energy, how much they emit, and how they share it. It is good for a sexy woman to know that she can radiate energy, not only through her chakras, but also through her hands. Our hands contain tremendous energy and are pathways through which energy flows. By merely using our hands to stroke someone's skin, we can deliver intense, delicious, and healing energy.

A sensual woman enjoys touching and doesn't hesitate to touch when touching is appropriate. In professional or casual occasions, for example, it is very acceptable to touch someone's arm or shoulder, though touching other body parts is inappropriate. In more intimate situations, touch is an important component of getting close. Holding hands, touching the face, stroking the arm are motions of connection. You share your energy through your hands, and you feel and receive the energy of your partner.

Touch Exercise

This exercise will help you become aware of the energy in your hands. It can be performed with a friend, your beloved, or one to whom you would like to give the gift of loving touch. This exercise is as effective while fully clothed as it is in the nude. If you're working through clothing, the energy in your hands will penetrate the fabric.

Have the other person sit or lie down. Open your heart as you feel this person's presence and energy. Take your time to feel his energy. Now reach out with your hands and slowly, gently lay your hands on his upper body. Let your hands go where they wish, to his arms, shoulders, chest, back, neck, face. Hold your hands ever so gently on the person and feel his skin, his energy. Your eyes can be open or closed, but your focus must be on what is happening in your hands. Now, slowly and gently move your hands over the person's body and skin, touching very lightly, not rubbing or pressing. The slower you move your hands, the better it is. Feel the skin or fabric move beneath your palms and fingers. Allow love to flow from your heart, down your arms, and out through the palms of your hands and into the other person. Simultaneously, stay aware of that person's body and energy. Feel his softness and innocence. Feel the vulnerability of that soul before you. Feelings will rise, and you will move into a bit of a trance state. Continue to move your hands over the other person's body slowly, gently, yet in focus the whole time. This mutual exchange of energy is intimate and healing for both the giver and the receiver. The recipient will feel safe with you, and safety is a basic ingredient of intimacy.

When you become aware of energetic touch, you can engage it at any time. Touching your beloved softly and slowly while watching TV or while he takes a break from the computer will calm and soothe him and connect the two of you. As a part of foreplay, the conscious radiating of love through your hands opens both of your hearts, and relaxes you into exquisite receptivity of each other, creating a loving bond.

Massage is a method of energetic touching, which is performed with focused intention to relax and heal the muscles. The best massage therapists aren't mere muscle technicians, but are masters of energy, and intuitively know where and how to touch the various parts of the body, and send healing energy into them. So when you feel the desire to massage a friend or beloved, don't worry about "doing it right," but rather focus on the energy you are radiating onto her or his body as you massage it.

Passion

Passion can be expressed in any situation. We can feel passionate about our work, our projects, our hobbies, our family, our friends, our sports teams. Passion is a very powerful expression of who we are and who our soul is.

We often look at passion as an indication of how connected we are to another person. We seek relationships that are filled with passion. And no wonder. In a passionate moment, our heart and soul are completely open and both radiating our energy and receiving the other's energy flow. When both parties are wide open with passionate energy, the world moves. Long, lingering kisses, moans, writhing bodies skin to skin, touching with the hands, gazing into each others' eyes, enthusiasm, trembling, verbal expression—these things are what sexual passion looks like. Passion is physical and emotional, and there is seldom any room in passion for logical thinking. Remember "going all the way" with someone and wondering afterward how you got there? In one word, it was passion. A sexy woman has no problem expressing passion with someone she feels love and sexual excitement for. In a long-term relationship, she can turn on her passion merely by looking at her partner as a divine representation of Shiva or God. Passion encourages returned passion, so when you become passionate with the one you love, passion will come back to you.

Expressing Appreciation

One powerful way in which to express passion is through words we speak in appreciation. Nothing is more of a turn-on than receiving a compliment, acknowledgement, or thanks. There is no greater gesture than to speak the words of appreciation. But please understand that appreciation is not to be limited to sexual situations. It can be expressed to all people in all aspects of our lives.

We all deeply desire love and appreciation. On some level, we crave acknowledgement and compliments. Receiving appreciation fills a deep desire. It's not that we *must* have appreciation in order to feel complete or good about ourselves, but when we receive positive feedback from our friends or our beloved, we are encouraged to continue whatever we are doing. Positive feedback helps us feel more confident. When we know this about ourselves, we can be sure that other people feel the same way.

In an intimate relationship (whether a first date or your husband of twenty years), appreciation deepens the intimacy. When you pay your beloved a compliment or express appreciation, you instill in him feelings of safety and self-acceptance within the relationship. He will feel good about himself for pleasing you. When a person feels good about himself, he will bring the best of himself into the relationship.

In a way, appreciation is a mini-prayer of gratitude. We thank God/dess for our blessings. Why not thank our beloved for his gestures. Think of your beloved as a divine being, and see what he does as a beautiful creation or magnificent gift. To him, it may be something simple. But to you, it is the most wonderful thing. So complimenting and appreciating is like saying a thank-you prayer. "You look so handsome in that shirt." Or, "Thank you for cooking us such a wonderful dinner." There is nothing too small, even taking out the trash, that doesn't deserve a "thank you."

Make it a practice to express appreciation every day. If you don't have a beloved, compliment everyone you meet. Express appreciation to your friends and neighbors. Call your parents and kids and tell them how happy you are they are in your life. By exuberantly showing your appreciation, you will create tremendous joy for yourself.

Eye Gazing

Looking deeply into someone's eyes is essential in creating a deep connection with that person. Eye gazing is an intimate gesture that connects you with the divine energy that dwells within your partner. It enhances the feelings of closeness you have with each other and intensifies your energetic connection. But looking deeply into someone's eyes can also be intimidating. Many of us fear others looking into our eyes. We're afraid our "real" selves will be discovered. Well, that's what happens. Your real self is your soul and the God/dess that dwells in you.

This exercise is simple. It can be a spontaneous gesture or as part of your sacred, loving foreplay, with sensual music, candles, etc. Sit close to your beloved, face to face.

Simply stare into the other's left eye, the eye also known as the Window to the Soul. Look deeply, and also see the beautiful face surrounding the eye. See the delightful being, the divine god or goddess before you. Stare into the eye and breathe deeply and slowly. Continue for several minutes, remaining connected and drinking in each other's beauty and essence. Don't look away, no matter how strange it may seem.

Now, place your left hands over each others' hearts. Cover your partner's hand with your right hand, as he will do to yours. Feel each other's heartbeat. Connect even more strongly and deeply. Maintain eye contact. Synchronize your breath as you sink ever deeper into each other's soul. Gaze and breathe.

After a few minutes, when you feel complete, release the heart-holding and eye gazing. Finish with a deep, lingering hug, still breathing together. Sink into the divine essence of each other.

Breathing Together

Breath can be an important component of an intimate, energetic connection. An awareness of your beloved's breath will deepen your connection and help you feel closer. It will strengthen your appreciation of his bodily form and his humanity.

Think of the intimacy of a long, lingering hug, in which you feel each other's breath on your neck and face, and feel your chests gently expand and contract against each other.

In Tantric practice, when couples breathe together, this ensures increased chakra energy and oxygenation of the cells, which results in deeper energetic connection and feelings of bliss and joy. With breathing practices, lovers can move their sexual energy up and down their spines and project their sexual energy toward the partner. They also practice breathing in unison, then out of unison (one inhaling while the other exhales), while hugging, sitting in the yab yum position (she sits in his lap facing him), and while making love.

You can practice the basic energy exercises found in Chapter 4 alone or with a partner. They are simple, but will intensify your intimacy and add greater dimension to your connection.

Part Three:

SPIRITED

8

SPIRITED

A Positive Energy Woman is a Spirited Woman. She is exuberant with love and joy. She finds beauty and meaning in everyone and everything. She appreciates her every blessing. She experiences glowing self-love and high self-esteem, for she knows she is a multi-dimensional being residing in a vehicle of flesh and bones. Keenly intuitive, she listens to her hunches and insights and pays attention to signs and messages others seldom notice. She sees beyond the surface of everyday things and accepts human challenges with ease and grace, perceiving each experience as a gift. She knows that she, herself, is a divine being and a channel for God/dess energy. She feels a responsibility to hone and use her natural-born gifts to benefit the planet, and she does so with fearlessness and zeal. Abundant with love, her vibration is light and loving and her energy welcomes us and draws us toward her. Her touch is comforting and filled with life, her laughter and her smiles are joyous and contagious. She selflessly gives and serves, wishing to uplift those around her. A spirited woman expresses, radiates, and *is* a positive vibration. Spirited is a state of being, and a manifestation of a life that includes spiritual living.

Spirited Defined

The dictionary defines the word *spirited* as an adjective: *full of spirit; lively, energetic, and animated.* This description of an outward expression is traditionally applied to people or animals, such as cheerleaders, who leap enthusiastically for their teams, or horses who gallop wildly in the wind. I believe this is a limited definition. I believe there is more to *spirited* than what we traditionally think. I would like to propose a new model of *spirited.*

First, let's explore the root word, *spirit.* Coming from the Latin *spiritus,* spirit means breath, vigor, courage, soul, life. It is related to *spirare,* "to breathe," and is also related to the Old French word *espirit,* meaning animating or vital principle in man and animals.

The dictionary defines spirit (noun) as follows:

1. a) The life principle, esp. in man, orig. regarded as inherent in the breath or as infused by a deity. b) Soul.
2. The thinking, motivating, feeling part of man, often as distinguished from the body; mind, intelligence.
3. Life, will, consciousness, thought, etc. regarded as separate from matter.
4. An individual person or personality thought of as showing or having some specific quality (the determined *spirit* of women libbers).
5. Disposition, frame of mind, mood, temper (in high *spirits*).
6. Vivacity, courage, vigor, enthusiasm, etc.[125]

Spirit is the most fundamental aspect of ourselves as living, breathing beings. It is the core of our existence. It is the expressive, thinking, creative, intuitive, and conscious aspect of our being that directs our physical body through life. All of us *have* spirit; all of us *are* spirits.

While everyone "is full of spirit," as defined by Webster's, are we all *spirited*? I don't think so. *Spirited* is a certain kind of expression of spirit. Let's look at the dictionary definition again: *lively, energetic, animated.* These three words characterize what appears to be joyful—a high-level, positive vibration expressing happiness, love, and exuberance for life. In my interpretation, a *spirited* person is full of joyful energy and expressive of that joy.

For many people, this *spirited* feeling occurs only occasionally in life, but for a Positive Energy Woman, *spirited* is a way of being. Joy remains fairly constant. Life is perceived as a wonderful gift, and her blissful attitude emanates as positive energy. *Spirited* becomes an aspect of who she is, and in fact, a facet of her personality.

So, how do we become spirited? I believe to raise our vibration to the level of joy at a near-constant state, it is important that we develop ourselves *spiritually.* So what does THAT mean?

The dictionary defines *spiritual* as follows:

1. Of the spirit or the soul as distinguished from the body or material matters.
2. Of or concerned with the intellect.
3. Characterized by the ascendancy of the spirit; showing much refinement in thought and feeling.
4. Of religion or the church; sacred, devotional or ecclesiastical, not lay or temporal.[126]

As defined thusly, the prevailing spirit of the word (pardon the pun) concerns the aspects of ourselves that resides beyond the body. This is the intangible essence of our being, the intellect and soul. Because we have souls, we are spiritual beings. We are thinkers and feelers who, at some point in our existence (if not every day) ponder life, its core meaning and nuances, and our purpose in it. Many associate *spiritual* with religion, but spiritual people aren't necessarily religious. Spiritual people are conscious of their spirit. They pay attention to it, feed it, nurture it. Just as our body thirsts for water, so does our spirit thirst for certain practices, usually labeled *spiritual* practices. Most often, these practices create a relationship between the earthly and the divine. It is this relationship that often fills one with joy and a high vibration of happiness. These practices assist us to become *spirited* people. *Spirited* is thus, I believe, a conscious refinement of our soul and spirit. It is an ecstatic manifestation of our soul or spirit. This is *spirit in action.*

The second side of our energetic triangle is thus the energy of the spirit. When we energize the Spirit side of the triangle, we attend to our spirit through certain practices and prepare our bodies to become vessels of pure love, peace, and joy, and thus express ourselves joyfully as spirited beings. Becoming a Spirited person asks that you cultivate the energy of the Spirit side of the triangle. It requires three simple, but life-altering, actions:

1. Know, nurture, and express your soul.
2. Create a relationship with the Higher Power or God/dess.
3. Invite the energy of the Higher Power to merge with your body and soul.

The equation looks like this:

Personal Soul + Universal Spirit = Spirited

I know, I know. This sounds a little New Agey, and you may feel uncomfortable with anything that has to do with the so-called Higher Power. But try what I suggest. You'll soon discover that these steps are as natural as breathing. None of these steps require you to commit to a religious path or a spiritual community. They ask you to have an open mind and a desire to expand spiritually. They ask you to give the project some of your time and do a few easy practices. The rewards are much greater than any new car or nice outfit will ever give you. Once you consciously open your mind and your soul to the highest vibration in existence, you will obtain all of the love, peace, and joy you could ever hope to experience.

Knowing, Nurturing, and Expressing Your Soul

Who you are is not your looks, your personality, your profession, the car you drive, or the possessions you own. Who you are is *your soul.* The human body is merely a vehicle for the soul, and the soul is on earth today to express itself through the body. Soul is the source of energy. It motivates the body. Your life is your opportunity to discover your soul. Through your life experiences, your soul expands and deepens. The first step to becoming a spirited person is to rise above your ego and mundane identity.

Spirit is the expression of the soul. Spirit is to soul as a painting is to paint. The soul is the fundamental material and color, and the spirit is the expressive use of the material and color that creates the beautiful painting. Expressing what exists in our soul can be an ecstatic experience in which we feel utter joy, a boost of self-love, and even a reverence for the gifts we possess. When a woman brings forth her soul's purpose, her spirit is cosmically joyful. She is a joyful human being.

Only by cracking the mysterious code of our soul and understanding our purpose on earth will we advance as human beings and create satisfying and meaningful lives. Life is a series of choices, and every day we can either choose to make material goods and high-tech stimulation our gods or focus on the treasures of spirit. When we are energized by our soul's calling, life becomes a thrilling adventure rather than an arduous trip. We feel fulfilled and joyful. Often we become unstoppable, taken by the fever of birthing a gift to the planet. Do you hear your soul calling? Is it asking you to write beautiful poetry? Heal the ill? Entertain the masses? When you listen and respond and learn who you are, you will experience a clarity and a love you have never felt before. You will begin to recognize yourself as a divine being. You will appreciate your precious soul and your life on the planet.

Carved into the walls of the temple of Apollo at Delphi were the words: *Know Thyself.* This is how we create a fulfilled life. When you know yourself, you will begin to move on a journey to discover yourself. When you know your soul, you can identify your values, your mission, your desires. Knowing these things will help you direct your life on the path of utter fulfillment.

When a woman is deaf to her inner calling or refuses to express the gifts of her soul, her spirit is choked and her energetic flow is blocked. Neglect of the soul can result in emptiness and depression. When we are empty of spirit, we turn to exterior sources of fulfillment and ignorantly seek life in drugs and consumption of consumer goodies.

Some of us know our life's purpose at a very young age, whereas others search their entire lifetimes. But some never look at all. Many people are blessed to know how to access the mysteries of the self. But many are clueless. For those of us who want to nurture the soul, we can find fulfillment by seeking answers outside of ourselves, through a higher power, often called God.

Creating a Relationship with a Higher Power

A Positive Energy Woman has a beautiful relationship with the Higher Power. She knows it is her nurturing mother, her fatherly guide, her best friend. Her relationship with God/dess is a minute-to-minute connection and an important aspect of her daily existence. She knows she is not alone, for from this beautiful energetic force, she receives all the love, guidance, and inspiration that she will ever need to manifest and create whatever she wants. She gains her strength, wisdom, and inner peace from her connection to Spirit.

Your religious upbringing may determine how you feel about and relate to a higher power today. If you are lucky, you had a good taste of who God/dess is at a young age and were made aware of his/her glorious aspects. Many of us, like me, however, received religious teachings when we were young that left us uncomfortable with, and even fearful of, God. He was intimidating, jealous, and intolerant unless we did things HIS way. Hoping to avoid an infinite afterlife in hell, we prayed out of duty or fear, but our prayers were only rote exercises and we had no feeling of connection with the Higher Power. Seeing the hypocrisy in the churches, singing joyless hymns, feeling empty as we prayed, many of us were completely turned off to religion.

If we want to create a positive relationship with the Higher Power, we need to understand who and what God/dess is.

Who is God/dess?

Goddess, God, Shiva, Shakti, Allah, Isis, Ashera, Aphrodite, Yahweh, Jehovah, the Universe, the Higher Power—whatever you choose to call the Higher Power, it is the divine presence that exists infinitely in the universe and is the source of love, inspiration, joy, and strength. This divine power is omnipresent (present in all places at the same time), omniscient (knowing all things), and omnipotent (all-powerful).

I believe the word "God/dess" is a perfect amalgam of masculine and feminine energies. While the English word "god" is considered to be a generic word, as "cat" applies to both male and female cats, the patriarchal religions have cast god as always masculine. We all learned to think of God as a big man in the sky. But my god is an equal opportunity deity, and God/dess is the all-inclusive, dual-gender nomenclature for this deity.

God/dess is omnipotent, omniscient, and omnipresent, in all things and all places at all times. God/dess is a mystical force that is the source of all energy of all things in existence. She is the source of creative life-force energy that dwells in each and every human being. God/dess is a limitless, creative, energizing entity that operates through us. She created nature on Earth and in all dimensions of existence. Through God/dess, we can access the highest energetic vibrations in existence: love, peace, joy, and enlightenment.

Worshipping, praying, honoring, and celebrating spirit seems to be an innate human desire. Archaeological findings dating as far back as 30,000 BCE indicate that early humans worshipped a higher power and perhaps gave thanks to it for food, fertility, and protection from danger. We can assume that these ancient people detected an energy that was greater than themselves and discovered that with certain methods they could not only manifest what they needed but also increase hope and joy.

The concept of God has always been a constant. Innumerable spiritual paths and practices have developed, and we have learned to touch and be touched by the divine. So profound are these experiences that millions of people around the globe became passionate followers of the various paths that came to define various cultures.

In the beginning, as primates evolved into humans, early hominids possibly recognized gods. We are not sure when this happened, but discoveries of fossils of the first upright-walking hominids around 1.5 million years old, make us ponder.

Humanity took a giant evolutionary leap when we developed intellect, conscious thought, and artistic expression. We learned to tame and make fire, to domesticate animals, to use tools. We invented agriculture and the wheel. We gathered in tribes, clans, and villages. Expanded consciousness transported humans into a level of existence above the primitive animal existence from which we evolved. The mysteries of life were demanding an explanation.

Our first spiritual leaders were shamans, the wise women and men of the tribe. With a deeply intuitive nature and innate connection with the mystical realms, shamans recognized that dimensions, worlds, and energies existed beyond consensual, everyday reality. Their relationship with God/dess was an active and communicative one. Recognizing the hand of God/dess in birth, death, sex, and other mysteries of life, the shaman made herself into a link between the divine and the human community, healing and blessing her people through rituals of dance and drumming. It was the shaman's ability to allow God/dess to flow through her that gave her great wisdom. Each of us has the potential to become a shaman. We can all learn to communicate, activate, and facilitate the workings of the divine.

We as God/dess

God/dess dwells within each of us. We are divine beings of love, light, and intelligence. We each have our own souls and spirits within us, but God/dess works through us. We are channels for divine ideas and faucets through which powerful, loving energy flows. Tantric practice asks us to see the god or goddess in each and every person, not just in ritual, but in everyday life. As we move through life, we will cross paths with thousands of people, and whether it's a brush past a stranger on the street, a light-hearted conversation with a casual acquaintance, or the drama of a full-blown love relationship, we are engaging with divine sparks of being. Every single person on the planet is divine. You, my friend, are a reflection of God/dess, a part of God/dess, a manifestation of God/dess in human form.

Religious Science, also known as Science of Mind, and other New Thought philosophies teach that each person is an emanation of God (as they refer to the Higher Power) and that each person has inside of us all of the creativity, love, and abilities of the Highest Energy.

When we tap into the energy of God/dess through prayer, meditation, and other practices, and truly believe that we are, indeed, a drop in the Universal Ocean with all of the capacities and skills of God/dess, we can charge the divine energy within us to do the things that will help us create joyful, productive, loving, and meaningful lives. We each have the capacity to attract to us all that we wish to manifest, as well as the wisdom and grace to accept and work through the challenges that life brings us along the way.

Think of the vastness and power of the ocean. The ocean is God/dess. Our soul is a drop of water in the ocean. Each drop, each soul, is its own entity of its own size and shape, but the essential makeup of the drop is the same as the makeup of the ocean. We all partake of the beauty, power, energy and life of God/dess.

By fully accepting and knowing that we are divine reflections of God/dess, we can comprehend the importance of our individual existence. By knowing that we are emanations of God/dess, we can feel more confident and loving toward ourselves. We have been given talents and skills that we can use to bring goodness to ourselves, our families, and the planet.

Creating a relationship with this all-knowing, all-powerful, ever-present spirit of the highest vibration is the source of our own happiness.

Belief

Believing is having the trust and confidence that something is true. Essential to becoming a spirited being and connecting with God/dess is believing that a benevolent, loving, and powerful Higher Power exists and is at our service. When we truly believe that God/dess can heal, comfort, and direct us, we will receive blessings and guidance. Likewise, believing you are *capable* of connecting with God/dess is vitally important. The traditional shamans were successful healers and advisors because they believed they were conduits of the Great Goddess, and their tribal family held the same belief. The priestesses of ancient Egypt and pre-classical Greece performed rituals for abundant crops, healthy babies, and the safe passage of the deceased because they believed the goddesses would respond kindly. The Hindus discovered enlightenment by merging the pranic energy of spirit with their own human spirit. The early Jews and Christians not only witnessed miracles, but also performed them in the forms of healings and multiplication of food.

When we connect with God/dess, we bare our souls, and release our ego, our personality, our earthly mask. Letting go of our ego allows us to release judgments and perceptions of ourselves so we may experience ourselves as pure spirit. We connect with a force that is greater than ourselves and allow the divine to work through us. We release control. The connection creates an alchemical reaction in our bodies. Our vibration rises, obstacles that stand in the way of our happiness are dissolved, and channels for great possibility are opened. We allow our own spirit and the spirit of God/dess to connect.

With connection to and belief in God/dess, we can manifest or create our deepest desires. Many miracles have occurred through belief: miraculous healings in which a wound or illness was cured by prayer or interface with a spiritual healer. We have also seen the transformations of people with addictions or living derelict lives who later became great women and men because they made a connection with a Higher Power and developed a belief in themselves. Marianne Williamson, spiritual activist and author of the popular *A Return to Love: Reflections on the Principles of A Course In Miracles* and many other books, admits to having experimented with drugs and alcohol, having unsuccessful relationships, and feeling lost before she discovered *A Course in Miracles*, a sacred scripture of the New Age movement. Today she speaks to and inspires audiences in the thousands with messages for positive living. Untold numbers of people have overcome great odds to gain good health, employment, and other achievements because of their belief in themselves and in spirit.

Conscious Awareness

Beginning in the 1960s in the West, a great expansion in the collective consciousness catapulted the evolution of the human mind to a new step. As if orchestrated by a cosmic conductor, numerous events pushed and stretched our minds to new limits, opening us to greater possibilities as human and spiritual beings. Along with the rise of a political counterculture that emerged during the Vietnam War and the organized push for women's liberation and civil rights, a wave of interest in ancient spiritual philosophies arose. More and more people investigated the paths of Hinduism, Buddhism, and other philosophies and learned practices that helped them transcend the mundane and attain expanded awareness and deeper awareness of the greater universe. Seeking a deeper meaning for life, people opened doors to a new consciousness that took fire in art, literature, music, and sexuality. Positive changes took place in popular attitudes toward women and ethnic groups. Concern for the environment arose, with the first Earth Day taking place in 1969. The awakening of our mostly Christian-Judeo culture continued, and by the 1970s, it had bloomed into the New Age movement. This expansion of mass consciousness continues to this day and invites us to perceive life beyond our three-dimensional reality and our individual lives. Now as quantum physics teaches us more about the true nature of the mysterious universe we live in, we are becoming more aware of the importance of our every thought and action.

I believe that maintaining conscious awareness is how we connect with the Higher Power. It's an important key to happiness. We may think "unconscious" means someone is in a coma or has passed out from drinking too much, but this kind of unconsciousness is only a state of sleep. A conscious person is awake and alert. Most people are conscious to a certain level, able to function in the world, earn a living, maintain relationships with friends and loved ones. But a high percentage of so-called conscious people are unconscious of the spiritual realms and of their own presence as a spiritual being on this planet. Those who are unconscious in this sense don't think of the results of their actions, the feelings of other people around them, or their own feelings. Unconscious people live in a limited three-dimensional world where daily life is carried on by rote and the greatest goal is to make it to Friday. This kind of consciousness, while pretty standard, is extremely limiting. It confines a person to a small and boring world. It diminishes the quantity of joy and minimizes our value on the planet.

True conscious awareness is living life in a variety of realms and dwelling every day in Heaven on Earth. True consciousness demands that we take off the blinders that keep us self-centered and trapped in our tiny, individual worlds that consist only of *me*. It allows us to expand our perceptions of spirit and the planet. Being truly conscious takes us beyond conditioning and helps us see through the filters of perception that conditioned us as we grew up. When we become truly conscious, we perceive things on a holistic level and understand the intertwining of the spiritual and earthly realms. We become less judgmental and view people and circumstances with compassion. We drop our victim consciousness and stop saying "me me me" and "my my my" and "it's *his* fault." We stop taking things personally and look at the larger situation. We receive every lesson with appreciation, no matter how painful the learning experience is. We see life as an adventure, and not as an arduous trek to slog through until we die.

When we become truly conscious, consciously aware, our life becomes richer. We appreciate the beauty of the planet. We really, for the first time since we were children, *really* hear the song of a bird. Birds have always been with us, but our total immersion in our "me" world has kept us from paying attention to them. We really feel the energy of other people and see beyond their masks. This helps us understand them better. We take time to smell the roses and break out of our head space.

Inviting the Higher Power to Merge with You

With an expanded awareness of life, we begin to see the results of our thoughts and our actions, not only within our bodies, but in our relationships and on the environment. When we are conscious of thoughts and words, we will strive to think and say things in a positive way. When we have a consciousness of our body's response to eating poorly, we strive to feed our bodies with nutritious foods. When we are conscious of the results of polluting the planet, we work to protect the environment. With a consciousness of the beliefs and conditioning of other people, we begin to practice acceptance and unconditional love. If everyone were to live a truly conscious existence, the world would be a better place. We would have a clean environment, less violence, and greater respect and cooperation among religions and nations. We would have peace on the planet.

Vibration

The vibration of our bodies ranges from low, depressed energy to high, loving, and joyful energy. Depending on our energetic health, our daily experiences, our state of mind, and, yes, our connection with spirit, our frequencies can slow down or speed up. For our personal energy fields to vibrate at the highest frequency, we must connect and merge with the highest Universal Energy. It is no surprise that when we consciously connect with a higher vibration, higher energy will penetrate our personal energy field. We transcend the lower vibrations that perpetuate unhappiness and depression and take on the highest, purest energy of love and light. Eventually we *become* a high vibration. By maintaining this connection, our frequencies will remain in the higher states, no matter what challenges we face.

In his book, *Power vs. Force: The Hidden Determinants of Human Behavior*, David R. Hawkins, MD, PhD, describes using the techniques of kinesiology on thousands of test subjects to measure the various vibrations of human consciousness. Shame, guilt, apathy, grief, and fear appear on this scale as the lowest vibrations. On the high end are love, joy, peace, and enlightenment. God/dess emanates the highest vibrations.[127]

We use our spiritual practices to invite the highest vibrations into our soul, which will actually merge with the divine energy of God/dess. We invite divine energy to enter into our body and fuse with our human life-force energy. The specific practice may last a short time, but the higher vibration will linger in our energy for a fairly long period. When we reenter the "real" world of consensual reality, we carry this higher vibration in us and radiate it. Human beings are, in fact, channels for spiritual energy. The more dedicated we are to a spiritual practice or conscious connection, the longer our higher vibration will endure. By creating a connection with God/dess, we are expanded with an infusion of conscious awareness and vibrations of love, peace, and joy. The ancient shaman is the perfect example. She knew how to surrender to a higher realm and become a channel or conduit for information and high vibration. As the shaman embodied the higher vibration, it was radiated to the community. As a mediator for God/dess, she took on Her qualities and played Her role. Sages throughout time have likewise encouraged their followers to practice to attain enlightenment.

The uplifting effects of spiritual tools are immediate and palpable. Prayer, meditation, dance, chanting, and other tools divorce us from the negative thoughts and emotions that keep us depressed, angry, and joyless. They lead us to a vibrational field of love, joy, peace, and enlightenment where lower level vibrations of shame, guilt, apathy, and fear are banished.

Energy attracts like energy. We attract whatever vibration or energy we emit. When we've been infused with the peace, joy, and love of spirit, we "wear" that vibration in our energy field. We create positive cause and effect and attract into our lives peaceful, joyful, and loving people, places, and situations. For example, if we feel very loving and generously give love to everyone we meet through a smile, a hug, some genuine attention, or kind words, this loving vibration ripples out into the universe and causes a positive affect on all that is. The universe responds by returning that vibration back to you.

Likewise, people with a low level of consciousness will attract other unconscious people with low vibrations, as well as situations that may get them into trouble or hurt them. Until their vibration shifts to a higher level, they will continue to attract the people and circumstances that will keep them at those low levels.

We can use prayer, meditation, and sacred texts or philosophies to shift our vibration. The congregations of churches, temples, and other spiritual gatherings generate an incredibly high vibration, as the number of people multiplies and amplifies the vibrations of love, peace, joy, and enlightenment to great levels.

While divine energy flows through all seven chakras, the upper four chakras—Anahata, Vishuddha, Ajna, and Sahasrara—are considered the portals through which the highest vibrations are channeled. (For a review of these chakras, refer back to Chapter 4.) When these chakras are nurtured and balanced, they will naturally vibrate at a high level, and their energy radiates from the body. This radiant, positive energy is the trademark of a spirited woman.

The World Is Not Three-Dimensional

Only in recent years have our scientists proved what mystics have known all along: the universe is not merely three-dimensional. Divine energy exists in all there is, and with intention and faith we can influence our reality by consciously connecting with this energy. In his book, *The*

Science of Mind, Ernest Holmes writes that "physics has revealed that this metaphysical abstraction is the thing that physics begins with— energy and intelligence."[128] Quantum physics is the study of atoms and subatomic systems of energy, discrete and indivisible units that behave like particles and waves, called quanta. Inexhaustible experiments to explore and explain quanta have been performed by scientists since the time of Isaac Newton (1643-1727), who tried to explain the behavior of light as particles, and Christian Huygens (1629-1695), who described light in terms of waves. Because of Newton's celebrity, his particle theory won the field and remained the accepted theory until the early 1800s, when scientists Thomas Young (1773-1829) and Augustin Fresnel (1788-1827) developed experiments that "proved" light was composed of waves.

The Stanford Encyclopedia of Philosophy differentiates classical physics (the study of energy and matter) and quantum physics: "Classical physics assumes that exact simultaneous values can be assigned to all physical quantities, and quantum mechanics disagrees, saying exact values cannot be assigned, the prime example being the position and momentum of a particle."[129]

Early twentieth century physicists Werner Heisenberg and Niels Bohr attempted to nail down and define the action of quantum units. But particles and waves make inexplicable actions and are filled with "quantum probabilities and organized chaos" that make them nearly impossible to measure. The more we know about the velocity of a particle, the less we know about its position, and vice versa. Experiments by Heisenberg and Bohr determined that the patterns and paths of particles can't be predicted by any known method. Sometimes a particle would act like a particle, and other times it acted like a wave. Bohr said, "The particle is what you measure it to be. When it looks like a particle, it *is* a particle, and when it looks like a wave, it *is* a wave. It is meaningless to ascribe any properties or even existence to anything that has not been measured." Heisenberg created the Uncertainty Principle, which states that one cannot assign exact simultaneous values to the position and momentum of a physical system. Albert Einstein, a contemporary of Heisenberg and Bohr's, was skeptical of their work. He famously said, "I cannot believe that God would choose to play dice with the universe."[130]

The particle's unpredictability opens up tremendous possibilities in the way quantum particles of energy work, for we are discovering that it isn't God who is playing dice, but us. Because our mere presence and intention to observe the movement of a particle influence the particle, we must know that our power goes beyond the laboratory and into our everyday lives. Scientists and philosophers recognize the power of our minds and its influence over our personal realities. They explore and deliver information that can help us become healthier, happier, and more prosperous. Movies like *What the Bleep Do We Know?* and *The Secret* are making their way into the mainstream and raising public consciousness. We are being empowered to take control of our destinies merely by being aware of and disciplining our thought processes. Biologist and stem cell scientist Robert Lanza sums it up beautifully. "As we have seen, the world appears to be designed for life, not just at the microscopic scale of the atom, but at the level of the universe itself."[131]

It is the inexplicable nature of quantum particles that helps to explain natural and spiritual phenomena. Free thinkers through the ages, knowing there is more to life than meets the eye, have studied the immutable laws of nature and their affect on the human and cosmic spirit. As early as the third century BCE, philosophers were awakening to the concept of quantum matter. The Greek philosopher Democritus (460-370 BCE) was the co-originator (with his teacher Leicippus) of the concept that all matter is composed of tiny, indivisible units called *atoma* that move about in an infinite void space.[132] Democritus was probably the first philosopher on record to believe that thought is caused by the physical movements of atoms.[133] A bit later, Aristotle opined that the atomist regarded the soul as composed of fire atoms. Life is associated with heat, and because fire atoms are readily mobile, the soul is regarded as causing motion.

A century or so before Democritus, however, Hindu mystics learned to meditate so deeply that their souls would leave their earthly bodies and enter the divine realms of expanded consciousness, and return to their body vehicle in a state of divine bliss. Records indicate that some Hindu adepts could levitate themselves above the ground and disappear and reappear instantly in another location. While these mystics may not have thought about the quantum force behind this phenomenon, they recognized the existence of cosmic influences beyond the perceived three-dimensional world. So did the Taoists. They discovered the existence of chi and learned to harness the vital energy from the atmosphere and merge it with life force energy within the body to revitalize the organs and live longer lives. Through the ages, in fact, spiritual practitioners from shamans to priestesses have employed prayer to obtain positive results from the Higher Power, including physical healings and securing ample food, and other necessities for survival.

Scientists have always been curious to see what the human body is composed of and have tried to measure the soul. Around 1900, Dr. Duncan MacDougall worked with the dying to obtain such measurements. He weighed patients seconds before and immediately following death. He discovered that the body weighs around three-quarters of an ounce less after death, suggesting the release of a measurable body of energy.[134] Is this the soul? If so, where was it in the living body? Where does it go when the body dies?

Our ancestors believed the soul of the deceased traveled to another place, such as the underworld, the stars, the Elysian Fields, or heaven. While some trusted that the soul would dwell in another dimension for eternity, others believed the afterlife location was a temporary stop-off before the soul returned to earth for another attempt at enlightenment. Does this explain reincarnation and the feeling you've always known someone you just met? Some people believe that only a thin veil exists between our three-dimensional world and other dimensions where angels, spirits, faeries, and other entities dwell. Some believe in psychic or astral planes where the living soul can travel to commune with the divine. We may think inspiration, prophecies, dreams, and intuitions come from within our physical brain, but many people believe they are messages from God/dess. Is it coincidence that so much of humanity has believed in a dimension that we can't see with our physical eyes? Is our soul the source of this innate knowing?

It is a fact that energy is in us and all around us. Kirlian photography can capture on film the aura, or electromagnetic energy, that surrounds a body or a leaf or anything else. It shows that energy changes form, color, and size, depending on one's health and outlook on life. It also reveals that a spiritual person's aura is much brighter, fuller, and colorful than the aura of a person with no spiritual beliefs or practices. With spiritual tools, a person can harness her own life force energy and merge with the energy of the divine to influence the energy of another person. Miraculous recoveries from illness have resulted from prayer, pranic (energy) healing, and strong belief. Likewise, the collective intention of a group of people may influence the energy of a larger crisis.

In 1993, quantum physicist John Hagelin, Director of the Institute of Science, Technology and Public Policy and Minister of Science and Technology at the Maharishi University of Management, along with other scholars of the Maharishi University, conducted an experiment to determine the effects of the group practice of the Transcendental Meditation program on preventing violent crime in Washington, D.C. The Project Review Board consisted of sociologists, criminologists, and police. In this two-month study, a group of up to four thousand participants in the TM program meditated at the nation's capital to increase coherence and reduce stress in the city. Results showed a drop in crime that was commensurate with the number of participants meditating during a period of time. Each day the group met, a measurable drop in crime was reported. When the group was its largest, crime dropped by 23.3 percent.[135] Is this coincidence? Or is it the result of a collective energetic focus that influenced the cosmic energetic web?

A spiritual woman understands the vastness of life on earth and the cosmic dimensions and learns to transcend her 3D limitations. She learns to use the tools that harness the positive influences over her life. With this ability, she can create a life of tremendous possibility, control her own destiny, and assist those who need her help.

To learn more about quantum physics and the application of theories to our lives, rent the movie *What the Bleep Do We Know?* This entertaining blend of documentary and drama features interviews with quantum physicists and others who study and implement the power of thought.

Spirituality vs. Religion

While the world religions and spiritual philosophies differ in their practices, they center around the common concept that a positive, energetic force dwells around us and in us and that this energy is accessible to human beings. Our religious and spiritual populations have grown into a glorious mélange of philosophies that range from worship of the ancient goddesses to Eastern mysticism, to Jewish, Christian, and Muslim fundamentalism and everything in between. Many of us journey to discover the treasures of religious and spiritual teachings.

When I was growing up, I was taught it was improper to talk about politics and religion. Today, I find that while people still get heated up over their political differences, many enjoy discussing religion and spirituality. People are eager to learn about new philosophies and share their insights. I feel that the migration of spiritual paths from around the world into the United States has increased our religious tolerance, expanded our vocabulary of God/dess, and increased our awareness of human beings as spiritual beings. We are blessed to live in a place and time when spiritual exploration is so widely accepted. In many times during history, diverting from a religious path was dangerous. Churches were very righteous about their beliefs and practices and greatly limited the opportunities people had for spiritual expansion.

My personal quest for a connection with God/dess is probably typical of many Americans about my age. I was raised in a Christian household and went to the local Methodist church with my mother. When I was older, I attended the churches of my friends. While I enjoyed the social aspect of church and embraced the teachings of Jesus Christ, I did not really feel comfortable attending church services or reading the Bible. No matter how much I wanted to be a Christian, no matter how often I read the Bible, no matter how many different Christian churches I attended, I never really "got it." I never *felt* God. In fact, I *feared* God. I never found the peace and upliftment from the Bible that so many other people seemed to feel. I never wanted to get baptized because, even at an early age, I knew I didn't want to commit to a specific church's path (although at the time I did not understand this). I was taught that the only way God would hear our prayers was if we prayed to Jesus, but I didn't want to pray to Jesus. I wanted to go straight to the source! I didn't like the vibe of the church, I never liked seeing Jesus hanging on the cross, I always felt depressed by the solemn hymns, and I thought Christmas was a ridiculous holiday. Because of how religion was taught to me, I could never establish a relationship with God.

In my late teens, I finally decided the Christian religion was not for me. I began to explore other paths. How grateful I am that I made that decision. Beautiful and meaningful spiritual paths opened up to me. Since that time, I have deepened my spiritual life by exploring other philosophies, practices, and communities. I've chanted with the Krishnas, meditated with the Buddhists, soul traveled with Eckankar groups, performed yoga at the Self-Realization Fellowship, participated in Native American sweat lodges, breathed with Kriya Yogis, participated in pujas with the Tantricas, danced to the Goddess with the Pagans, learned the Universal Principles through Science of Mind, and much more. Each and every ceremony, ritual, and sacred text has deeply affected me in a positive way. I was able to create a connection with God/dess! At last, my soul was fed and my spirit expanded. Finally, I could merge with the Highest Power and feel the presence of spirit in my life. I wanted to do the things that would help me connect with the universe.

Learning about spirit and God/dess became my passion. I experienced the glorious feelings I could never find as a young Christian. I have built an outstanding relationship with God/dess. In my studies, I have discovered many of the practices and principles that help me to connect with spirit and live a deeply fulfilling life.

As I explored various religions and spiritual teachings, I discovered that God/dess is joyful, bright, friendly, loving, and nonjudgmental. God/dess is creative, intelligent, and loving energy. God/dess does not want to punish us, no matter what we do. God/dess is a friend, completely accepting and loving. Connecting with God/dess is as natural as uniting with a human loved one.

I am not at all a religious person, but I am a tremendously spiritual person. The moment I realized the Christian religion was not the most suitable path for me was the moment I could more readily connect to God/dess through other practices. That's when I became spiritual. I learned that while all spiritual and religion paths and practices have a similar goal—to enter into a relationship with God/dess—there is a vast difference between spirituality and religion.

Religion, especially organized religion, embodies a dogma (doctrine, belief, moral codes) that its followers must practice in order to get to God. In the Middle Ages in Europe, the Church was as political as it was sacred and enforced laws and rules to keep people under its control. People were taught that God was "out there" and that following the rules of the Church assured them of a place in heaven. The sacred scriptures and texts provided guidance on living the proper life. Deviation resulted in damnation and hellfire. Still today, many religions adhere to the belief that their way is the only way and their god is the only god.

Many religious people, even many who belong to a church, are spiritual. They merge energetically with the Source of Love and all there is. Other religious people are not at all spiritual and don't have a spiritual connection. They attend church out of obligation, habit, or community pressure. I witness religion as a separation of people. Too many paths proclaim that their path is the only way to God and that every other religion is wrong.

Spirituality is different from religion. Spirituality is an awareness of ourselves and others as spiritual beings. It is consciously connecting with Spirit. There is an understanding that our body and soul is an aspect of God/dess, and mystical practices and tools are used to create a spiritual awakening on both physical and spiritual levels. An energetic relationship exists between the Divine Spirit and human spirit. The seeker not only venerates the Universal Power of Love with gratitude, but also offers his or her body as a channel for spirit to enter into and work through.

Many spiritual people are seekers who enthusiastically explore various methods and techniques that enable them to create and maintain a connection with spirit during this lifetime and beyond. They have a conscious awareness of spirit every minute of every day. Spirit truly becomes a part of them and guides them. Spiritual seekers may or may not follow a particular path, and a great many (like me) will delight in the rich practices of various paths. Many use a variety of esoteric and mystical tools borrowed from any number of spiritual paths to dive into the river of Universal Love.

Mystical Practices

As spiritual beings dwelling in human bodies, we can easily tap into the omnipotent, omniscient, and omnipresent energy of God/dess. Some of us may have forgotten how to (or never really believed we could) create a sacred relationship with spirit. But some of us may have been taught that performing any spiritual practice other than prayer is evil; it's playing with black magic. As a young Christian, when I completely bought into the notion that "Thou shalt have no other gods before me" (Exodus 20:3), I turned a blind eye to the practices of our ancient priestesses, shamans and spiritual mystics. I was denied the rich and beautiful aspects of spirit. The fact is, the spiritual tools of the sages are divine and carry a positive vibration.

Since this book is about becoming a positive life-force energy for the planet, I believe it is critical for us to incorporate some form of spiritual practice, or at least awareness, in our daily lives. This does not mean practicing for an hour a day or committing to a single religion or path. It means expanding our consciousness and creating an awareness of ourselves as God/dess and connecting with the higher vibration. It can be as simple as spending a moment listening to the birds singing in the morning or as elaborate as a participating in multi-dimensional rituals.

Ahead are some introductory tools, derived from various spiritual paths, that can assist you in making your spiritual connection.

Suggested Reading to explore the topic of the soul:

Care of the Soul: A Guide to Cultivating Depth and Sacredness in Everyday Life, by Thomas Moore
The Soul's Code: In Search of Character and Calling, by James Hillman
Anatomy of the Spirit and *Sacred Contracts*, both by Caroline Myss
A Return to Love, by Marianne Williamson

9

TOOLS TO CONNECT SOUL AND UNIVERSAL SPIRIT

The method for becoming a Spirited woman is to engage in practices that enable us to connect with the highest vibration in existence—a Higher Power or Universal Energy, or God/dess.

In the equation *Personal Soul + Universal Spirit = Spirited*, the + means "connecting with." Just as connecting with another person takes place energetically (as illustrated in Chapter 4), so does connecting with a higher power. Connecting is a conscious action in which you are willing to give and receive energy. An infusion of the highest vibration will raise the vibration of a personal soul profoundly.

Nature

The ancient Japanese religion, Shinto, taught that rocks, plants, and animals were actually *kami*, or spirits. Tribes of North and South America traditionally honor the wisdom of plants, listen to messages in the wind and the calls of birds, and perform spiritual ceremonies among the trees and rocks. Prince Siddhartha mediated under a huge Bodhi tree until he became the enlightened Buddha. Jesus Christ proved his faith in God as he wandered the Judean desert.

I, too, believe that nature is a pathway to spirit, and that we connect with the Universal Light through its creations. Nature is an energetic carrier of divine vibrations that enter and heal our energy body. Nature is the medium through which we can tune into our inner wisdom and receive divine guidance. Making a practice of spending time in nature can help you on your path to becoming a Spirited woman by showing you how to be at one with your divine Self while uniting yourself with the healing, high vibrations of the Universe.

The untouched places—meadows, woods, wetlands, desert, and ocean—are thus sanctuaries for Divine communion. But we don't always need to trek out into the wilderness to connect with God/dess. Simply stopping to marvel at the simple creations that are in front of us is an act of spiritual union. Observing the zigzag flight pattern of a moth, feeling the texture of a rock, smelling the sweetness of moist soil, and drinking in the exquisite colors of the sky are moments of expanded awareness and transcendence from the mundane, and gestures of gratitude to the Great Creator.

I firmly believe that spending time in the countryside or wilderness is greatly beneficial. I recommend you do so whenever you can. Those of us who live in urban areas don't recognize how the din of people, tasks, our frenetic schedules and traffic, and the electronic energy waves from power lines, computers, and cell phone signals all interfere with our connection to our inner selves and spirit. Leaving the civilized world and absorbing the peaceful vibration of the earth helps us to feel a higher planetary vibration that we don't feel as easily inside a building in the city. Leaving behind our societal activities and perceptions of self invites us to empty our minds of the trivia that stands between us and joy. We become reacquainted with our truest essence.

Fully experiencing the sun, clean air, the land, animals, and plants calms and heals our over-stimulated systems. The earth exudes pure, positive energy. Clean air is filled with the vital life-force energy that purifies our cells and bloodstream and helps us function in our highest capacity. Replacing the buzz of electrical interference with the hum of a bee calms and rejuvenates our nervous system. Experiencing the vastness of the universe can help us put the minutia of our lives into proper perspective.

When we spend time alone in nature, we embark on an inner journey. We can explore the emotions and thoughts we have ignored or not expressed. We can process, without interruption, those things that are waiting to be released. We can channel new information, receive inspiration and guidance from within, more clearly hear our intuitive mind, and receive messages from the greatest Energy. We reunite with our soul's calling so that we can go forth in positive directions.

Being in nature can be hiking in the woods, camping in the wild lands, or gardening in your flower patch. Bird-watching and star-gazing, both with guidebooks, will help you see the limitless splendor of nature and expand your knowledge of it. Contemplating an ant will inspire awe of our own miraculous human bodies. Praying, singing and chanting out loud all create a powerful connection with the highest vibrations of all. Journaling and drawing will yield thoughts and pictures you didn't know existed inside you. I will often take my camera and make feeble attempts at capturing the depth and inexplicable greatness of the land. Photos are limited in what they can capture of nature's beauty, but photography is a fantastic exercise for truly seeing what is before you.

I most wholeheartedly recommend venturing into parkland. The U.S. National Park system protects our country's greatest natural treasures of unique geology and ecosystems, which offer infinite opportunities to explore your inner, as well as outer, landscapes.

I frequently go on solo camping trips in national or state parks, where I hike, explore, and meditate during the day, and then feast, sit by my fire, and gaze at the stars at night. For me, dwelling in the celestial temple of earth and sky is where I feel the closest to God/dess.

Experience the feeling of total solitude in nature by taking time to be totally alone. Another person's energy can be distracting from total immersion and communion with God/dess. However, if you are with a friend or group with the intention of communing with nature and God/dess through meditation, a drum circle, and other ritual, your own connection can escalate.

My Experience in Nature

The most profound and palpable connections I have had with God/dess, or Spirit, have come when I have been alone in nature. I truly feel that I merge with high energy, the highest, purest vibration, as I sit quietly on some friendly rocks or lie on the grass and watch the birds and listen to them warble, when I gaze up at the sky and the stars. A bright, starlit night sky instantly sends me into worship and connects me to my ancestors, who gazed at that same night sky and were possessed by the mystery of the cosmos. In nature, I feel so small and yet so large because I become a piece of the whole. We are all connected, and I truly feel the energy of the rocks as I touch them. I hug trees and feel their energy, and, yes, love. I admire the flowers and thank them for their beauty and scent. I feel myself, and thank myself for being the amazing creature and spiritual being that I am. I am in awe of who I am in the scheme of things. I am a part of the vastness of life and of the universe that I get to observe and participate in.

I have had many religious experiences while in nature. Once, when I was camping in Joshua Tree National Park in Southern California, I sat on a huge bolder and gazed at the sun as it set over distant, surreal, rock formations. As the golden ball sank slowly to the horizon, I sat and watched as the orange sky slowly faded into dark blue and the stars began to appear. The silhouettes of the rocks on the horizon looked like unearthly beings visiting earth. The dim landscape became celestial. For a moment, I became confused. Had I been transported to another planet? Was I on alien turf? Or was I a being from another planet, suddenly sitting in a desert on Earth? For an instant, I was both. My mind and soul had expanded. I could step outside my body and my preconceived notions of who I was, what I was, and where I was. I saw things from the perspective of a fully conscious and alive being. I felt intense gratitude for that moment of being present. I felt the true gift of being human and having the faculties to experience such a beautiful place in the universe. I expanded with intense love and appreciation for the gifts of God/dess/the universe and for my ability to receive them. As I felt the wonders of God/dess and the universe, my mind opened to the vastness of it all. I had briefly awakened from my tiny world of projects and limited thoughts into gigantic, unfamiliar, and yet very safe feelings that don't come from interactions with other humans in daily life.

Gratitude

Once upon a time, it is said, a Zen monk was walking through the woods. Two tigers began chasing him. The monk ran to the edge of a cliff, where he saw a vine he could climb down and escape. As he descended, he saw two more tigers waiting for him below. He looked up and saw a mouse nibbling the vine. In front of him, he noticed a big, ripe strawberry. He plucked the strawberry and ate it. It was the best strawberry he had ever eaten, and for that he felt extreme gratitude. Though he was facing his demise, the monk was able to be in the here and now and experience a pleasant morsel of life.

This little story shows us how even in the direst circumstances, life offers us morsels upon which we can focus and be grateful. When you maintain an *attitude of gratitude*, you will be energized by the beauty of existence, even in the midst of troublesome challenges.

I read somewhere that gratitude is the flame that sparks the cosmic consciousness. Cosmic consciousness is an understanding that all aspects of life are expressions of being. It helps us become aware of the beauty and vastness of life that is much grander than our personal lives on earth. Marsha Sinetar, author of *Ordinary People as Monks and Mystics*, refers to cosmic consciousness as a "peak experience," in which a person enters the absolute, if only for a second, and experiences himself *being*, rather than *becoming*. The individual's consciousness expands, causing him to feel he has everything because "he experiences everything within."[136] Through gratitude, we transcend our limited perceptions of a limited life, and experience the grandness of existence.

Gratitude is a high vibration radiated from the heart chakra, an expression of love and honor, an acknowledgment of the good in your life. Gratitude is appreciation for all you have and all you are. When you see the good in your life, your mood and vibration remain in a positive state. Lightness and joy are a part of your being. They allow harmony to reign over your daily life and relationships. Your self-esteem and self-love remain robust.

Maintaining an attitude of gratitude doesn't take any time. It requires no special mantras or exercises. But it does require you to be aware of your thoughts. Even on your worst day, there is so much for which to be grateful—your life on the planet Earth, your body, your health, your friends, your home, the flowers, the stars. Focusing on the treasures of life and expressing gratitude for them, especially during the challenging times, will energize your spiritual body, and positively affect your physical and mental being. You will become more resilient in life and not crumble under the slightest mishap. When you feel gratitude, your love energy is fueled and radiant. It sends out and attracts back both love and support.

When we focus on what we *don't* have, what we *aren't* gaining, and *what went wrong*, we become blind to the good in our life. When our mind wraps around lack, we feel frustrated, unhappy, helpless, and hopeless. We radiate a "downer vibration." We attract more negativity. Our relationships and self-esteem suffer. But shifting into a higher vibration of gratitude is as easy as switching your thoughts. Gratitude will help you deflect the affects of focusing on the negative.

With an attitude of gratitude, you may eventually find the gifts within your challenges. There is purpose in all things, and grateful thoughts will help you become more accepting and understanding of the mysteries of life. You will see what really is and understand it as a part of the human experience that enables the soul to grow. Things that cause doubt and worry can be seen as valuable lessons for growth, for which we can be thankful. In fact, you may begin to see no difference between "good" and "bad." You may stop making judgments about an event being good or bad.

My friend Sonja is an example. From a young age, Sonja was active and motivated. After college, she built a career in environmental biology with employment at a great company. She also volunteered in several ecological programs. Then, at the age of twenty-four, she was diagnosed with a retinal deterioration disease. Her eyesight was slowly fading. It became more and more difficult for her to perform her job and her daily tasks. Filled with fear, anxiety, and anger, she left her job.

Hearing that yoga would help reduce stress, she took a yoga class. There she found the inner peace she so greatly needed. She loved yoga and became filled with gratitude that she had been guided to discover her new passion. Her spirit became lighter and more joyful. Sonja soon made it her mission to become a yoga teacher and help others relieve their anxieties. With that decision, her whole life blossomed. Now she has a huge client list and is one of the premier yoga teachers in Los Angeles. She is joyful and focused, a deeper and more philosophical person. She can see the grand scheme of existence and is grateful for her life. She is surrounded by friends and appreciated by strangers who are attracted by her positive nature. Most impressive is her ability to manifest her desires. With a cosmically positive attitude and a heart filled with raw desire, she has attracted into her life an adoring and supportive husband, and after years of trying to get pregnant and then miscarrying, she finally conceived and gave birth to their first child. Sonja's connection to spirit enabled her to rise above frustration and anger to gratitude, joy and the manifestation of dreams. Amazingly, the deterioration of her eyesight slowed, and she still maintains some ability to see. She is a true inspiration for all who know her.

Like Sonja, we can learn that focusing on good brings good to us. When you see the rising sun or bring home a paycheck or cook a delicious meal, it's good to feel gratitude. Every day you jump out of bed with glowing health and a beautiful, feminine body, express your appreciation. Being aware of your blessings every minute of every day will lead you to a joyful life and create a higher vibrational spirit within you.

Gratitude Exercise

How do we express gratitude? By being aware of our blessings and expressing love and appreciation from our heart. Prayers of gratitude, even simple, one-sentence prayers, are powerful and can be uttered throughout the day. When I see a fantastic sunset, I say, "Wow! Thank you, God/dess!" Gratitude is like a cosmic hug.

In the morning as you drink your coffee, eat breakfast, or drive to work, express your gratitude for the day to come. Thank God/dess for the good things that you expect to happen that day. Thank God/dess for your loving and harmonious family, for a great day at work, for your efficiency and sharp thinking throughout the day, for your friendships and adventures. I guarantee you will have a great day. It is almost as if expecting a harmonious life creates it. In the book, *Ask and It Is Given: Learning to Manifest Your Desires* (the teachings of Abraham), by Esther and Jerry Hicks, the Law of Attraction is explained as "That which is like unto itself is drawn."[137] We receive that which we are grateful for.

At bedtime, express thanks, either orally or in writing, for every little good thing that happened for you during the day. Give thanks for the most mundane things, like clean water, food, good health, your apartment, your car, for the opportunity for your gifts to come through. Your list will help you see how really blessed you are and will fill your heart with joy as you drift off to sleep.

Ritual

I find it interesting that the word "ritual" resides within the word "spiritual." Perhaps it is only a coincidence that one of the greatest spiritual practices is ritual.

A ritual is a ceremonial act, religious or otherwise, that follows a prescribed rule or custom, through which an intention is set into place. Saying grace before eating blesses our food. Blowing out the candles on a birthday cake helps make a wish come true. Dressing up for a special date sets into motion the intention of having a good time.

As a spiritual activity, ritual can be a multi-dimensional, possibly participatory performance in which the body, mind, and spirit are engaged in an energy exchange with God/dess. Singing, dancing, drumming, praying, meditating, breathing, chanting, reenacting a myth, and reciting poetry or other inspirational literature all come together to create a sacred environment that welcomes the Highest Energy, communicates with divine spirit, and energizes the intention of an individual or a group. In ritual, human spirit unites with Cosmic Spirit. The intention settles deeply within the soul and is set aloft into the universe. This co-mingling of divine and earthly spirit is palpable, and creates a lasting impression on our soul, shifting our consciousness, raising our energetic body, and empowering the manifestation of our intention. Ritual is magical.

Ritual can be done unconsciously, but the most effective ritual is one of conscious design. Xia Moon, priestess and director of Temple of the Goddess in Los Angeles, describes ritual as "the formula, the recipe, for cellular alchemy. It provides a psychic pathway for transmutation to take place." She explains that during ritual, every aspect of the self is involved, including the physical, emotional, mental, and spiritual bodies. This is full-bodied experience that "encompasses the totality of the human expression, and the layers of meaningful action amplify the experience, thereby creating the potential for a deeper, cellular transformation than could ever be accomplished from, say, simply repeating an affirmation alone."[138]

Ritual is also a manifestation of the evolution of human consciousness. In *Primitive Mythology: The Masks of God*, Joseph Campbell surmises that the more advanced Neanderthal Man (who lived around 30,000-10,000 BCE) was the first to establish myth and ritual in a spiritual context. In the earliest temple caves, discovered in Ukraine, Spain, and France, there are inner and outer caves, hearths where fire glowed, and illustrations of "wizard beasts," dancing humans, and nude goddesses. Perhaps these caves were places where people connected with a greater spirit and where shamans performed ritual magic for successful and safe hunts.[139] Sculptures and cave paintings of feminine forms indicate a system of rites dedicated to the worship of the divine feminine, and perhaps these rituals were performed by both women and men.[140]

As human beings evolved, they became aware of phenomena over which they had no control. Life was filled with the inexplicable. Yet, somehow, the early mind discovered that the mysterious forces of nature could be controlled (to a certain extent) by the magic created through ritual. Rituals were performed to assure an easy birth, a successful hunt, the safe passage of the spirit of the dead to the underworld.

As spirituality became more sophisticated and deities were established as the masters of specific domains of nature, such as weather, fertility, and death, ritual practices were designed specifically for that deity. In the Eleusinian mysteries, for example, Greek priestesses engaged in elaborate rituals that lasted for days and included sacred drama, dance, and liturgy to please the goddess Demeter, ask her for healthy crops. Their intention may also have been for union with the goddess for power and a rewarding afterlife. Buddhists engage in rituals of chanting and meditation to energize peace and understanding in the universal spirit and end all suffering of sentient beings. Hindus breathe, meditate, and recite mantras for enlightenment. Tantric ritual uses energy exchange and breathing techniques to create divine union and achieve enlightenment. In their sweat lodge ceremonies, Native American tribes pray, chant, and pass the sacred pipe as they purify body and spirit. The rituals of Jewish synagogues and Christian churches incorporate choirs, scripture readings, and prayers to God.

Ritual amplifies our intention and transmits it into the cosmos. Because we are all connected in an infinite web of energy, the cosmos often responds. Intention is mindful direction, determination, and action toward a specified thing or purpose. As our intention vibrates into the universe, it attracts like energy and builds to a force of great influence, often manifesting the focus of the intention. As the pulse of intentional love energy soars into the collective energy field, for example, the entire planet benefits from a single ritual. Intention can take the form of a request for support, guidance, or healing, an expression of gratitude, or ascension into enlightenment.

Performing a Ritual

A ritual can be a simple, solo event or a group performance of epic proportions with hundreds of participants. You can plan your own ritual and fill it with eclectic elements from many sources or you can follow a pre-set formula as prescribed by a specific spiritual group. (You can find ritual formulas on the Internet and in books.)

It is interesting to note that most cultures share similar ritual tools to create a sacred space, focus the mind, and invoke spiritual energy. These tools can include the following:

- Tools needed to create a ritual environment:
1. An altar upon which to set sacred objects, such as statues of deities and items that symbolize deities. Christians use the cross to symbolize Jesus. Goddess worshippers may use a statue of one of the goddesses (Aphrodite, for example) or any of the objects that symbolize her, such as roses, doves, and conch shells.
2. Fire, including candles and bonfires
3. Incense

- Tools needed to raise energy and set intention:
4. Music, such as drumming and singing
5. Praying
6. Chanting
7. Dancing or other movement
8. Mudras, asanas, or other poses
9. Readings of poetry, sacred texts, or original works
10. Sacred libation (in some cultures)
11. Water for purification

- Tools needed for celebrations include a sacramental feast or potluck dinner.

Following is a basic ritual formula that invokes Spirit, energizes intention, merges human and Cosmic Spirit, and sets intention aloft. Whether used in solo or community ceremony, this ritual will create harmony in your soul and in the cosmic energetic web.

1. *Invocation.* Welcome the presence of God/dess to your ceremony. Your invocation can be an informal, "God/dess, please join us in celebration," or a more elaborate invitation with the lighting of candles, dancing, the ringing of a bell or playing a singing bowl, chanting *OM* three times, or whatever you'd like to do.
2. *Worship.* Recognize the divine spirit and express your reverence and appreciation with dance, poetry, and singing or chanting. Acknowledge the creative force of God/dess, and let Her know you honor Her greatness. Remember, as an emanation of Goddess, you are also expressing reverence and appreciation for yourself.
3. *Intentional prayer or meditation.* Speak your intention. In prayer, through song, or in writing, state what you wish to accomplish or bring to life, be it inner peace, world peace, enlightenment, assistance for someone in need, good health, abundance, or a new job. Whether you are alone or in a group, the power of intention is greatly amplified in ritual. When a common intention is set by a group, huge surges of intense energy are generated and sent into the cosmos. This positive energy will set off a reaction that greatly influences the outcome.
4. *Energizing your intention.* Focus to further energize your intention. Dancing, drumming or playing instruments, chanting, prayer, mediation, etc., with your intention in mind will breathe life into your intention.
5. *Expressing gratitude.* Give thanks for the presence and action of the God/dess, usually expressed as prayer. Give thanks that your intention has been heard and know it will come to life. Then expand the gratitude to include all of your blessings and everything that you are, have, have done, and will do. Finally, give thanks for the presence of the higher spirit among you at this time.
6. *Celebration.* Knowing your intention has been heard and is set into motion, engage in joyful activity that honors the God/dess and all of life. This can be drumming, singing, dancing, playing instruments, or any other activity that is highly spirited.
7. *Closure.* Thanking the benevolent spirits for their presence and releasing them. Prayer, song, applause, hugs, blowing out of candles, chanting *OM*.

I have participated in many different kinds of rituals, from minor gestures to major productions, and each time I experience a deep peace and closeness to Universal Power, which is always described as love. There is no wrong way to perform ritual. If the intent is pure and good, it will be received by the cosmos.

For more information on ritual and the Temple of the Goddess, log onto www.templeofthegoddess.com. *The Mysteries of Demeter* by Jennifer Reif delivers the history of worship of Greek goddess Demeter and describes what may have been the ritual services performed at the sacred temple of Eleusis near Athens, which operated from the Mycenaean era (1,900-1,100 BCE) until the 4th century CE. Another recommended book is *The Spiral Dance*, by Starhawk, which introduces the ancient Goddess religion as it has been revived through pagan and Wiccan practices and explains how to create and perform rituals.

Sacred Dance

We'll never know when humans first began to dance, but evidence points to the possibility of dance as a part of ritual and worship since the time humans first acknowledged a spiritual force. The early shaman danced until she entered a trance state. At ancient Egyptian religious festivals, priestesses danced for the goddess Hathor in celebration of her arrival. Ancient Sumerian priestesses danced and twirled with snakes in hand. Every gesture of the Hindu Bharata Natyam dance was one of veneration to one of many goddesses. All through history, we have seen evidence of people of various spiritual and religious paths who have danced to connect with God/dess in celebration of birth, death, woman, and manhood initiations. Of the religious mysteries, or ancient, special rituals, Andrew Lang, author of *Myth, Ritual and Religion*, wrote that we "cannot find a single ancient mystery in which there is no dancing… Of those who reveal the mysteries, they 'dance them out.'"[141]

Dance is prayer in motion, a way to communicate with the divine. Dance is an expression of gratitude, a request for guidance, a pact of partnership to assure success of a pursuit. When we dance, God/dess energy is present. The vibration of the dancer rises to a joyful level and radiates it to her community and the world. Dance is our reunion with spirit. It's an invitation to the divine to dwell within us. When we invite the divine to dwell in us, we usually release control over our body and mind and act as a channel for spirit. The body may move in ways the dancer never thought she could. She feels the ecstasy of surrender to divine energy. Negativity is released, and passion, joy, and inner peace are experienced. This infusion of spiritual energy is an emotionally, mentally, and physically healing, meditative experience. In trance dance, we are dancing to ask the divine spirit to enter our body and work through us. Our mind becomes free of meaningless thoughts. Our third eye is energized and more receptive to insights, inspirations, and intuitions. In ancient religions, priestesses received oracles, or divine messages, while dancing. Trance dancers of ancient times and in contemporary Native American cultures danced to the beat of a drum for hours and days, non-stop and without food and water, to create the deepest connection with spirit and gain an understanding and appreciation of life. According to Frank Natale, author of *Trance Dance*, drum beats at 120 per minute will send the dancer into an altered state of consciousness and separate the mind from the body, allowing the body to become a channel of spirit energy.

Sacred dance is a creative expression of soul. When a dancer allows her spirit to express what is within, she is creating a dimension of ethereal beauty that entertains and raises the vibration of the audience. Dance as expression will energize the throat chakra and clear it of any negative energy that stands in the way of your ability to communicate. It enables you to convey the feelings inside you.

Dance Exercise

With the intention of connecting with or worshipping the Higher Power, dancing as a form of worship can be performed anytime and anywhere, alone or with a group. Either way, first set your intention for the dance. Do you wish to express gratitude? Channel spirit and receive its energy and messages? Both? In dance, you are free to give and receive as you please.

Ancient dancers moved to drumbeats and the music of simple string and wind instruments, but we have the benefit of worlds of music. In fact, world music is a wonderful aid for dancing. Its tunes swirl and move with exotic instrumentation and motivating rhythms. Find several selections that you like, a mixture of fast and slow.

If you are expressing worship of the God/dess, let your body take beautiful shapes and positions and move with joy and gratitude. It is vital that you release all judgment of your dancing abilities and just enjoy your physical being. Dance with appreciation, celebration, and reverence with all your heart and soul. Project your energy toward the heavenly realms. Soon you will feel the loving vibration of the God/dess resonating with you. As you dance in partnership with the divine, your energies mingle. You receive the joyful electricity of the God/dess while she gleefully experiences your brilliant light.

For trance dance, you need a CD that has continuous rhythmic music, preferably with strong percussion. Trance dance invites Spirit to fill you as you empty your mind and release control over your physical body. It may take awhile to enter into a trance state, but there is great benefit if you dance in a surrendered state for half an hour.

For the first few minutes of your dance, move with purpose and creativity. After you have warmed up and feel ready to let go, release all effort and allow your body to move on its own. Release all thoughts. It may take several minutes to an hour to become fully entranced and become a channel for spirit, at which point you may enter a meditative state when your conscious mind empties to make room for divine thoughts and inspiration. Your body will move on its own, moving slowly and gracefully or frenetically and wildly. Let yourself enjoy the ecstasy and freedom of spirit flowing through you. Continue for as long as you would like or are able. Be receptive to cosmic or God/dess energy, and you will feel the buzz of a high vibration penetrate you. You may receive important information or physical healing. After you feel satisfied and full of spirit energy, release the movement and sit quietly to feel the generous love of the benevolent God/dess shower over you.

I encourage you to dance as much as you can. Not only will you feel more feminine and joyful, but it is a wonderful workout for the body. If possible, work with a teacher of ecstatic dance. In the Los Angeles area, I recommend a divine dancer named Heaven who teaches Spirit Dancing. Her gatherings encourage participants to express through movement what is in their souls while inviting in the energy of God/dess to enter and merge to create a dance of spirited celebration. Learn more at www.spiritdancing.org.

Tara Dance, a dance of devotion and peace, is presented worldwide by Prema Dasara and Anahata Iradah. Performed in the spirit of Tara, the Tibetan Goddess of Compassion and Wisdom, Tara Dance is empowering and inspiring. It is endorsed by the Dalai Lama himself. For more information, log onto www.taradhatu.com or www.traveling-light.net.

Prayer

Prayer is the outwardly directed communication of our soul to the Highest Benevolent Power, God/dess. Prayer can be presented as an elaborate liturgy of words and verse, with the physical emphasis of prostrations, or as simple thoughts and feelings that vibrate from the heart. However prayer is expressed, miracles are activated, outcomes influenced, and requests manifested into reality.

As children in the Western world, we may have been encouraged to say grace at dinner—"God is great, God is good, and we thank him for our food. Amen"—recite simple prayers at bedtime, or memorize the Lord's Prayer. These may be sweet introductions to God, but they are not very effective as a means of communication. Prayer is more than mere memorization and reciting of rote verse. It is a full-body, spiritual experience in which we merge with God/dess energy, and transmit our worship and our heart's expression to it.

Because we are energetic beings, our thoughts and emotions are transmitted into the cosmos. Positive thoughts or vibrations unconsciously sent to the universe fuel the good that we then experience. However, our thoughts fluctuate day to day, and even minute to minute, from faith to doubt, from positive to negative, which results in manifestations that are scattered or completely nullified. Prayer is a clear, unwavering message that is communicated with focused intention to God/dess. It is the cause of deep desire, emphatic mindfulness, and firm belief that assures the desired effect from the Highest Power.

Looking at the grand scheme of human evolution, unspoken prayer probably preceded language. Cave paintings of stags, bison, and ponies led early archaeologists to believe that animals were perceived as divine. Some paintings show a shaman interacting with the animals. These images are found on several continents, with drawings in caves in North Africa decorated with similar imagery to caves in France, of men with arms upraised before a buffalo, and couples dancing before bulls.[142]

Female figures found in Paleolithic caves lead us to believe that the female body was also experienced as a divine force. Woman may have been perceived as an "effective magical force" during menstruation and pregnancy.[143] Were thoughts and emotions transmitted in community rituals to the beasts and goddesses symbolized on the cave walls to ask for a successful hunt or a safe birth? Did images of beasts or women appear in the minds of our ancient sisters and brothers? In the depths of despair, did they send out emotional pleas for comfort and guidance?

Today, we are beginning to recognize the science behind prayer and learning how prayer can become more effective as a spiritual tool. Gregg Braden, author of *The Isaiah Effect: Decoding the Lost Science of Prayer and Prophecy*, studied the texts of ancient religions and contemporary science. In his exploration of the Dead Sea Scrolls, believed to have been written by the Essenes, a group of spiritual mystics who lived in Judea between the second century BCE and the first century CE, Braden deciphered the ancient secrets of effective prayer that corroborate many of the findings of today's scientists. Prayer is a single, strong vibration that results from the unification of thoughts, feelings and emotions, experienced as heart, mind, and body, whose effects are manifested in our outer world.[144] When thoughts, feelings, and emotions remain constant in our thoughts and prayer, we can create abundance and healings, experience peace during chaos, and produce good in our lives and the lives of others.

In his book, *The Science of Mind*, Ernest Holmes writes that "Prayer is not an act of overcoming God's reluctance, but should be an *active* acceptance of Its highest willingness."[145] I, too, believe God and the Universe are benevolent and of unlimited good. Because the good already exists within us and around us, our prayers become more than a plea to a God that is "out there." Instead, when we pray, it is an activation of the good that already exists within us and around us. In a universe of infinite possibility, we can influence the world as our creation with our strong belief. As thoughts, feelings and emotions, prayer translates into belief, and belief can manifest our deepest desires. As Jesus said, "Therefore, I tell you, whatever you ask in prayer, believe that you receive it, and you will."[146]

Modes of Prayer

Prayer activates the third eye and crown chakras and opens the throat chakra, creating a mode of communication that resonates at the highest vibration. Prayer doesn't need to be a big, formal affair. It can be short and sweet, but it does require sincerity, focus, and true desire to connect and be heard. While prayers can be traditional verses written centuries ago for particular purposes, they can also be expressed in song. When sung with heart and soul, songs directed to High Spirit have all the meaning of a spoken prayer. Christian hymns are such a form of prayer, as are popular songs with spiritual intention, such as George Harrison's songs "My Sweet Lord" and "Give Me Love," both of which speak of his devotion to the spiritual path of Krishna.

Best of all, prayer can be expressed at any time, anywhere, with free-form, flowing words, and positive intention. If you aren't used to praying, this may be a good time to practice.

To pray, take a moment to close your eyes and focus on spiritual energy. Acknowledge that God/dess is with you, all around you, and within you. Then connect with all of your heart, opening to love and receiving love. Connect as if you are with a dear girlfriend or your beloved. This connection of love energy with Spirit is the "juice" with which your prayer is activated. Speak unabashedly and without inhibition. Be yourself and be real. Pray with all of your heart. Don't be ashamed to cry, whether you are in desperate need for help or shedding tears of joy. The benevolent God/dess is nonjudgmental. Releasing what you may be unable to share with any human may provide intense relief and stir great emotion. When your prayer is complete, know that it is heard and then release it into the Universe. This release represents your full faith that God/dess has heard you and that action will be taken. After praying, you will feel lightness, inner peace, and joy. Your energy will vibrate at a much higher level.

Prayer is not limited. There are infinite reasons for prayer. Here are a few of the most common purposes of prayer.

Prayer of Gratitude. We know that an expression of gratitude is key to living a joyful existence. Please perform regularly. (See Gratitude section.)

Prayer for Guidance. Acknowledging that we can't do it on our own and asking the God/dess to take our hand and lead us in the right direction is both humbling and (ironically) empowering. We live in a world of infinite possibilities and options, and sometimes we must admit that we have taken a wrong turn, and we are not sure of what other road to travel. By "letting go and letting God/dess," we can release expectations and open our mind to other possibilities. When we ask for guidance, we are making way for divine intervention. Inspiring thoughts may awaken us to a path or direction we have never before considered.

When you are given divine guidance, it is likely you are being led to something that serves you and/or is an expression of your soul. In this case, you will know in your heart that this is exactly what is right for you to do. You will feel grateful for the inspiration and opportunities that show up. Please know that often the guidance may not be what you think it should be, but your soul will respond in a strong, positive way that your personality will find difficult to resist.

Prayer Asking for Comfort. There is no better way to cope or find comfort than by connecting with Spirit. Spirit helps to put things into perspective by reminding us, on a deep, subconscious level, that the vastness of life includes things we don't understand. If you are suffering from grief, spirit will help you detach from the pain and help you become aware of peace. Taking a moment to commune with a power that is greater than yourself and asking for comfort will help you to relax and even escape from discomfort.

Prayer for Compassion and the Healing of Others. I learned from Buddhists that there is no greater expression of love or service than to ease the suffering of all sentient beings. Indeed, letting go of our own existence and being consciously aware of others' pain is in itself a spiritual experience. Transmitting our positive energy into the situation and requesting the assistance of the Higher Power to provide healing and comfort will indeed energize the healing, comforting energy of the universe.

Science has proved that prayer has healed people of disease. Studies have shown that long-distance praying is effective at reducing pain and illness in a subject. Christian Scientists believe in prayer as the sole healing tool. Most spiritual communities and churches have prayer groups that meet regularly, if not daily, to fulfill prayer requests to ease pain or to focus on a national or world-wide crisis.

Affirmative Prayer. An affirmation is a statement of something as if it were true. An affirmative prayer is a prayer in which you affirm that the result is *already* manifest. This is the trickiest kind of prayer, because to truly affirm that something already is so, you must believe it with all your heart. Half-hearted, "kinda think so" believing is ineffective. You must embody the feeling of the desired outcome as if you already know how it feels. Deeply connecting with spirit, stating what you want or need as if it already is, being grateful that it is done, and then releasing it into the universe *knowing it is done* will make it so. As prescribed by the Essenes, affirmative prayer unites thoughts, feelings, and emotions to manifest a desire or need.

The Science of Mind, by Ernest Holmes, explains in depth the science of affirmative prayer. In the following paragraphs, I've distilled a few of the essential elements of effective affirmative prayer from this book.

First, embody the greater good. We must realize the spiritual universe is perfect, and God is complete and perfect. Recognize the presence of God and Good. Know that God sees you as perfect. Know that you, a creation of God, are perfect. When saying affirmative prayer, understand that the perfection of God is embodied within you. When praying affirmatively, start by acknowledging absolutely, "Perfect God within me, Perfect Life within me, come forth into expression through me as that which I am; lead me ever into the paths of perfection and cause me to see only the Good."[147]

Next, turn away from the condition that you wish to change by conceiving the opposite in your mind and prayer. For example, if a health issue causes you concern, pray *for* the good that you wish for, not *against* the ill you wish to heal. Speak knowing that you have a capacity to fully experience the good that you wish. Conceive of the outcome as if it has already happened. Focus on what you want.[148]

Pray with feeling and emotion. "The more exalted, the more heavenly, the more boundless . . . the thought is, the more power it will have."[149] You must know within your very being that your word is received, and not merely intellectually accept it.[150] Know that God/dess is present and fully receiving your words and your feelings. Passion will solidify your prayer.

Give gratitude for all of the blessings that abound in your life right now. Know, without a doubt, that some action will result from your prayer.[151] A traditional ending of a prayer as spoken by Science of Mind followers is, "And So It Is. Amen." You know in your heart it is done.

For more details on affirmative prayer, I recommend *The Science of Mind*, where you can read all of the principles of the Science of Mind, a blend of ancient wisdom and New Thought philosophies. On-line courses that teach the fundamentals of Science of Mind, including detailed techniques of affirmative prayer, can be found at http://enhancing.com/foundational/.

Mantras and Chanting

A mantra is similar to prayer in that both are verbal communications directed to God/dess to manifest tremendous joy, freedom, and spiritual enlightenment. While a prayer can be a free-form flow of words and emotion, a mantra is a formally designed, sacred sound or phrase that works scientifically with the energy centers of the body and Universal Spirit to stimulate specific responses and effects.

As you learned in the Human Energy chapter, ancient Hindu spiritual adepts discovered that the vibrations of certain sounds create frequencies that influence the energies in our chakras. They also determined that stringing together various sounds and phrases would resonate with universal energy and create a cosmic connection. These dual effects of chanting mantras fill our subtle bodies with positive, balanced energy and attract positive universal energy to us. Buddha also discovered the power of the mantra and incorporated it into the Buddhist practice. Chanting mantras is a deeply engrained traditional Buddhist practice.

The positive affects of mantras are numerous. Chanting brings our energy back into balance and opens our consciousness to our true selves, freeing us from ego, false identity, and attachments to the material, all of which can bring us dissatisfaction and sadness when we place too much importance upon them.

Mantras can also clean up our karma. Karma is the Sanskrit word for "action." Buddhist philosophy takes the concept a step further and includes the motivation or intention while taking the action as karma. Buddha said of karma, "If a person commits an act of good or evil, he himself becomes the heir to that action. This is because that action actually never disappears." A dormant force that is activated by mental, verbal, and physical actions, karma can lead to a potentially good or bad result that can appear in the present, the future and even future lifetimes.[152]

Hindus have a similar take on karma. *Chant and Be Happy*, a book based on the Krishna teachings of Bhaktivedanta Swami Prabhupada, explains karma this way. "For every material action performed, nature forces an equivalent reaction upon the performer."[153] The *Bhagavad Gita: As It Is,* the sacred text of Krishna Consciousness, calls karma "fruitive activities." According to one's karma, in material nature, he is manifested into an animal or man. Otherwise, he reaches immortality and transcends the wheel of life, and ascends to the "material heavenly planets."[154]

Chanting positive sounds will dissolve negativity that we may hold within us and that may be manifesting now or in the future. When we chant a mantra over and over, our mind transcends the mundane and unites with spirit of Self and with Spirit of the universe, becoming one. Chanting a mantra will fill you with God/dess Consciousness, which will fill you with pure love, joy, and inner peace. This positive essence transmits from the body and ripples out into the universe, to which the universe responds by returning blessings and more positive energy.

The Hindu believed that Universal Spirit is both feminine (Shakti) and masculine (Shiva). These divine names personify the various aspects of divine nature in a pantheon of goddesses and gods, each of whom represented a particular aspect of divine and human nature, such as love, creativity, abundance, and spiritual enlightenment. Mantras were devised to address each deity directly, to energize his or her particular aspect, and draw that aspect to us. For example, chanting mantras directed to Laxshmi, the goddess of abundance, attracts the energy of prosperity and money. Chanting to Shakti awakens the feminine aspects of the Self. There are hundreds, if not thousands, of mantras praising the deities, expressing gratitude, or invoking blessings. These mantras have survived the centuries and are still used in spiritual practice today.

Adepts recommend that a mantra be chanted 108 times per session, starting with one or two sessions a day. It is recommended that serious students chant a minimum of sixteen sessions a day. Mala beads (a string of beads that looks somewhat like a rosary) are recommended to keep track of your counting. They can be purchased at any New Age shop, Krishna temple, or from sources found on the Internet. You can also create your own mala by stringing together 108 beads of the same size, with one large bead, called the master bead, at one point in the circle of beads. Chanting while sitting quietly with the eyes closed will help you to focus completely on the energy of the mantra. Holding the beads in your hand, with the bead between the thumb and forefinger, begin chanting the mantra with the first bead after the master bead. Continue with the rest of the beads. You will know you have completed a full round when you return to the master bead.

If you are committed to healing or energizing a particular aspect of your life, such as opening for transformation or drawing in love, some gurus advise that the mantra be repeated for forty days. However, you can create a beautiful connection with Spirit even if you chant less. Seven is a mystical number, and when you chant seven, fourteen, or twenty-one times (or in more multiples of seven), your consciousness and beingness will shift.

Hundreds of Hindu and Buddhist mantras, each designed to create a particular vibration for specific purposes, have been chanted for centuries. Following are but a few classic mantras that will open your heart and mind to Universal Spirit. If, because of your religious upbringing, you feel resistant to communicating with a deity other than the Judeo-Christian God, please remember that we're working with *energy*. The Goddess, God, us—we're ALL spirit and ALL a form of God/dess. Chanting to a God/dess is a prayer to God.

OM
The sound of Universal Spirit, and the highest vibration of all of existence, *OM* will draw Universal Spirit to you to raise your own spiritual vibration.

Mantra for Truth and Bliss
Sat Chit Ananda Namaha
(Pronounced *Sat Chit An nan da Na ma ha*)
Translation: May our minds be filled with Truth. And may Bliss be our only reality.

Mantra to Shakti to reveal the true nature of reality and purify feminine energy.
Hrim Shrim Klim Parameshwari Swaha
(Pronounced *Hreem Shreem Kleem Para-mesh-wari Swa-ha*)
Translation: "Salutations to the Supreme Feminine. May that abundant principle which hides the nature of ultimate reality be attracted to me."

Mantra to invoke Shiva and prepare his union with Shakti
Om Shiva Hum
(Pronounced *Om Shee Vah Hoom*)

Mantra to Tara, the Divine Mother of Tibetan Buddhists, for Universal Peace
Om Tare Tuttare Ture Sarva Shantim Kuru Swaha
(Pronounced *Om Tah-rei Too-tah-rei Too-rei Sahr-vah Shahn-teem Koo-roo Swah-hah*)
Translation: "Om and salutation to She who is the source of all blessings, please bring peace to all."[155]

If you are interested in learning more and discovering more mantras, I recommend a book titled *Shakti Mantras: Tapping into the Great Goddess Energy Within*, by Thomas Ashley-Farrand. This book delivers in-depth information on the history of mantras and an in-depth study of various Hindu goddesses for whom numerous mantras are given.

Meditation

Millennia ago in India, early Hindu spiritual adepts seeking enlightenment discovered the powerful benefits of sitting still, watching the breath, and emptying the mind. They learned that by tuning out the distractions of the three-dimensional world and suspending awareness of all thought, they could create an unobstructed channel primed to connect them with the Highest Cosmic Power to receive energy, wisdom, and guidance. This connection would yield a greater understanding of Self and an expanded awareness of all that is. Through meditation, one could attain liberation from the mortal body, freeing it from rebirth in the world of humanity.

The Upanishads is a collection of sacred Hindu scriptures written by the seers and saints of ancient India as long ago as the seventh century BCE. They are the first texts to introduce the concept of meditation. By merging the prana, or primal energy, of the soul of the universe, and the life force energy of the human body, divine union is made. The texts express the importance of the mantra *OM*, the sound of the Brahman, or the energy of the Divine Spirit that dwells in everything and within the Self. Meditating on and chanting *OM* helps us transcend our mundane thoughts and tap into cosmic consciousness, which is an understanding that all aspects of life are expressions of being. Through meditation, we can become the receiver of divine energy, resulting in wisdom, inner peace, and love.

In the fifth century BCE, the young Prince Siddhartha, wishing to attain enlightenment, earnestly meditated under the Bodhi tree. After several months, he awakened as the Buddha, or spiritual master. Henceforth, he prescribed meditation as a tool for gaining insight and wisdom in understanding the reality of life. Meditation is used to release ego-centeredness and those things that make us unhappy, such as attachment, delusion, ignorance, greed, hate, and false belief in self. When ego is released and enlightenment, or awakening, is attained, we become free from karma and the cycle of birth, suffering, death, and rebirth.

Ever since those long-ago days in India, meditation has remained a vital spiritual tool, and many contemporary spiritual paths around the world incorporate meditation and contemplation in their practices. Meditation is similar to prayer in that it is a vehicle for connecting with God/dess. However, while prayer is active communication that we direct to God/dess, meditation is passive and receptive, allowing us to hear God/dess's message. It's said that prayer speaks and meditation listens.

To meditate, you must release your awareness of your chattering mind and the over-stimulated world and tap into silence and nothingness, which is the true spirit of your being. Meditation is not a shutting down of awareness, but a hyper-awareness of the All that is beyond your human existence. In this spiritual space, we are open to receive divine guidance and inspirations that we would otherwise never hear.

Sitting in silence helps us transcend daily life and enter higher realms of higher consciousness. In the modern-day world, meditation is recommended for stress relief and a path to physical and mental well-being. When left unchecked, stress can be the source of many illnesses, including heart disease, insomnia, and depression. Stress, the primal "fight-or-flight" response our bodies enter during a fearful moment, stimulates the adrenal glands, which increase the production of adrenaline to prepare us for action. In our hyperactive American lifestyle, with stressful jobs, families, and more, our adrenal glands may function all day in hyper-drive. So stressful is our normal life, in fact, that many of us barely notice the detrimental effects stress has on our bodies, minds, and souls. Meditation lets us "drop out" for a while and relax, which enables us to become centered again. In fact, many doctors recommend meditation to their overstressed patients. The muscles relax, the adrenal glands return to normal, the heart rate slows, and the eyes rest. We are restored to physical and mental well-being. Taking as little as a few minutes to meditate, even closing your eyes for a few minutes at work, thus brings benefits. Longer meditation sessions create a deeper rest and more powerful connection to spirit.

There are numerous methods of meditation, from Transcendental Meditation (TM) to Buddhist Vipasssana, from walking meditation to waking meditation, from empty mind to guided imagery. Through meditation, the crown and throat chakras become open channels for spirit, enabling us to receive vibrations of the Highest Power while simultaneously becoming a transmitter of positive vibrations into the cosmos to benefit all. By disengaging awareness of the physical body, we become open to inspiring messages that may really be our own intuitions. Below are meditation techniques that you can perform at home or in nature.

Transcendental Meditation

In 1958, Maharishi Mahesh Yogi introduced Transcendental Meditation (also called TM), which is based on ancient Hindu practices, to the world. Maharishi taught that by meditating twenty minutes a day, twice a day, we can transcend to a "quieter" place. His prescribed practice doesn't ask you to concentrate or contemplate, but to let your mind naturally let go. When we transcend thought, he says, we enter a state of pure consciousness. A commitment to the practice will result in a constant feeling of lightness, peace, and restfulness. Ultimately, unity consciousness is attained, in which we feel a love and devotion to God/dess and gain an understanding of all of creation.

To practice TM, find a quiet place and get comfortable. Sit upright with your back straight, either on the floor with your legs crossed, or in a chair, hands in lap, palms up. Now simply relax and let your mind go. Release all thoughts. Eventually your mind will slow down, and body functions, such as breathing, will also become slower. Practice TM for at least twenty minutes twice a day, in the morning and evening, every day. For more information, including teachers and TM groups in your area, visit their website at http://tm.org/.

Vipassana Meditation

A Buddhist meditation, Vipassana, means "to see things as they really are." Like TM, this practice teaches us to release the chatter and impure thoughts from our mind and focus on the body and observation of the Self. While the essence of this meditation is simple, the practice is not easy. With our addictions to our lists of things to do, reruns of emotionally-charged situations, and worry about the future, it takes great discipline to relax the mind and concentrate on the most mundane of actions, just breathing.

Sit on the floor with your legs crossed and your back straight. Concentrate on your breath, focusing on the slow inhalation and exhalation of air into the lungs. In and out, in and out. Maintain your focus on your breath. Should any thoughts enter your mind, gently ask them to leave, mentally wave them away, and return your focus to your breathing. After a time, you will enter a zone in which your mind is completely empty of thought. This is similar to sleep, but devoid of any visions or thoughts. Deepak Chopra calls this "the gap," "the state of pure awareness, that silent space between thoughts, that inner stillness that connects you to true power."[156] Maintain your breathing and your empty mind for an hour or more. While this sounds like a long time, on Vipassana retreats, people do the meditation for several hours during the day or over an entire weekend with just a few breaks.

Walking Meditation

Thich Nhat Hanh, a contemporary Zen Buddhist master and author of *The Miracle of Mindfulness* and *A Guide to Walking Meditation*, teaches a walking meditation practice in which inner peace is attained through full awareness of every move we make. This is an excellent exercise for becoming fully present, as it asks that we become aware of every aspect of our being and all that is around us in every step we take. With each step, feel your foot as it touches the ground and your muscles as they flex with your steps. Feel your arms as they swing past your hips. Notice the sound under your feet. You will be amazed at how easy it is to release mundane worries and thoughts when you become fully present.

Thich Nhat Hanh's meditative technique can be applied to everyday activities from washing the dishes to drinking a cup of tea. It takes us out of states of worry about the future and things that don't even exist and helps us become more conscious of the life at each present moment, with full awareness of our body and the world. This is truly living. While there is great benefit to performing the walking exercise for as little as a half hour, the recommendation is to hold this expanded consciousness all day, and all through your life.

Breathing Meditation

As you know from the Human Energy chapter, breathing exercises are vital to raising the energy in the body. The Hindus, who first identified the transcendental nature of breathing, incorporate breathing exercises in their mediations. See the Complete Breath exercise in the Human Energy chapter.

Sit on the floor, on a pillow, or on a chair with your legs crossed and back straight. Take a moment to relax. Chant *OM*, allowing the word to extend the length of the exhalation of your breath. Allow it to last as long as is comfortable. For the first half of the breath, allow the O to be the main sound, and on the second half of the breath let M be the main sound. Feel the vibration of the O in your heart, and M in your third eye. Repeat two more times for a total of three *OM*s. Sit for a moment and feel the reverberation in and around your body.

Now perform the Complete Breath exercise, slowly and meditatively. Really focus on your breath as it enters your lungs. Feel your ribs and back expand. Hold your breath as long as is comfortable. Allow your mind to be empty during this moment. Then exhale slowly, maintaining keen presence on the departure of your breath from your lungs and the contraction of your ribs. Perform this breath seven times, total.

Now your body and mind are prepared to enter a deep meditation. Sit still and relish the peace in your body and mind. Do all you can to allow your mind to remain free of chatter and allow divine energy to fill your body and soul. Maintain your meditation for a minimum of twenty minutes.

Yantras

A yantra, also known as a mandala, is a visual pattern or design in which the shapes and lines create a vibration that resonate with the energy of the universe and the energy within the body. Similar to, and as powerful as, a mantra, the design of a yantra corresponds to the chakras and energy centers in the body and attracts positive energy from the universe. When used in meditation, yantras balance the chakras and create a connection with the great universal energy. During meditation, a yantra is used as a companion tool with a mantra. This powerful combination of visual and sound vibrations can invoke intense peace, love, and spiritual connection.

While there are many yantras with various design and line combinations, many powerful designs remain constant and have been used for centuries in their true form. The Sri Yantra is one such design. (You'll find a Sri Yantra in Chapter 6, *Yoni Magic*.) With converging upward and downward triangles, and often surrounded by a circle of lotus petals, the Sri Yantra symbolizes the merging of the energies of the feminine (downward triangle) and masculine (upward triangle). The dot in the center of the design is the point at which focus is directed during meditation.

You can find many colorful and beautiful yantras on the Internet. (Use the Google search engine and the key word Yantra.) You will be presented with an array of various patterns. Print one out and stare into it for a lovely shift in your consciousness.

To meditate on the Sri Yantra, use one of the most powerful mantras with it, *Om Mani Padme Hum* (see Chapter 4). While gazing at the center point of the yantra, chant the mantra 108 times. This meditation will attract, stimulate, and balance the feminine and masculine energies within you. This practice can transport you into a state of bliss, joy, and expansion.

Kali Yantra

*In Hindu tradition, Kali is the fierce and benevolent mother goddess
and destroyer of negative ego.*

Mudras

Our hands are powerful energy radiators and receivers. A mudra is a
hand gesture, with the fingers and palm positioned in a certain way
to create an energy vortex used to connect with Universal Energy. You
may be familiar with some mudras, such as the prayer position, with
the palms of hands together and fingers straight up, or the hand gesture
of Buddha in meditation, with index finger and thumb touching
each other to make a circle. Even a simple hand up with the palm
facing a person as you say, "Hi," is a kind of mudra in which your
positive energy sprays out of your palm to the other person. These, and
hundreds of other simple hand postures, energize the subtle energy in
the body while attracting divine energy from the universe.

Mudras were developed by Hindu spiritualists and later fully embraced by Buddhist mystics, who discovered that the pure essence of spirit can be generated by simple positions of the fingers, hands, and arms. Just as each mantra and yantra creates a specific vibration and yields a subtly different effect, so does each mudra. Mudras work with all of the energy centers in the body, including chakras, meridians, and nadis, to energize the entire body and create transmitter-like action for drawing positive energy in from the universe.

Within our fingers exist about 4,000 nerve endings,[157] so think of the energy that flows through them. Now consider that each finger represents one of the five elements, and is influenced by a planet:

- *Thumb:* Fire and Mars, influencing willpower, logic, and ego.
- *Forefinger:* Air and Jupiter, influencing knowledge.
- *Middle finger:* Ether and Saturn, influencing patience and emotional control.
- *Ring finger:* Earth and the Sun, influencing vitality, health, and matters of the heart.
- *Little finger:* Water and Mercury, influencing spoken and written communication, beauty, and creativity.[158]

With the chakra energy of our palms and the energetic influence of each finger, placing the hands, fingers, and arms in certain gestures creates a variety of positive results that range from physical rejuvenation, to emotional balancing, expanded consciousness, and keener intuition, to the most delicious spiritual connections.

As symbolic gestures, mudras are used to communicate with God/dess. The sacred Indian dance, Bharata Natyam, incorporates a variety of mudras to express the love for the God/dess and desire to connect with Her. While the dancer herself often enters states of ecstasy during the dance, the entire audience will experience the divine vibration generated by the dancer's mudras.

You may incorporate mudras into your meditation and make them a small part of your session, or you can center your meditation specifically around the mudras. Either way, mudras will enhance the spiritual energy in your session.

As with mantras, there are dozens of mudras, each used for a specific purpose. Below are a few basic mudras that will amplify the energy of your meditation.

Guyan Mudra

Creates receptivity and calm.

How to form: Bring the tips of the thumb and index fingers together to make a circle. Extend the rest of the fingers. During meditation, rest the hands on the knees with palms facing upward.

Uttararbodhi Mudra

Symbolizes perfection and connection with a supreme power.

How to form: Bring palms together. Index fingers touch and point upwards. Thumbs can cross or are held next to each other. Other fingers are interlaced. During meditation, hands are held at the heart area or over the head.

Adi Shakti Primal Power Mudra

Also known as the Yoni Mudra, this helps us get in touch with female energy.

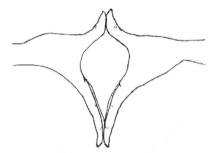

How to form: Bring the tips of the fingers and thumbs of each hand together. Thumbs point upward, while fingers point down, the hands form an almond shape. During meditation, hold hands at the lower abdomen.

To further explore more mudras, I recommend *Power Mudras: Yoga Hand Postures for Women*, by Sabrina Mesko, a master of mudras who learned the techniques from Hindu masters who gave her permission to disseminate this mystical technique to the masses. Her book explains and demonstrates dozens of mudras that raise the energy to make you feel more beautiful, emotionally centered, powerful, spirited, and much, much more.

Yoga

Probably the most popular spiritual practice today, outside of attending church services, is yoga, a full-body mudra in which breathing, asanas (whole-body poses), and meditation are incorporated into a dynamic mind/body/spirit exercise. Yoga, which means "union with the infinite," stimulates physical functions and energy centers and opens the channels of the subtle bodies (chakras and meridians). The suspension of all thought while posing allows a deep connection with the inner self, and a union with Universal Spirit.

No one really knows when the yoga originated, but some evidence indicates that it may have been as long ago as 3,300 BCE, among the people of the Indus Valley Civilization of India. Excavations in the sites of ancient cities have produced coin-like seals carved with figures and symbols, some bearing figures in yoga-like positions.

Yoga was introduced to the United States only a little more than a hundred years ago, when Swami Vivekananda presented the concept of yoga to the World Parliament of Religions held in Chicago in 1893. He then traveled around the United States for three years to share the philosophies and techniques of yoga.[159]

Perhaps the greatest force for introducing yoga to the people of the West was Parmahansa Yogananda. When he arrived in Boston in 1920 to serve as India's delegate to an international congress of religious leaders, he spoke on the science of religion, or the science and philosophy of yoga and meditation. That same year, he founded the Self-Realization Fellowship and toured the country to lecture to packed stadiums and halls. People were turned away by the hundreds only hours after his lectures were advertised. Thousands of people became members of the Fellowship and adopted yoga as their spiritual path, including renowned artists, scientists, and business people like George Eastman (of Eastman Kodak), poet Edwin Markham, and conductor Leopold Stokowski.[160]

Indra Devi, also known as Mataji, or the First Lady of Yoga, popularized yoga and meditation in Hollywood in the 1940s and '50s, when she taught it to such silver screen luminaries as Greta Garbo, Rita Hayworth, Gloria Swanson, and Yul Brynner. Mataji had studied under yoga master Krishnamacharya in the late 1920s, becoming his first female student and the first foreign woman to ever enter an Indian ashram. Throughout her life, she taught around the globe and wrote several books on yoga, including *Yoga* (1948) and *Forever Young,*

Forever Healthy (1955). She died at her yoga center in Buenos Aires in 2002, just two weeks short of her 103rd birthday.[161]

Several of the most influential thinkers of the 1950s were also practitioners of yoga and attribute their spiritual awakenings to their practice. Dr. Richard Alpert, a successful psychology professor in the early 1960s, was an early experimenter with, and later an authority on, psychedelic drugs, such as LSD. Dissatisfied with the trappings of success, he used LSD and other hallucinogens as a means of heightening his state of consciousness in pursuit of happiness and wholeness. But it was when he traveled to India and learned the practices of yoga masters that he found true peace and mind expansion he could never attain on LSD. Dr. Alpert became Baba Ram Dass, and in 1971 wrote *Be Here Now*, which became one of the greatest spiritual books in print. Soon many seekers were traveling to India to learn yoga and bringing the practices back to America. Hundreds of students became certified yoga instructors. Today, yoga is a million-dollar industry in the United States, attracting hordes of people wishing to strengthen their bodies and souls.

While many people believe yoga is primarily physical exercise, it is much more than that. The various stretches and poses stimulate the chakras and meridians to clear and purify both the subtle energy body and the physical body. Like mudras, these poses, called asanas, attract beneficial energy from the cosmos. Breathing, an essential component of yoga, oxygenates the body. With an empty mind, cosmic awareness is expanded. The results are inner peace, emotional balance, and divine bliss. The side benefit is a physical body that is more limber, healthier, and better toned.

There are several forms of yoga, each with its own set of benefits and effects.

Hatha yoga creates a harmonious balance in the body by employing various asanas. This is the practice we most often associate with yoga.[162]

Kundalini yoga is the balance of the chakras, primarily through breathing and with some asanas. The breathing practices described in the Human Energy chapter are a form of Kundalini yoga.[163]

Bhakti yoga is the devotional yoga in which every movement and action performed is with God/dess in mind.[164]

Tantra yoga, "expansion through liberation," seeks to unify Shakti and Shiva energy through individual and couples practices involving meditation and ritual.

From these basic forms of yoga, numerous teachers have developed their own practices. Yoga is a deep and vast subject, best understood by actually doing it. I am not including any yoga positions in this book, but if you are interested in yoga, I highly recommend that you find a qualified teacher and attend classes. Even one class a week, which normally lasts an hour, will produce tremendous benefit in your body and soul.

Giving Service

Perhaps one of the most powerful ways to strengthen your spirit is to give of yourself. Giving selflessly to assist individuals or support spiritual communities is a powerful way to connect with God/dess, share your gifts, and raise your vibration and perceptions of yourself and your life. Taking time to leave the comfort of your own head and your comfortable life and reaching out to focus on another in need creates a tremendous energetic exchange. In and of itself, radiating your positive energy to someone in need is a spiritual gesture. Service can be something as minor as a smile to a stranger or offering your seat to an elderly person. When you step out of your own life to express care to others, such as visiting an elderly neighbor or donating money to a needy person's hospital bills, this generates highly positive vibrations that fill you and radiate into the universe, positively affecting all that is.

Volunteering and giving service in churches, spiritual groups, and organizations that help others, like soup kitchens, the Red Cross, and the March of Dimes, is also powerful spiritual service. Serving food, cleaning up after an event, even taking out the trash—nothing is too small. Your energy merges with the high vibrations of others, and this amplified healing energy radiates toward the subject, into the universe, and back to you.

Embarking on a Spiritual Odyssey

There are times in our lives when we are so busy, so overwhelmed with things to do, worried about bills, and stressing to reach the finish line that we lose sight of the reason for the race. Making the motions, rather than being fully present, we listen to the world instead of our soul's desire. To regain balance in life, sometimes we must do exactly what we believe we don't have the time or money to do—take a break from ordinary life and embark on a spiritual odyssey.

When we reduce our life to a routine filled with work and obligations, we lose sight of our true selves and our soul. We squelch our soul's callings. If we ignore our inspirations, intuitions, and soulful desires, our lives become filled with physical and emotional ailments. Like radar, our health and feelings indicate how close or far off we are from our soul's desire. When we ignore the signal that we are not moving in the right direction, or not moving at all, we may feel depressed, lost, and stressed. Sometimes we get sick. Until we wake up, take notice, and make changes in our life, our quality of life will be challenged.

Unable to endure the agony of watching us, sometimes the universe will step in and create opportunities that will force us to make changes. We may be fired from a job (often one in which we are miserable), we may become ill, we may experience what seems like a personal failure. While these events may appear to be catastrophic, in reality, they are positive and force us to stop and listen to our soul. When we pay attention, this "time out" becomes an opportunity to meditate and listen to our soul, recharge, commit to a new life, and make positive changes in our lives.

Waiting for a wakeup call from the universe is one option. I have a better solution—don't wait for the universe to call. Take action yourself. Set out on a spiritual odyssey. A spiritual odyssey is a personal journey in which our sole (soul) purpose is to disconnect from the mundane world and explore the unfamiliar, whether it is a geographical location or the depths of our soul. It is during this odyssey that we connect to a power much greater than ourself. We should listen carefully for the inspirations, intuitions and callings that suggest our next steps to a more fulfilling and joyful life.

Some of the most profound teachings, philosophies, and art were created by those who took time out to refuel with cosmic energy. The Buddha sat under the Bodhi tree for many months to discover his soul through meditation. Jesus Christ wandered in the Judean desert for forty days and forty nights, examining his soul and his god. What these two men found changed the planet. The priestesses of the ancient goddess religions retreated with the seasons to worship and meditate and thus influence abundance on the earth.

A spiritual odyssey takes time. While for some, the clouds of the mind clear and insights shine through in as little as a weekend, for others, the journey can take weeks or months. Many spiritual organizations have monasteries and retreat centers to which we may travel, but some people prefer to trek into unfamiliar areas to gain a new perspective and learn new ways of living. Many a person has backpacked around Europe to "find himself or herself."

I embarked on a spiritual odyssey not long ago. It was an experience that changed my life for the better. Here's my story.

In 2002, I was living "on the edge" in Los Angeles. I had been living in L.A. for about a year and had created a couple of friendships, but I felt very empty. I had searched for community, but I wasn't really sure what to look for or where to find it. I had also allowed all of my spiritual practices to fall away, so my life was devoid of any spiritual connection. After 9/11, when business was slumping all across America, I lost my cool job with a production company and ended up working with a temp agency to get administrative jobs. I moved from my own apartment into a roommate situation. I was struggling financially and worrying about my credit card debt. For several months, I searched for production jobs and used the time to develop documentary television show ideas, which I pitched to production companies, but with no success. After nearly a year of dead-ends, I felt lost and lonely. I was drowning financially. My soul felt empty. Soon the questions emerged. *What is my life's purpose? What should I do now? Should I leave L.A.?*

One morning, while taking a walk on the Venice Beach boardwalk where many artists and vendors display their wares, I was drawn to a man painting beautiful pictures that depicted tiny humans in the vastness of the cosmos. These paintings were powerfully spiritual and familiar to me on some level. They touched my soul. I introduced myself to the artist, whose name is David, and expressed appreciation for his beautiful paintings. David is a peaceful man with a wise and loving vibration, and I felt a connection with him, not a physical attraction, but a spiritual, sisterly one. He asked to give me an astrological reading, which I joyfully accepted. His reading was surprisingly accurate. As he read that I was moving into a time in which I needed to take action to discover what I would be doing in the future, I took the reading seriously. I told him about my feelings of loss and lack of direction. I also shared my deep desire to paint and create art, a desire I had ignored for years.

"You need to go out into the wilderness and paint your heart out," he said.

Hmmmm. This message felt real. It hit a nerve. I listened more. He suggested that I attend the Rainbow Gathering held on Michigan's Upper Peninsula as a part of a journey of self-discovery. He described the joyful community and events of the gatherings, the kinds of people I would meet, many of them on their own spiritual quests. He declared that this journey would give me what I needed to move into the right direction in my life. Should I deny myself any kind of spiritual quest, whether it was the Rainbow gathering or any other kind of trip, he said, I would continue to face the challenges I was currently facing. He recommended that I quit my temp job, leave L.A., and have faith that I would discover what I needed to advance in my soul's work.

Wow. I left that reading with an amazing buzz. Something about that message hit home. It seemed so right to me. My soul was stirred. I went home and thought about it. And thought and thought. Logically, the idea seemed crazy and impetuous. But my soul took hold and wouldn't let go, no matter how much my mind resisted. Turns out, sometimes the nonsensical is the most sensible.

The Rainbow Gathering was four weeks away. I looked at a map to find out where the Upper Peninsula of Michigan was. Holy crow! Three quarters the way across the country! Drive to a Rainbow Gathering? Me? Alone? I panicked as I thought about it. I hadn't even made the decision to go, and my body was responding as if I were going. I thought, No, I can't do this. My car would never make it. I have no money. Plus, listen to a stranger? A sidewalk artist? Shouldn't I be listening to a career counselor or a financial advisor? This is nuts!

But my soul would not rest. It pushed me toward both painting and the Rainbow Gathering. It was as if I had no say in the decision. After a week of contemplation, I decided to do it. I put in my two-weeks' notice at work, sold a few personal belongings, put the rest of my stuff in storage. With the $600 security deposit from the room I was renting, I bought a roll of raw canvas, paint brushes, and several large tubes of paint. I was ready to paint and do some serious soul searching. I couldn't believe I was doing this, but I couldn't NOT do it. My soul was much stronger than me.

I went back to Venice Beach and met David and told him about my decision. He was pleased and assured me I was doing the right thing. I knew it, too.

At the end of June, I hit the road. My goal was to get to the Rainbow Gathering by July 4 for their huge peace meditation. My plan was to travel as a free spirit for one month and search my soul. Not only that, I made a deal with the universe that if any town along the way called me to live there or if my car broke down, I would live there.

It took me three days to drive to Michigan. The whole way I was in disbelief. What the hell was I doing? Was I crazy? As I drove up Interstate 15 in Utah and across the 70 through Colorado, I felt the intense strangeness of taking a gigantic risk. As I drove through the surreal canyon landscape of Utah, I was filled more with doubt than with joyful spirit. But I knew I was embarking on an important mission for my soul. I knew God/dess was with me. As I drove through the plains and mountains each day, I sang, and after I pitched my tent in nature at night, I prayed. The entire time, I felt safe.

On July 3, I arrived at the national forest of the Upper Peninsula. I carried my tent and some supplies into the forest and drank in the cool beauty of the towering pine trees and grassy open spaces occupied by hundreds of colorful tents. After pitching my own tent, I wandered around to meet people. It took me a while to get my bearings in this giant commune, but after a few friendly encounters, I began to settle in.

The next day, at the peace meditation, thousands of people united on a hillside and meditated and prayed for peace. The spiritual energy was both palpable and powerful. After an hour of meditation, a beautiful rainbow appeared in the sky, though there was no sign of rain. Afterward, there was a great celebration with dancing and drumming.

In the week that followed, I communed with the most interesting and conscious group of people I had ever met in my life. I realized this was a giant tribe connected by a common thread—conscious living as directed by their soul's desires. Most had lives that did not conform to society's expectations. They shunned the nine-to-five paradigm and had found more meaningful modes of living that honored the earth and its people. There were healers, spiritual followers and leaders, performers, environmentalists, and artists at the Rainbow Gathering. Many were what we might call hippies, living in their vans, creating and selling their wares. Others lived with the seasons, traveling from one organic farm to another to cultivate and harvest crops in exchange for living space. Many were activists with missions to raise mass consciousness for a cleaner planet. I even met mainstream people taking a break from the corporate world. Communing with these kindred spirits helped me see more clearly that I had been ignoring my soul's callings and focusing on mere survival in the material world.

I witnessed another way of life at the Rainbow Gathering. I prayed to be completely present in a situation I had never experienced before—living in a tent in the woods and communing with 10,000 hippies. I wanted to completely immerse myself in feeling the spirit there and become a totally free spirit. I wanted to live life as a river and flow where life took me, without expectation, judgment, or fear. I volunteered to work in one of the many community kitchens, where I served food donated by generous Rainbow people to every kind of human being I could have ever imagined. Before eating, we gathered in groups to pray and express our gratitude.

During the day, we communed and talked about life. We swam in the river and walked through the woods. At night, singers and fire dancers performed for an appreciative audience. Practically non-stop around the clock, highly-skilled drummers beat out tribal rhythms, inspiring our primal spirits to emerge, asking for us to dance and trance. I was taken into a spiritual place. I felt very present, connected to spirit and the earth

Nine days after I arrived, the Gathering ended and I hit the road. But my spiritual trip was by no means over. I had experienced the ultimate community. Now it was time for an intimate, one-on-one relationship with God/dess.

Not sure where I would go next, I left Michigan and camped in the verdant Wisconsin landscape for a couple of days. As I gazed at the infinite possibilities on my map, South Dakota jumped out at me. I had visited the Badlands National Park nearly fifteen years earlier and had wonderful memories of camping in the nearby Black Hills. South Dakota was a magical place that remained in my heart. Now it was calling me back.

It was mid-July. The sun was scorching hot. I sang and prayed as I drove across Wisconsin and South Dakota. At the Black Hills, I found the campground at the reservoir where I had camped many years before and set up my tent under a glorious tree at the water's edge. There were only one or two other campers at the huge reservoir, so I was in complete solitude. I felt no fear. I was on a mission to commune with God/dess and "paint my heart out."

Over the next several days, I immersed myself in total spirituality. I fasted, meditated, and prayed, asking for guidance and offered my soul to service. I practiced Tantric breath exercises that I'd practiced years before and filled my lungs with fresh air while charging my body with energy. I swam in the reservoir to cool down and bathe.

At night I contemplated the stars. I felt safe.

Obeying my mission to paint my heart out each day, I focused on claiming the images that lived in my soul. In my meditation, I received an image of an indigenous woman in her power, her naked body covered in ancient designs. She came to life on my canvas. Inspired by my own primal awakening at the Rainbow gathering, I painted her as if I were illustrating various days of her life. I painted her sitting in her power, praying, dancing, flying over the mountain. With each painting I was astonished that my hands were bringing this mystic image to life. It was as if God/dess Herself had taken possession of my hands to paint these powerful images. My spirit was ecstatic as I expressed on canvas what wanted to take life. I painted twelve paintings in one week. I felt complete. I had accomplished my mission.

Then it was time to leave the Black Hills. But to go where? I wasn't sure. I wasn't getting the calling I thought I'd get. Deciding to go to Taos, New Mexico, onward I traveled in my little Honda Civic, down Route 385 through the plains of Nebraska and into Colorado. I kept my ears and soul open for a calling for my next residence. Funny thing: while I was open to any location, Los Angeles seemed to keep whispering to me. *Come back.* Hmmmmm.

In Taos, I found a campground next to the Rio Grande. The vibe was very different from the expansiveness of South Dakota. The canyon, which towered over me, seemed to block out creative inspiration. However, my soul's work was far from complete, and I experienced a different kind of spiritual expression, this time in the form of journaling. For hours each day, I wrote and wrote and wrote. I wrote about my life, my worries, desires, my gifts, what was next, who I was to become. With each page came more clarity. I realized my career path was correct, but that life is more than work. I was awakened to the fact that there was an absence of spirit in my life. I came to understand that I needed to bring it back. I found my need to keep alive the feminine spirit that was born in my paintings and to engage in work to further explore this spirit. With each word I wrote came more joy and more faith in my life. I became stronger, more sure, alive and awake each passing day.

All this time, I heard no callings to live in any of the towns I was driving through or finding on the map. But I did continue to hear a very faint invitation from Los Angeles: "Please come back." Trusting the voice, I drove back to L.A.

Returning to Los Angeles with a rejuvenated soul and empowered spirit, I was welcomed by friends with open arms, tremendous love, and unconditional support. They offered me places to stay and opportunities for work. They shared their souls with me like never before. I had changed. I was able to see the preciousness of these dear friends of mine.

Opportunities began to present themselves immediately. Within the first week of my return to L.A., a former co-worker called me to paint a picture for a book written by political pundit Bill Maher. Later, I met a woman whose company was on a search for an associate producer. I gave her my resume and immediately got the gig. A friend soon recommended I check out the Agape Spiritual Center, a spiritual community where the Science of Mind philosophy was practiced. I followed her advice, experienced a powerful sense of community, and discovered a spiritual path that resonated with my soul and stimulated my entire being.

Things started falling into place for me. I became reacquainted with my soul and began to recognize the kinds of opportunities that would allow me to express and expand it. I trusted my inner spirit and began to fearlessly express it. I created a very intimate relationship with God/dess, with whom I feel instinctive trust and from whom I receive an endless supply of joy. I felt more joyful, clearer than I had ever felt before in my life.

I have learned that when we say to the God/dess and ourselves, "I am here to serve. What is it you wish me to do?" we discover those things that will bring us our greatest joy and the most fulfilling life. Sometimes we'll be asked to embark on a spiritual odyssey. Other times, we may be asked to sit still and take notes.

One day I went back to the Venice Beach boardwalk and found David, the artist, and showed him my paintings. As I shared with him my spiritual journey, he smiled. I am eternally grateful for this beautiful man. God/dess was working through him to deliver the message I needed to hear most.

By the way, you can see David's art at www.davidalexanderenglish. com.

Recommended reading and watching:

Tantra Bliss, by Bodhi Avinasha

Jewel in the Lotus, by Sunyata Saraswati and Bodhi Avinasha
Shakti Woman, by Vicki Noble
Double Goddess: Women Sharing Power, by Vicki Noble
Power Mudras: Yoga Hand Postures for Women, by Sabrina Mesko
Shakti Mantras: Tapping into the Great Goddess Energy Within, by Thomas Ashley-Farrand
The Once and Future Goddess, by Elinor W. Gadon
The Miracle of Mindfulness: A Manual on Meditation, by Thich Nhat Hanh
Be Here Now, by Ram Dass
The Art of Tantra, by Philip Rawson
Women and Spirituality DVD series, directed by Donna Read
What the Bleep do We Know? (DVD)
The Secret (DVD)

Part Four:

STRONG

10

STRONG

At the dawn of the third millennium, *Anno Domini*, women have begun to gain a foothold in the power structure of many nations around the world. Our demand for respect has brought a response, and we've made great strides in the political and corporate arenas. An eye-opening report presented by *Forbes Magazine* in 2007, "The World's Most Powerful Women," indicates that several countries are led by women presidents and other high officials, including Angela Merkel, Chancellor of Germany; Sonia Gandhi, President of the Congress Party of India; Michelle Bachelet, President of Chile; Helen Clark, Prime Minister of New Zealand; Queen Rania of Jordan; and Queen Elizabeth II of the United Kingdom. The list also includes corporate giants headed by women, including PepsiCo's chairwoman, Indra K. Nooyi; Xerox's chief executive, Anne M. Mulcahy; WellPoint's president, Angela Braly; Morgan Stanley's co-president, Zoe Cruz; and eBay's Margaret Whitman, chief executive and president.

Women in the Western world, particularly in the United States, are at this time not only the most privileged on the planet but probably also the most fortunate in history. Thanks to the hard work of our foremothers, society has evolved from one of limitations and inequality to freedom and near equality.

Statistics show that women aspire to attain higher education. In the United States, women were not allowed to enroll in colleges until 1833, when Oberlin College first opened its doors to women. According to a National Center for Education Statistics report, "Trends in Educational Equality of Girls and Women," by 1930, 40 percent of the college's enrollment was female.[165] Today, more women than men are enrolling in institutions of higher education. In a report by the U.S. Department of Labor, Bureau of Labor Statistics, in 2006, 66.0 percent of female high school graduates enrolled in college, versus 65.5 percent of men.[166] According to the U.S. Census conducted in

2000, 21 percent of married women had more education than their husbands, and 28 percent of unmarried women had more education than their partners in unmarried-partner households.[167]

Women are also the fastest-growing consumer market. The U.S. Census Bureau indicates that of the 66 million working women in America,[168] women between the ages of 24 and 54, are the country's most potent consumers and have the greatest purchasing power. And while women continue to earn about 22 percent less than men, they make more than 80 percent of the purchasing decisions at home. They thus influence how the market designs, positions, and sells its products to them.[169]

A general trend indicates that both women and men are postponing marriage. In 2000, the median age at first marriage was 25.1 years, up from 20.8 years in 1970. The number of women between the ages of 20 to 24 who had never married doubled between 1970 to 2000, up from 36 percent to 73 percent.[170] Many attribute this to women's desire to pursue higher education and/or establish their careers before they tie the knot.

And more women are choosing to be "childfree," a term referring to people who make the conscious decision not to have children. The 2003 U.S. Census found that 44 percent of women ages 15 to 44 in the United States didn't have children. This is a record number. The National Center of Health Statistics confirms that the number of American women of childbearing age who define themselves as childfree rose from 2.4 percent in 1982 to 6.6 percent in 1995.[171]

At the same time, more women are choosing to become single mothers. The U.S. Census Bureau reported that in 2004, 32 percent of all women between the ages of 15 and 44 were unmarried and that 83 percent of them were never-married.[172]

The U.S. Census Bureau also indicates that in 2000, 40 percent of never-married women in their 30s have a child. In 1970, there were 3.4 million single mothers in the U.S., whereas in 2000 there were 10 million.[173] An article by Larry Bumpass and Hsien-Hen Lu, "Trends in Cohabitation and Implications for Children's Family Contexts in the United States," reveals that 41 percent of births to unmarried women are actually born to cohabitating couples, not "single" women.[174] Stephanie Countz, author of *The Way We Really Are: Coming to Terms with America's Changing Families*, states that because there is now less stigma toward unmarried mothers in the U.S., women no longer feel they are locked into marriage.[175]

Society is thus responding to women's strides to take greater control of their lives. Now women can enjoy opportunities once reserved for men only, and even situations that were once altogether unacceptable by society, such as single women choosing to become pregnant through artificial insemination and raising the child alone—and running for President of the United States—are now acceptable.

Evolution is survival to the tenth power. A species' survival is dependent on sustenance, protection, and procreation, with natural instincts and innate drives guiding each individual to stay alive. Evolution is a naturally occurring tweak to those components that make the species stronger and better. But I believe that with the right tools and positive attitudes, many people can take evolution into their own hands, by pushing and advancing their own minds and bodies to higher and higher levels of mental acuity and creativity. But the human experience can become richer and more meaningful than mere survival. Evolution improves the way humans live. It is also changing the face of the planet, for better and for worse.

A strong and powerful woman is an example of evolution in action. She is driven to harness her natural faculties and high-level tools and information to better herself and empower herself to advance in the world. An evolved woman is easy to identify. She is a talented, charismatic, and creative woman who exemplifies the possibilities of human life. Inspired and driven, she expands the boundaries of human potential. Earliest woman was strong enough to bear children and adapt to the elements so that the species could survive. Shamanic women were the glue of their tribe. Warrior women, queens, and priestesses displayed physical and mental strength in their determination to maintain justice and harmony in their societies. Contemporary figures of strength include Oprah Winfrey, Hillary Clinton, the singer Madonna, and an untold number of corporate presidents, scientists, doctors, artists, and politicians.

I define the subtle and differing qualities of strength and power a few paragraphs further into this chapter. A strong woman projects confidence (high self-esteem) and exudes positive energy. Because she has identified her mission or purpose, employs every internal and external resource to make it real, and finds great fulfillment in bringing it to fruition, a strong woman can be a very happy woman. She's unstoppable. She is valuable and valued. She pursues her dreams with a sharp mind, physical fortitude, and spiritual passion, overcoming every obstacle and succeeding against all odds. With clarity, guts, and drive, she has closed the door on self-doubt, limiting beliefs, and negativity.

She educates herself so that she can make the best choices and perform most effectively. She heeds her inner voice and divine inspiration. A strong woman deals honestly with others, achieving her goals through integrity, not anger, manipulation, or dishonesty.

While we may feel inspired by strong women, few of us feel that we have what they have. We tend to think we are limited in what we can create. Well, I don't buy into this mindset. Each and every one of us has the ingredients to create great relationships and enriching work, to contribute to society and the planet. As Naomi Wolf said in her book, *Fire with Fire*, "Women are far more powerful than they know, have far more leverage than they are using, and can raise their voices to make rapid, sweeping irrefutable changes in the conditions of their lives."[176]

We have at our fingertips infinite external and internal resources to help us attain our every dream. Externally, we have education, information, people, and money, while internally we have the intelligence, desire, and instincts. All of these things are available to even the most seemingly disadvantaged person. When intention and desire for personal growth are strong, we still need, however, to overcome any number of obstacles. But who is most likely to take advantage of all that life has to offer to create the life she wants? Strong women are, for they have cultivated the inner and outer energetic forces to create a life that expresses who they are.

The ultimate manifestation of strength in a woman lies in her successful and satisfying life. Success doesn't necessarily mean monetary riches, however; it can be a life rich in experiences, positive relationships, comfortable surroundings, glowing health, and fulfillment from the expression of self. To become a positive force on the planet and to create the life you want, we must have strength.

Strong and Powerful Defined

Strength is the third side of our Energetic Triangle. In order for us to become authentic Positive Energy Women, the Strength side of our Triangle must to be equal to the Sexy and Spirited sides. Although for many of us, strength and power mean the same thing, there are subtle differences. The source of our power energy is the Manipura, or solar plexus chakra, located at the navel area. Authentic power arises from inner strength, which we can only obtain by refining and balancing all of our chakras. A person can have the most balanced Manipura chakra in the world, but if, for example, the Muladara, survival, chakra is out of whack, power may rise out of desperation. Likewise, if the heart chakra is deficient, power may be wielded with unkindness. Positively balanced inner strength will help us to become truly powerful.

Strength is the physical and mental energy we exert to live life. Strength motivates us to take action and gives us the fortitude to stay on track. Strength is the cultivation of mental intelligence, physical vigor, will, and charisma. Power is strength manifested as high self-esteem, charisma, and positive influence.

We tend to see strength and power as nearly the same. We often interchange the words, and call strong women powerful or empowered. But while the general concepts of strength and power are similar, the two words have different nuances. *Webster's New World College Dictionary* offers numerous definitions for strong. Listed below are a few of them.

Strong is an adjective:
1. Physically powerful, having great muscular strength, robust.
2. Performing well or in a normal manner.
3. Morally powerful; having strength of character or will.
4. (a) Intellectually powerful; able to think vigorously and clearly, (b) having special competence or ability.
5. Governing or leading with firm authority.
6. Holding firmly, tenacious.
7. (a) Hard to capture, able to resist and endure attack, (b) not easily defeated; formidable, (c) not easily dislodged.
8. Having many resources; powerful in wealth, numbers and supplies.
9. Having a powerful effect.
10. Having a large amount of its essential quality.
11. Intense in degree or quality. Ardent, passionate, warm.

Webster's defines "powerful" as an adjective meaning "having much power, strong or influential."

Power is a noun:
1. Ability to do, act or produce.
2. A specific ability or faculty.

3. Great ability to do, act, or affect strongly; vigor; force; strength.
4. The ability to control others, authority, sway, influence, special authority. assigned to or exercised by a person or group holding office.
5. The rate at which work is done.
6. A person or thing having great influence, force or authority.
7. A nation, esp. one having influence or domination over other nations.
8. National might or political strength.
9. A spirit or divinity.

Let's compare the two words. *Strength* is our internal energy. Strength is the personal cultivation of various aspects of our human form and character, such as muscles, robustness, morals, intelligence, and tenacity. Every human being possesses these expressions of nature, and as beings of free will, we can develop them to the extent we desire. But to live fully to our highest potential, high levels of strength in every aspect of our character are necessary.

Power is strength in action. It is a perceivable manifestation of strength. Power is outward energy that is observable, often with an effect on others.

So let's review. Strength is the *internal* energy that we use to cultivate our natural human characteristics. Strength thus is a high degree of cultivation of each characteristic. Our empowered nature helps us survive and prosper. Power is both *internal and external energy.* It's the result of strength and an outward expression of strength.

Each and every one of us has the potential to be STRONG. Strength does, however, require energy and development. Please don't let this turn you off. Developing your strength can be one of the most enjoyable and rewarding endeavors of your life. It can certainly be the foundation of your future.

A human being is the most advanced creature in the universe (that we're aware of). We're made of a physical and energetic body, mind, spirit, and emotions. Becoming a strong woman requires us to condition and maximize these human elements. The physical, mental, spiritual, and emotional makeup of a Strong woman is thus:

1. A hearty physical body
2. Clear and balanced energy centers (chakras)
3. An inspired mind (inspiration, inner, and divine guidance)

4. A cultivated mind (knowledge and learning)
5. Balanced emotions

The energy necessary to engage to strengthen our physical, mental, spiritual, and emotional elements comes from deep within. These energy forces of strength include:

1. Creativity
2. Passion
3. Commitment
4. Self-discipline
5. Courage
6. Motivation and volition (will)

Once you become strong, power naturally follows. Since power is the result of strength, there is nothing you can really *do* to cultivate power itself; it is a natural result of strength. Thus, a person with power is characterized by having:

1. Inner strength
2. Positive energy (charisma)
3. High self-esteem (confidence)
4. Clear expression of self

Power is different flavors of energy that arise from strength. When you're powerful, you are:

1. Giving and benevolent
2. Caring and compassionate
3. Supportive
4. Empowering and encouraging
5. Inspiring
6. Positive

A weightlifter is strong. Jeannette is an amateur weightlifter. Through weight training, she conditions her muscles to function at their greatest ability, and then she pushes them further to become even stronger. Jeannette doesn't compete. She trains for her own pleasure and satisfaction. Her self-discipline to train regularly, as a form of strength in its own right, will make her body as strong as it can be. This will increase her self-esteem and self-confidence. Now Jeannette is also the president of the Valkyrie Women's Fitness Club. She loves the workout and is passionate about sharing the benefits of strengthening the muscles with everyone, young and old. Her own muscle strength and knowledge of weightlifting makes her valuable to the club. A picture of self-confidence and self-esteem, Jeannette exudes positive energy to the club members. She walks her talk. Her power energy motivates and inspires her club members and attracts new members constantly. Power is thus an outward projection of energy with a foundation of strength.

If Jeannette were not committed to her workouts and passionate about knowing human anatomy, would she have developed the self-confidence to become an effective club president? Probably not. Which illustrates why power is based on strength fueled by commitment, knowledge, and passion. (You don't need to lift weights in order to become energetically strong, but it doesn't hurt. In fact, many scientific studies show that weight-bearing exercises, including weightlifting, will help women prevent osteoporosis and other physical ailments.)

An evolved, positively energetic woman is strong in mind, body, and spirit. She has the internal energy and fortitude to do what is needed to live life easily and create the results she wants. And she exudes positive energy to create mutually supportive friendships and business associates. A strong and powerful woman maintains high self-esteem. As she becomes physically stronger, her self-esteem rises, which in return makes her even stronger. Strength comes from preparation and legwork, from discovering your mission, healing old wounds, developing physical strength, and cultivating knowledge to achieve the power to influence people or events.

A strong woman is motivated. She has a *can-do* attitude and ample self-discipline. She doesn't dwell on the past, but is firmly planted in the present and works toward a future of comfort and riches, both financially and experientially. As she becomes stronger, her self-esteem and charisma rise to new heights. Her self-esteem motivates her to walk confidently in the world. Her charisma helps her easily connect with people in relationships of mutual love and support.

Let's look at the life of a very powerful woman, the entertainer Madonna. Before she soared to the top of the *Billboard* charts and become a star, she spent years honing her skills. Early in life, she identified her mission to be a dancer and singer, and it was only through tremendous commitment to become the best singer, dancer, and businesswoman possible that she was able to get the attention of record producers and then the public. Clear, focused, and highly skilled, Madonna rallied those around her to support her mission and vision. Because of her foundation of strength, Madonna became and has remained an icon of entertainment for over twenty years. She is a hera (female hero) for many women today.

I, myself, have always been a pretty strong woman, but I haven't always been powerful. I've always been clear about my career and missions, and I have been focused on developing my career skills. Sometimes I have been a near workaholic, mostly because I love what I do, but also because I set lofty goals for myself. I've also always been committed to glowing physical health and have always maintained a workout regime, so physical energy was never a problem for me. But in spite of my inner strength, my low self-esteem used to get in the way of my success. I couldn't live the life I wanted. I didn't feel my talents or skills were good enough, so I didn't heartily pursue great jobs with solid companies that offered great pay. And since I didn't feel I was worth much, I never asked for raises. I loved my work. I was good at it. For me, that was enough. Unfortunately, I never learned how to manage the money I did make, so I was always struggling financially. Not only that, but I also constantly talked about how broke I was. I connected well with people in social situations, but I lacked the confidence to speak with professionals and often didn't express my feelings or ideas. And on top of all that, I kept finding myself in unfulfilling relationships with men, which not only made me unhappy, but also caused me to doubt myself and even go against my own principles as I struggled to maintain the relationships, thus lowering my self-esteem even more.

The sources of my low self-esteem and disempowerment were old wounds and negative conditioning from my early years. It was only through healing and reprogramming myself that I learned to raise my self-esteem. That's when my power became greater.

If you have true, honest, positive strength and power, you will attain your goals. Your dreams will come true. Your power will make you attractive and inspiring. People around you will be willing, if not excited, to listen to your message and return positive energy to you, which will further energize you to meet your objectives.

Commitment is a critical ingredient to living to your highest potential and creating the life you desire. Women tend to be people pleasers, easily influenced by those they love, including family and significant others. Such a woman may forget herself and her goals in order to maintain harmony in her relationships. But while it appears to be noble to compromise or to put a goal on hold to tend to a family matter, it also compromises your power. It is essential to hold your vision, especially if it is a vision that incorporates your mission on the planet today. If you are a mom and need to work to put food on the table, but you desire to be an artist, you MUST carve out time whenever possible to create your art.

People who have false power will get what they want by being overpowering, manipulative, and/or threatening. They resort to bullying and false confidence to gain a desired result from people. *This is not real power.* This is an indication of insecurity and low self-esteem. Truly powerful people are engaging and inspiring. While they may have a strong energy, they don't use force or manipulation to rally others.

Except in the physical fitness section, there are too few books on the bookstore shelves about strong women. But there are quite a few books about women's power. Strong or powerful, it doesn't really matter. The information is good for us women. Priscilla V. Marotta, Ph.D., author of *Power Versus Wisdom: The New Path for Women*, describes positive power as "the ability to implement adequate life strategies. Positive power allows an individual to be effective, to manage fears, to activate their energies, and to act with confidence."[177] In her book *Now It's Our Turn*, Alana Lyons tells us that power, among other things, "is energy, an awareness of self. Internal power can be stretched outward to the world. ... Power is knowledge that you are able to act."[178]

The Energy of Strength and Power

Strength and power are *all* about energy. Unless your physical and energy bodies (chakras) are healthy and strong, you will limp through life, perhaps wander aimlessly and never fully express who you are. You know from the Energy chapter that as an energetic being, you have full control over the degree to which you build and express your energy. You also have control over how healthy and strong you are. To develop the ultimate self-love and self-esteem, it is up to you to make sure your energy centers are clear and potent.

Power energy exists in Manipura, the third chakra, which is in the belly area where your "guts" live. You've used the expression, "She had guts to do that." Well, your guts are the source of your courage and will. When defeated, you may feel "sick to the stomach." This is your power shrinking and pulling back. An energized Manipura chakra enables you to recover quickly from setbacks and returns you to your way. This energy motivates a person to lead or to courageously pursue an idea or mission. A strong woman has a perfect balance of power with the courage to pursue her dreams, but she is not overpowered. She does not risk abuse, manipulation, and selfishness.

But it isn't only Manipura that will make you strong. Every chakra in your body contributes to your strength. If even one chakra runs at less than efficient levels, your strength and power may be limited.

Without strong survival energy, a woman may sacrifice herself and her mission just to pay the bills. Strong sexual energy will keep her vital and radiant. Motivation and action influenced by heart energy will ensure that her journey in life is fulfilling and rewarding. People in power who omit love can become evil. Unconscious leadership yields chaos and devastation. Communication energy empowers our ability to express or demonstrate our life's purpose. The third eye is the source of intuition and psychic insights that are critical to our travels through life, as they are the hunches that encourage us to take risks or avoid something at all costs. Life-altering inspiration comes through a clear sixth chakra. And finally, by connecting with God/dess or the Higher Power through our crown chakra, you will be inspired, energized and nurtured every minute of your life and filled with clarity, joy, and satisfaction.

Please refer to Chapter 4 for the exercises that heal and stimulate the chakras.

Women and Power

In her book, *Power Versus Wisdom: The New Path for Women*, Priscilla V. Marotta asks the reader to perform an easy exercise. Write down the words that you equate with Power. When I took the test a few years ago, I wrote these words: "aggressive, domineering, self-righteous, selfish, demanding, take charge, masculine." And more. Pretty negative, eh? Well, Marotta explains that it is common for women to perceive power as a negative characteristic. This belief prevents us from becoming powerful. After all, who wants to become self-righteous, aggressive, and domineering? Women are often hesitant to own their power because they don't want to appear powerful in a negative sense. But Marotta explains that power can be implemented in positive ways. Power liberates, rather than oppresses; it inspires action, rather than forces it; it eliminates stress, does not create it; it fosters personal growth, rather than limiting it.[179]

To become effective in the world, we need to change our beliefs about power and strength. Many powerful people do employ negative energy to get their way, but this is destructive power that is detrimental to our world. These people are *over*-powering and use their strength to lord it over others to get what that want. Truly powerful people don't seek to dominate or manipulate. They strive to inspire and generously give of themselves. They rally cooperation through enthusiastic pursuit of a positive cause.

In her book *Truth or Dare: Encounters with Power, Authority and Mystery*, author Starhawk describes three different forms of power: *power-over*, *power-from-within*, and *power-with*. Power-over is the attitude of authority or supremacy that uses fear tactics to obtain compliance.[180] In this system, no one "has inherent worth; it must be earned or granted." Systems and rules are enforced to control the people. This kind of iron-fisted domination damages the human spirit, and often spurs disharmony and violence.[181] Subtle-levels of power-over have shaped nearly every institution in our society, including families, in which parents punish their children with spanking when they're "bad," the workplace, where the boss demands that the employees work overtime without pay or be fired, and politics, where a leader can institute hubristic policies and threaten anyone who opposes them.

Power-from-within, Starhawk writes, "stems from a . . . consciousness. . . that sees the world itself as a living being . . . where there are no solid separations and no simple causes and effects."[182] In this context, each and every person is equal in value, without the need to earn worth. We are awakened to our own abilities and potential. Power-from-within "arises from our sense of connection, our bonding with other human beings, and with the environment." We identify and master our gifts within. This form of power is exuded in acts of creation and cooperation, such as writing, building and, healing.[183] Power-from-within is "the art of changing consciousness," which is communicated through action, "which speaks in the body and to all of the senses in ways that can never be completely conveyed in words."[184] Its motivation is to "experience and share pleasure, to connect, to create, to see our impact on others and on the world."[185]

Power-with, she further writes, combines the philosophies of power-over and power-from-within. Power-with is "social power, the influence we wield among equals."[186] It is spiritual power that acknowledges a pattern of relationships and is interested in how the patterns are formed. It recognizes the inherent value of everyone, but also "rates and compares, valuing some more highly than others."[187] Power-with is the social influence we exercise among our peers. In a group, someone may take a leadership role, but it is not a position of demanding authority, but of guidance, inspiring the best from each individual in a group. "It is," Starhawk writes, "dependent on personal responsibility, on our own creativity and daring, and on the willingness of others to respond."[188] An example of this model is the spiritual ministry in which a leader takes a non-dominant role, identifies the strengths of each person, and inspires each individual and group to work cooperatively to fulfill the mission.

Riane Eisler, author of *The Chalice & the Blade*, has also developed philosophies about power and has defined two different approaches: the dominator and partnership models of power. The dominator model is "the ranking of one half of humanity over the other." The dominator model has a system of hierarchy, in which the person at the top holds all authority and forces those at lower levels to respond to his demands. This model is "psychologically a function *not* of a feeling of power, but rather of a feeling of powerlessness."[189] In this paradigm, under which most societies on the planet currently function, the masses are governed by fear, and "male dominance and male warfare are inevitable."[190] Partnership, on the other hand, is "the linking, rather than ranking, of social relations." This system is based on equality, and the cooperation of the members of society, each person contributing her or his strengths for the good of the group.[191] Some would consider this model a more "feminine" way of power, in that it is more holistic and intuitive, ". . . tending to draw conclusions from a totality of simultaneous impressions rather than through step-by-step logical thinking."[192] The "destructive conflict" of the dominate model could be replaced by less violent or "passive" approaches, which "offer concrete hope for change."[193]

With a common mission of inspiring peace and harmony in our societies, Starhawk and Eisler write about similar concepts of power and work to inspire us to move into a direction of cooperation for the betterment of ourselves and the planet.

We need to better understand power. When it is used to inspire, evoke the best in individuals, and motivate us to bring out the best in ourselves, it is positive energy in action. It is critical to a fulfilled life and evolved species.

Look at your own attitudes about power. How do you perceive power? Positively or negatively? By making it positive, you may be more willing to become powerful. If you feel you need to grow your positive power, I recommend *Power Versus Wisdom: The New Path for Women*, by Priscilla V. Marotta. I also recommend *Now It's Our Turn: How Women Can Transform Their Lives and Save the Planet*, by Alana Lyons.

Strong and Sexy

Strength is third side of the Positive Energy Woman's makeup. It complements our Sexy and Spirited sides. Some women believe that a strong woman can't be sexy. *Au contraire!* Strong women are extremely sexy. Powerful woman are as feminine as they want to be. They employ their natural feminine gifts—with integrity—to achieve their goals. Women who are sexy, spirited, *and* strong contain balanced feminine energy. They do exactly as they please while maintaining a feminine demeanor, not subduing themselves or consciously acting like a man to accomplish a goal or a mission. The very qualities of femininity—cooperation, compassion, intuition, and nurturing—will help to empower a woman. Many men find strong and powerful women very sexy. They will give energy to a relationship, rather than rely on a man for his energy.

To live in a female body, we need to possess a tremendous amount of strength. Like a man, a woman can build muscles and condition her body to perform great athletic feats. But beyond the functions we share with the male, a woman has the capability to conceive, grow, and give birth to a baby human. The vast fluctuations of emotions and physical comfort that occur each month, not to mention pregnancy and the birthing process, would challenge even the strongest man. Yet women move fairly easily through life with this magnificent, multidimensional body and use their minds, skills, and passions to create art, science, technology, and systems to improve and evolve our species. So how is it that women are considered the weaker sex?

Men have always feared and admired the feminine body, emotions, and power. Eventually, they could only cope by controlling women. At times, I feel compassion for men, for many of them never fully understand our mysterious, magnificent beingness. It is up to women to lovingly and compassionately demonstrate to men that we are strong and powerful beings fully expressing ourselves and that we can—in a feminine way—fulfill missions of joy and planetary goodness.

Inner Expansion and Outer Manifestations of Strength

Each and every human is born with a body, a mind, and a soul, plus unique capabilities and talents. We are also given the inherent gift of energy to propel us to develop each aspect of ourselves so that we may realize our potential greatness.

It takes focus and intention to become strong, but when we realize that the gift of life is to expand and evolve as a human being, we find it a pleasure to do what it takes to become the best we can be as a positive force on the planet.

Perhaps the most challenging aspect of the Energetic Triangle, strength, requires a commitment to healing and improving every aspect of our being, so that we may fully express our soul and life's purpose. Unlike a light bulb, human power doesn't turn on with the flick of a switch. It takes work.

To become a strong and powerful woman, two actions must happen: Inner Expansion and Outer Manifestation. These actions help us to *feel* that we can face opportunities and challenges, and make us capable of *doing* so.

Inner Expansion addresses:

1. Emotional healing
2. Physical health
3. Clarity of our gifts and life's purpose (an aspect of spirit)
4. Positive mindsets and mind expansion

These four actions help to clear and strengthen the energy centers, so that you can perform optimally in life and eliminate the clouding of obstacles that often stop us in our tracks when we are emotionally, physically and spiritually weak.

Outer Manifestation is power in practice. The components of this category are:

1. Taking action
2. Connecting and communicating
3. Service and community

The strength and power energy cultivated from Inner Expansion are projected into our work, our relationships and the way we design our life. As we work to expand and improve our body and mind, our outer manifestations become more effective, focused and clear. We will become more charismatic, function with greater fortitude, and create a life that we desire.

11

INNER EXPANSION

Weak women are wounded, fearful, and negative. Low self-esteem prevents them from trusting themselves and believing they deserve full and abundant lives. A weak woman will repeat patterns of self-sabotage and attract the negative situations and people into her life. She will be satisfied with low-level jobs, she will eat poorly, and she will park herself in front of the TV for hours on end. She may be angry, depressed, and hateful. Low self-esteem and negative beliefs are the results of wounds that lie deep in the body and soul and absolutely disempower a woman.

Healing our wounds is essential, therefore, to creating a foundation of positive emotional strength, and until her wounds are healed, a woman will remain limited and powerless. As in the garden, unless the soil is tilled and rocks are removed, the seeds of positive beliefs, information, and positive energy will never grow. We must perform the inner work to remove the rocks and weeds that stand in the way of our self-esteem.

Emotional Health

While inner work is not exactly fun, it will take you on a journey that is as full of adventure as world travel. Think of it as self-discovery where you are exploring your own inner sanctums and the secrets caves of your psyche. Your exploration can be as exhilarating as a hike in the woods or a white-water rafting trip. Your psyche *is* a natural wonder!

Your psyche is *you*. It is all of your beliefs, which were formed by all the hurts and wounds you experienced in childhood and bad relationships. These wounds are stored in your precious body, including your organs, your muscles, your skin, your brain, and even in your soul, and they come forth as negative emotions and low self-esteem, denying you happiness. If you want to feel love and joy and are ready to be released, reprogrammed, and retrained, you must work on healing yourself.

In this chapter I offer suggestions and books to get you started on your inner journey. However, total healing often requires working with professionals and teachers who have devised methods of healing. For this reason, I also suggest several wonderful teachers and healers. Some of these methods cost money, but healing is a highly worthwhile investment. I've spent thousands of dollars on healing, and I don't regret a single penny. I have also gained intense healing from certain books and practices that have cost very little to no money.

Forgiveness

The world's wisest people and spiritual leaders agree that forgiveness is an act that contributes to a positive life. The Dalai Lama, for example, has said that forgiveness "is crucial. It's one of the most important thing[s]. It can change hatred. To reduce hatred and other destructive emotions, you must develop their opposites—compassion and kindness. . . . Forgiveness allows you to be in touch with the positive emotions. This will help with spiritual development."[194] Madame H.P. Blavatsky, one of the founders of Theosophy, likewise wrote in *The Key to Theosophy* that a man "who, believing in karma, still revenges himself and refuses to forgive an injury, thereby rendering good for evil, is a criminal and hurts only himself."[195] And part of the Christian philosophy is based on Jesus' teachings of forgiveness of our sins.

New Age teachings repeat the ancient wisdom. As Catherine Ponder, author of *The Dynamic Laws of Prosperity*, writes, "when a stubborn problem does not yield, it is because there is a need for forgiveness," and advises we "need to practice forgiveness every day because of many negative, subconscious attitudes stored in our emotions of which we are not even consciously aware."[196] Gerald G. Jampolsky, M.D., likewise writes in *Love Is Letting Go of Fear* that "inner peace can be reached only when we practice forgiveness."[197] And Louise Hay, author of *You Can Heal Your Life*, writes that "whenever we are ill, we need to search our hearts to see who it is we need to forgive."[198] Finally, relationship master and author John Gray concurs. In *Mars and Venus on a Date*, he writes that "how you end a relationship has an enormous impact on the quality of your next relationship."[199]

Is there someone from your past or present toward whom you feel resentment and anger because you feel they did something wrong to you? Does your blood boil when you think about the negative experiences you had with that person? Are you also noticing that your life isn't exactly working the way you want it to? Are you distrustful of others? If you are, then perhaps it is time to practice a little forgiveness. Anger, resentment, and guilt stand in the way of—and may destroy—your strength and power. Self-righteousness may be blocking your energy.

But for some of us, even when what we're angry about is something small, forgiveness may be difficult, and for victims of trauma, forgiveness may seem impossible. Forgiving someone is a highly conscious exercise, almost saintly, and to effectively forgive, we practically have to leave our bodies and go into our most soulful self. Forgiveness takes letting go of the ego, letting go of the negative energy we have toward the offending person. Forgiveness is seeing the other person as being human and capable of making mistakes. Forgiveness is stepping away from our life in the three-dimensional world, rising above it, and looking at it from a universal perspective. It's seeing the offending person as a soul just trying to make its own way around the world. In a word, *forgiveness is love*.

Our anger toward a person doesn't hurt that person. It hurts us, the person who is angry. Our negative emotions diminish our self-love and inner peace. You can be oh, so angry with your mother, and she probably doesn't even know it. Here you are, thinking your anger is hurting her, but it's not doing a thing to her. It's hurting you by raising your blood pressure, increasing the acids in your stomach, increasing your heart rate, giving you zits. But is your mother aware of your anger? Probably not. When you get into the same room with her and your negative vibe just shoots out of you, that's when she'll know. She'll feel uncomfortable and want to avoid you, which will make you even angrier.

Forgiveness stops the cycle of negative energy.

Forgiveness Exercises

The act of forgiveness is amazingly simple. It doesn't even require that you talk to the person directly. It can be a simple statement to the universe. "It is OK that you [the offending person] did that to me. I understand that was the best you knew how to do at that time."

Forgiveness can also come in direct contact when you connect just to say that everything is OK and wish to apologize for how you have been holding negative energy.

You may also need to forgive yourself for having hurt others or for allowing someone to hurt you. Forgiving yourself can be more difficult, but if you are willing to open your heart to yourself and (once again) acknowledge yourself as a soul in a body vehicle just trying to make its way the best you know how on this planet, then you can forgive yourself.

If hurt is deep, anger strong, and forgiveness difficult, you may wish to engage in a more serious practice of releasing the negativity. One very effective practice is to write a letter to that person, spelling out in detail the way she or he hurt you and describing your deepest feelings, then declaring your forgiveness. But beware. Writing your feelings may cause intense emotional release. This can be painful, but it's also a *good thing*. After you finish writing this letter, *burn it*. Release the negative energy, release your anger, release your bitterness, release your thoughts of revenge. The burning sends your positive forgiving energy out into the universe. If your hurt is deep or long-standing and forgiveness is difficult, write another letter and burn it, too. Continue the practice until the pain begins to ease and you begin to find lightness in your heart.

Another very powerful exercise is to meditate and imagine your offender sitting in front of you. See her or his face, feel his or her vibration. Speak to that person, either out loud or silently in your mind, and express your hurt. Eventually, you will release the hurt and begin to feel love and compassion for that person. Then you can send vibrations of forgiveness toward her or him. This exercise may help break through your most hard-core anger. But please know that sometimes forgiveness doesn't happen with one affirmation or one thought. It may require many, many sessions, perhaps years, to finally truly feel that you have forgiven that person and that your negativity toward her or him is banished. The act of forgiving is itself extremely healing and empowering. It raises your vibration to higher levels.

Reciting the Buddhist mantra of compassion, *Om Mani Peme Hung* (which is different from the *Om Mani Padme Hum* mantra in Chapter 4), will help to purify you of negative emotions and transform pride, anger, jealousy and other negative emotions into wisdom and enlightenment. Or simply praying for forgiveness is another powerful healing tool. By asking the Universe to open your heart and see the pure essence of the one who offended you, to accept and forgive the transgression, you will heal negative emotions.

The Dalai Lama is perhaps one of our greatest teachers of forgiveness. Though for more than fifty years, his homeland, Tibet, has been occupied and ravaged by the Chinese government, which has massacred up to a million people, including thousands of Buddhist monks, and destroyed over a thousand monasteries, and forced the Dali Lama himself to him to flee, this man is able to see the Chinese with compassionate and forgiving eyes. He performs a simple forgiveness meditation called "giving and taking." He visualizes sending positive emotions, like happiness and affection, to others, breathing out compassion and forgiveness. He receives their sufferings and their negative emotions, breathing in the poisons of hatred, fear, and cruelty and replaces them with "fresh air, converting the fresh air to compassion and forgiveness, and sending it out again.[200]

Simple prayers asking for compassion and forgiveness are also helpful.

Emotional Healing

Emotional wounds, and the various ways they manifest into our daily lives, can disempower us. A strong and powerful woman doesn't cry when her opponent wins, she doesn't pout in the office when her coworker gets the promotion, she doesn't fly into a fit when the butcher sells the last lamb chop, the one she was eyeing for her own dinner. Nor is she emotionless. She does not repress her joy when her friend announces her engagement, she is not stoic when she discovers she's been betrayed, and she does not frown when others are laughing and having a good time. Denying and ignoring our hurts and wounds will not make them go away. They remain and fester. They interfere insidiously with our happiness throughout our lives. Multiply one specific hurt by months and years of minor events that have also been buried, and you have quite a landfill of emotions that get in the way of joy, happiness, and power. Under your strong, stoic exterior, you may be a boiling cauldron of emotions, constantly stewing with anger and frustration and easily ignited into a hissy fit by the slightest insult.

If you find that you sabotage yourself or damage your relationships because you are "over-emotional" or that you are frequently unhappy about the things that life dishes up for you, you may have unresolved emotional issues. The goal of emotional healing is to explore and release the pent-up, negative emotions that are the result of childhood programming, hurtful relationships, and other painful life events. With proper facilitation, these emotions can be cleared for good.

Emotions are often stored in the body, so clearing them can be a physical process as well as a mental and/or emotional one. As you know from the Energy chapter, clogged chakras block our energetic flow, resulting in disharmony and a range of unsettling emotions and general dissatisfaction. Until your chakras are empty of negative energy, joy, inner peace, and self-love will always remain elusive to you. In emotional clearing, your emotions can be expressed as screaming, crying, kicking, beating pillows with the fists. In recent years, emotional clearing therapies have been created to release negative energy stored in the body. One such therapy is Core Energetics, developed by John Pierrakos and based on Wilhelm Reich's Bio-Energetics. Another is Primal Screaming, developed by Arthur Janov in the late 1960s. While these two techniques are greatly beneficial, there are other, often less dramatic, methods of clearing emotions. I have experienced numerous emotional healing processes, including those discussed below.

The Healing Power of Journaling

Journaling, or regularly writing down our thoughts and feelings, is an effective method of healing old and recent wounds. In a journal, we can express our deepest thoughts, dreams, ideas, and feelings privately and without being censored, unless we censor ourselves, which would defeat the purpose of this exercise. The only things you need to journal are a notebook used specifically for this purpose (I usually use the wire-bound kind), a pen, the willingness to be open, and time to write. You can journal any time and any place—at a coffee shop, at the kitchen table, in bed. While journaling is no replacement for psychotherapy for deeply-rooted psychological issues, it does help identify the source of our hurt and allows us to access our true feelings about it. Understanding the source of our pain may potentially help to clear away the negativity. But one of the greatest gifts of journaling is the opportunity we have to explore and clear our emotions. Only by healing and releasing negative emotions can we become a clear energy body and radiate positive energy.

We often deny our feelings and bury them, saying, "It's OK," when it really isn't OK. Perhaps we were raised to not express ourselves. Or we didn't speak our truth to avoid hurting someone's feelings. There are numerous reasons for denying our feelings, and we have all done it throughout our lives. Some of us have such deeply buried feelings that we don't even realize they exist. But, boy, they do, and they manifest in any number of ways. Disconnecting from our feelings, both old and recent ones, can lead to depression, confusion, poor decision-making, low self-esteem, poor relationships, and more.

Journaling is a way to review old events and residual feelings so they can be healed and released. Writing about an event that occurred long ago may help you explore the situation and come to terms with it. Perhaps you will come to understand something you never thought about before. Or maybe looking at it for the first time in years will help you see that it wasn't really as insignificant as you thought, or, conversely, that it was much greater than you remember it. It may also help you see your role in the event more clearly, and the event may have contributed to who you are today. You can express exactly how you felt about the experience without holding back. You can record your feelings toward a person or event and write things you may have never had the courage to say, or even think, before.

Sometimes reviewing a hurtful event will trigger old emotions and make you sad or angry. You may curse, cry, and stab your journal with your pen, purge your emotions like never before. Let this release happen. This is a good sign. It can be a healing moment. Let your emotions fly! Releasing feelings can clear out your emotional body and lighten your vibration. You may even decide to forgive the person who hurt you so badly.

You can also process feelings from more recent experiences, perhaps reviewing a hurtful comment someone made at work yesterday. You can release the emotions and resentment in your journal that would otherwise fester inside you and return to a positive attitude. You may even see truth in that formerly hurtful comment, and learn from it; this is a sign of a strong person well on her way to greater power.

But journaling isn't just a process for releasing negative emotions. It's also useful for exploring the positive parts of our lives. Writing about the good elements of our lives creates cheerful feelings, which will not only help us feel uplifted, but will counter any negative residue you may feel from exploring old wounds. I recently reviewed some old journals from years ago. During those days, I filled my journals with negativity, so in rereading them, I was now faced with page after page of angst around old boyfriends, lousy jobs, and disdain for myself. Yuck! I had a decent life then, but all I focused on was negative stuff. No wonder I was a miserable and depressed woman during those days! Seeing how I refused to acknowledge anything positive in my life helped me realize that I had actually perpetuated my bad feelings.

Don't be like I was. Use your journal to explore the good in your life. Install positive vibrations in your energy field and draw positive energy toward you. This will enhance your healing experience.

In her book, *The Artist's Way*, Julia Cameron recommends that we write three pages of stream-of-consciousness thoughts every day, starting the minute we wake up. Writing whatever comes to mind helps to eliminate foggy thoughts and cut through the miasma of swirling, chaotic mental bits and pieces and get to your deepest, truest feelings. Writing every day helps us sort through the bugs of our days and express our thoughts about them. Just writing *I feel overwhelmed by the things I have to do* and then listing those things, along with our feelings about them, can lighten our mental load considerably. We may find ourselves feeling more able to manage our to-do list. We can also use our journal as a "problem and solution" guide. Write down the problem, express our feelings about it, and then write ways to solve the problem or resolve the issue. This puts us in a powerful position. Likewise, if we're confused about something or having a difficult time making a decision, writing down the pros and cons of the situation and our feelings about each can help us see more clearly what to do.

Neuro-Linguistic Programming

Neuro-Linguistic Programming, or NLP, was founded in the 1970s by Richard Bandler and linguist John Grinder as a tool for personal change. NLP began as an exploration between neurology, linguistics, and "programs," or observable patterns. Concepts from hypnotherapy were added. Through a process of visualizing, we are coached to change our perception of an event and experience so that it becomes less immobilizing, frightening, or threatening. NLP has proven to be highly effective, and often works in one session.

I belive NLP is one of the most powerful tools for positive change on the earth today. Negative beliefs about any part of who we are can get in the way of living up to our highest potential. As we reprogram our mind, negative beliefs are replaced by positive ones.

Negative beliefs are planted in childhood, when we perceive an event or situation as negative and internalize it to make it a part of who we believe we are. For example, Maya's alcoholic mother kept telling her she was "bad" and would never amount to anything. Maya believed it. She was an underachiever all through school and didn't even attempt to enroll in college. She struggled on the job, was afraid of every move, and never made suggestions, even when her ideas were valid. About the time she decided life was not worth living, she agreed to allow a friend who was working toward her certification as an NLP practitioner to practice on her. The results were astounding. Maya identified the first moment she had allowed her mother's voice to influence the way she thought about herself as "bad" and "worthless." The practitioner then guided her to hear the voice differently, change the meaning of her mother's words. While it's difficult to imagine turning a negative moment into something more positive, Maya succeeded. After three sessions, her self-esteem and self-assurance were increasing and she no longer believed she was worthless. She began to see herself as a valuable and talented being. She gained tremendous confidence at work. She began to take classes, greatly surprising herself with her level of intelligence. Thanks to NLP, Maya is now enjoying her life and looking forward to reaching her highest potential.

Working with an NLP practitioner is most beneficial. You can find one in your area via the Internet or alternative news publications. If you wish to try it on your own, a good source of information and techniques is *NLP: The New Technology of Achievement*, by Steve Andreas and Charles Faulkner

Emotional Freedom Technique (EFT)

Emotional Freedom Technique is a surprisingly easy healing technique that we can perform on ourselves to eliminate phobias, fears, emotional triggers, and even some diseases. It is so effective that a problem can often be resolved after just one session. Developed in the 1990s by Gary

Craig, EFT is a simplified version of Thought Field Therapy, a healing technique developed in the 1980s by Roger Callahan. EFT consists of systematically tapping certain meridians in the body (the "veins" through which our life force energy flows) with our fingertips while thinking or speaking about the problem we wish to heal. The theory behind EFT is that negative emotions are caused by disturbances in the body's energy field. Tapping on the meridians while thinking of the negative emotion restores balance back into the energy field. The technique is used by numerous healers across the country. You can even download the technique from the Internet to try it on your own. See www.emofree.com.

Personal Growth Workshops and Seminars

I attribute much of my current strength and power to healings that have occurred in the various personal growth workshops and seminars I've attended. I have traveled far and wide to attend certain workshops, and even when I was financially challenged, managed to pay for tuition and hotels. I'm grateful for every penny I spent. I identified my purpose in life, reprogrammed negative beliefs into positive ones, healed old wounds, and learned the practices and techniques that are still helping me to reach my highest potential. I attribute my current happiness, high self-esteem, prosperity, strength, and power to the healings facilitated by the brilliant facilitators and teachers of the workshops I attended.

These workshops and seminars are experiential classes facilitated by experts who are extremely effective in making positive shifts in our life and psyche. We actively participate in exercises to "get" the lesson to transform and change an aspect of our lives. There are innumerable workshops and seminars that focus on spiritual, psychological, emotional, and physical healing, all with the goal of resolving the issues that stand in the way of our highest potential. The effectiveness of the workshops comes from the total immersion we are invited to make in the practice. Workshops can last anywhere from two hours to two years, with an average length of three to seven days. The results are increased confidence, expansion of consciousness (because we are introduced to new ways of thinking about ourselves and our lives), breaking through old beliefs and paradigms, and so much more.

If you're interested in seeing what kinds of personal growth and empowerment workshops are available, pick up any New Age or health magazine or one of the alternative free publications. The Internet is also an excellent place to find information. (While workshops are becoming more mainstream, they aren't usually advertised in the major newspapers.) You will be surprised at the kinds of workshops available. Below is a list with descriptions of a few of the more popular seminars that are presented both in the USA and internationally. I have attended several of these workshops and can attest to their positive influence on my personal growth. Please note that while this book is about women and for women, in the realms of personal growth, I believe both women and men are equally gifted and valuable resources for healing.

Insight Seminars. Developed by spiritual teacher John Roger, the Insight Seminar is a weekend-long experiential workshop designed to open your heart and heal the wounds that prevent self-love. Wise and loving facilitators interact with the group through lectures and mind-expanding individual and group exercises that assist us in learning about ourselves and confronting the parts of ourselves we wish to change and/or heal. Emotional release is encouraged and supported. Learn more at www.insightseminars.com.

Landmark Forum. Landmark is an incarnation of the Erhard Seminars Training (est), which was popular in the 1970s. Landmark is less about the heart and more about the intellect. Though it's not warm and fuzzy, but rather stiff and cold, it yields highly positive results in many of its participants. In a three-day seminar, a facilitator delivers exclusive Landmark concepts for living, growing, and leading. She or he processes with individuals and the group and helps them confront and overcome limiting perceptions of the self. The Forum has made a profound and positive impact on thousands of people, including many of my friends. Landmark offers numerous other seminars for leadership, communication, and more. Learn more at www.landmarkseminars.com.

The Work of Byron Katie, Workshops and Seminars. In 1986, Byron Katie experienced a life-changing realization that ended years of deep depression. She became conscious of the fact that suffering is optional and that joy is in everyone, always. She became instantly aware of a process of self-inquiry that led her to the cause of her suffering. Byron's life shifted overnight and she emerged from a hopeless life to a life of joy. Now she travels the country and shares her process, called The Work, helping thousands of people find their own joy. She has written several books, including *Loving What Is: Four Questions That Can Change Your Life*, and *A Thousand Names for Joy: Living In Harmony with the Way Things Are*. To learn more about The Work, log onto www.thework.com.

Christopher Howard Seminars. The foundation of Chris Howard's work is NLP (see above). Chris travels the world to present the techniques to help lead us to our success. He is the author of *Turning Passions into Profits* and *Three Steps to Wealth and Power: Unleash Your Potential for Unlimited Achievement*. Reading these books, you can learn the excellent techniques for healing, empowering, and stepping on the right path to a great life. Chris's website is www.chrishoward.com.

Anthony Robbins Seminars. Tony Robbins has been at the forefront of personal growth for many years and has empowered hundreds of thousands of people through his seminars, books, and audio/video series. He is highly charismatic, motivating, and hope-instilling, with the sole purpose of helping us increase our power and potential in the world. He is one of the first personal growth authorities to use NLP for reprogramming negative beliefs. You can learn about his seminars at www.tonyrobbins.com. You can also learn many of his techniques from his motivating book, *Awakening the Giant Within: How to Take Immediate Control of Your Mental, Emotional, Physical and Financial Destiny.*

The Pathwork of Self-Transformation. Eva Pierrakos learned at a young age to listen to her inner voice, which she accessed through automatic writing and later through speaking in a trance state. Her inner guide gave her tools to overcome the obstacles that got in the way of living fully in our true nature and led her to create a system for self-purification, self-transformation, and spiritual self-realization. Eva lectured in the United States from 1957 to 1979 (the year she died) and delivered spiritual guidance to great numbers of teachers, healers, and therapists. Over 250 of her lectures were recorded and transcribed and have been made available at no cost by The International Pathwork Foundation. These mind-expanding lectures give us information that spurs our spiritual transformation. An on-line community offers an opportunity to connect with others on the Path. Their web site is www.pathwork.org. Many of Pierrakos' lectures that don't appear on the web site have been compiled in a book titled *The Pathwork of Self-Transformation.*

Alternative Healers

There are dozens of excellent modalities for dealing with emotional issues, and healers are not difficult to find these days. Practices such as Rolfing, theta healing, rebirthing, shamanic journeying, hypnotherapy, Eye Movement Desensitization and Reprocessing (EMDR), and other techniques are all useful. If you live near a city or even a reasonable-sized town, you can find an alternative healer. Use your instincts to identify the kind of healing that calls to you. It's also good to get referrals from friends and then call and ask the healer questions.

Get a Therapist: Traditional Psychotherapy

If you are not attracted to the alternative healing methods and you recognize issues in your life that are standing in the way of your happiness, healthy relationships, physical health, prosperity, and everything else that you desire, then perhaps traditional therapy is the thing for you. In the olden days, being in therapy seemed almost shameful, but today it is practically a status symbol. There is nothing to be ashamed of. People will openly admit they see a therapist. I honor those in therapy, because it shows that the person wants to change for the better and is taking action. Strong and powerful women are all about change for the better and taking action!

Physical Health

You have full control over your body and health. How can you be powerful in your work if you don't have the clarity and energy to do the work? How can you survive your daily life if you don't have the physical strength to lift, carry, go long distances? How can you feel sexy if you're tired and don't like the way your body looks? How can you be inspired and experience inner peace if you're constantly stressed and don't feel good? In two words—YOU CAN'T. To be sexy, spirited, and strong, you must be glowingly healthy.

Traits of a Healthy Woman

A healthy woman is a strong woman. She is vibrant, happy, alert, energized, and free from pain and disease. Her eyes are bright and sparkly, her skin is clear and glowing, and her teeth and gums in good condition. Her body and muscles are toned, her mind and focus are sharp. She has perpetual energy and enthusiasm and rarely experiences aches or pains. She gives herself ample rest and has control over stress. She's self-confident and often looks years younger than her age. She loves her body and treats it with care and respect. Her radiant energy is strong because her energy centers are working at capacity. She remains healthy and vital throughout life and into her more mature years, maintaining an energetic bounce in her step and superior functioning of her brain.

The way a woman takes care of her body is a reflection of her attitude toward everything in her life. A healthy woman has a lifestyle of commitment, self-love, self-discipline, and will power. These same dynamic forms of strength are used in the way she does her work and maintains her relationships and other personal endeavors. She's the kind of woman we want in our social circle, on our team, and as our leader.

Health for Survival and Evolution

America's recent passion for good health and strong bodies reflects a step in our evolution. Before the 1960s, we were virtually clueless about the connection between health and disease. During the 1960s, simple concepts for diet and exercise began to be promoted as elements of healthy living. Today, health and fitness is a billion-dollar industry supported by scientists, medical doctors, exercise physiologists, nutritionists, and other experts who research and share the secrets to maximum strength and eternal youth. Science is linking the affects of nutrition to every function of our body, including brain chemicals, hormones, and cellular makeup. It has proved that exercise, even something as simple as walking, makes the heart stronger. Likewise, a few daily servings of vegetables can help prevent disease.

Thanks to the declining rate of infectious diseases, public health efforts, improved health care, and healthier lifestyles, our life expectancy has increased dramatically over the past century. According to a 2002 study by the Centers for Disease Control, the age expectancy of American women has reached nearly eighty years, up by twenty-nine years from 1900, when the age expectancy was age fifty-one. (Today, life expectancy for men is age seventy-four, up from age forty-eight in 1900.)[201]

Health and fitness are fully integrated into the American culture. Health food stores have evolved from tiny, hippie-run shops into gigantic, mainstream super markets. Health clubs and yoga studios thrive in even the smallest towns. We have easy access to workout videos, alternative health practitioners, nutritional supplements, and innumerable books and magazines. There is no barrier to stop any woman from learning, obtaining, and practicing those things that contribute to maximum health.

Health and Disease Are Choices

Our personal health insurance is health *assurance*. Taking care of our bodies with high-nutrient foods and regular workouts can potentially reduce our trips to the doctor's office. Even a moderately good diet and minimal exercise will maintain our health to a certain level and ensure a high quality of life, even in old age. In other words, if we take good care of ourselves, we won't end up as little old ladies who can't open a jar without assistance. We'll still be dancing and running, participating in Senior Olympics, traveling, thinking, and living independent lives. In fact, Martha Graham, pioneer of modern dance, performed until the age of seventy-six; she lived to the ripe old age of ninety-seven.

With such easy access to information and healthy options, we might think the population of the United States is the healthiest and fittest on the planet. But statistics show that we have more heart disease, diabetes, obesity than any other country. It is a fact that Americans are more obese than any other people on earth, a condition that is directly related to cardiovascular disease, diabetes, and stroke. Dr. Jennifer Zebrack of the Medical College of Wisconsin states that obesity is the most common nutritional disorder in the developed world and the second most preventable cause of death after smoking.[202]

Heart disease and diabetes are manmade diseases, created by lifestyle habits that lead to obesity. Let's look at the typical American lifestyle. Overwhelmed by the demands of work (Americans work harder for more hours per week than any other country), we default to a fast-food diet that lacks all nutritional value. Our exercise plan is the "couch potato workout," that is, pushing buttons on the remote. We push ourselves to work longer hours and endure great stress. We get too little sleep. We drink lots of coffee and soft drinks for energy to get through the day and snack on steady doses of junk food. No wonder Americans are fat and sick!

But we don't have to live like this. Americans have healthier options, and we can all decide what kind of lifestyle to choose. Your choices determine your future. Will you choose health or disease?

Every day, several times a day, we can make decisions that are good for our bodies. We can decide what to consume and how to much to move our body. We can decide to eat steamed vegetables or French fries. To walk after work or crash on the couch to watch TV. To stay up till 2 a.m. or get eight hours of sleep. To swallow a diet pill or cut down on pasta and bread. When we are committed to becoming healthy, there's no hesitation. We choose what contributes to good health.

Yes, good health is a choice and a commitment. Choices will eventually become habits, and soon we're not choosing anymore. We've changed our lifestyle and just live it. We don't think twice. We automatically go for a run after work and habitually buy fresh salad greens and broccoli.

Natural Lifestyle vs. Typical American Lifestyle

As American women, we are blessed to live in a time when we have numerous options that lead to optimal health and healing. But when it really comes down to it, there are two basic American lifestyles: the healthy, natural lifestyle or the typical American couch-potato lifestyle.

The goals of the healthy, natural lifestyle are to feed and condition the body to function most efficiently, feel good, and be free of disease. This lifestyle incorporates the following elements:

1. Enthusiastically learning about the body and health
2. Consuming whole foods (fruit, vegetables, and unprocessed foods)
3. Taking proper nutritional supplements

4. Exercising the body for strength, endurance, and stress reduction
5. Getting adequate sleep
6. Sticking to a moderate to no intake of unhealthy or toxic foods and substances (such as sweets, alcohol, and caffeine)

What we get from our healthy, natural lifestyle are healthy organs. Our physiology is highly functional and our immune system, hormones, circulation, and brain chemistry are healthy. We have strong muscles and bones. We have greater resistance to disease, higher life-force energy, and an overall feeling of well-being.

When we maintain a healthy, natural lifestyle, if we succumb to illness, it is usually less severe and quicker to pass. Our choices of treatments are natural and/or alternative, which work on the body on a holistic level to strengthen and rejuvenate both the problem area and entire body. We may seek one of a variety of natural healers, including specialists in nutrition, acupuncture, herbal remedies, homeopathy, Ayurveda (Eastern Indian healing), and Chinese medicine. A single healing modality can be greatly beneficial, and two or more used together may speed up the healing process.

The goals of the typical American couch-potato lifestyle, by contrast, are focused on the here and now satisfaction of just surviving one more stressful day. Americans typically consume foods that merely taste good, but sometimes, to control their weight, they don't eat at all. They avoid physical activity that challenges the body. This lifestyle includes little sleep, high stress, and over-consumption of caffeine, alcohol, and sugar. There is no thought to the body's future or the results of lifestyle choices, let alone disease prevention.

If (*when*) illness sets in, the follower of the typical American lifestyle automatically seeks medical attention from a doctor of standard Western, or allopathic, medicine. Western medicine is a mixed blessing. It repairs the damage created by unhealthy living with drugs and surgeries, but the cure often comes at the *expense* of another aspect of our health. (Think about those television ads for prescription drugs and the lengthy lists of health risks and side-effects associated with the drugs. And people still want to take them?) Educated just to fix and repair, allopathic physicians automatically prescribe drugs to heal symptoms, but they seldom address the *source* of the disease. Sometimes they prescribe a second drug to cure the uncomfortable side-effects of the primary drug. Uneducated in diet and exercise, standard medical doctors offer little advice for healthy living. This is, however, beginning to change.

Let's look at the treatment of cardiovascular disease from these two perspectives. The healthy, natural lifestyle will help to prevent cardiovascular disease from developing in the first place. But if we were to develop cardiovascular disease, it would be treated, and very often cured, with lifestyle changes. Dr. Nathan Pritikin and Dr. Dean Ornish have proved it can be done. They have developed and prescribed disease-reversing lifestyle programs to thousands of post-heart attack patients who regained their cardiovascular health. Their programs consist mainly of healthy eating and exercise habits without the use of drugs or surgery. (For more information, read *The Program for Reversing Heart Disease* by Dr. Dean Ornish and *The Pritikin Program*, by Dr. Nathan Pritikin.)

Conversely, allopathic physicians most typically treat heart disease with prescription drugs and surgeries. They may encourage their patients to lose weight and exercise, but they offer little practical advice on how to do so. (The average typical American lifestyle patient is unlikely to make any lifestyle changes, anyway.) Not only are the drugs extremely expensive, but they often harm other organs, like the liver and kidneys, and they often leave the patient feeling sluggish. If the drugs don't work, the doctors turn to surgery, at the cost of hundreds of thousands of dollars.

Mind you, I honor and am grateful to the American medical system for its ability to repair our bodies. But we have the power and resources to avoid many radical treatments and surgeries. The Strong and Powerful Woman chooses the natural, healthy lifestyle to prevent disease and to maintain maximum performance throughout her life. She's in life for the long haul and thus honors her body and treats it well.

Attitude

Good health is one result of having a positive attitude toward life. Our attitudes influence our choices. Our attitude about our body and health directly relates to our level of health. When we see the correlation of a positive attitude about health and the resulting good health, it is easier to make lifestyle changes. When we respect our body and see the value in health and longevity, we will think positively about committing to a healthier lifestyle.

Too many Americans have a negative attitude about things that are good for them. Sometimes we sound like little kids. Say the word "vegetables," and we scowl and say, "Yuck!" Ask us to take a walk or exercise, and we say, "I don't feel like it. I'm too tired." Many of us don't realize how detrimental a negative attitude toward health is, how it can stand in the way of a feeling good. Luckily, we have within us the power to change our attitudes, especially if we make it a priority to become glowingly healthy. Instead of seeing broccoli as a slimy green vegetable that tastes bad (because so many Americans cook broccoli to death), let's think about its benefits: its high vitamin and cellulose content, the fact that it feeds every cell of the body and aids digestion, that it's filled with vitamin C, which boosts the immune system, and that as a cruciferous vegetable broccoli defends the body against cancer. Do you feel more like eating broccoli now?

In fact, research shows that we can actually psych ourselves into making better food choices. When debating between a not-so-healthy food choice and a nutritious one, telling yourself that the nutritious one tastes just as good as the junk food can sway you to make the better choice. Likewise, the more you know about good food, such as vitamin content, the more you may like it and choose it.[203]

The same goes for exercise. Negative thinking sounds like this: "What a drag. I feel so tired. I don't have the energy to get off this couch. I'll exercise tomorrow." By thinking positively about the benefits of exercise, we're more motivated to get moving. If we knew and experienced the positive affects of exercise, we might be more motivated to do it. The Mayo Clinic advises that even minimal exercise will help us feel better and become healthier. The positive effects of exercise are noticeable almost immediately. You feel more confident. Your self-esteem rises. Evidence suggests this is due to both the increased levels of mood-enhancing neurotransmitters in the brain and the reduced level of the stress hormone, cortisol.[204] You know the long-term effects of exercise: increased strength of the muscles and bones, increased strengthening of the heart and lungs, lowering of cholesterol, diminished risk of diabetes, burning of calories (and thus weight loss), and so much more.

Now do you feel like exercising? Often the most strenuous part of your workout is psyching yourself up to do it. But once you get off the couch and make the first move, the good feelings kick in immediately, and continuing the workout becomes easier. Once you recognize the good feelings that come from exercise, the decision to exercise on a regular basis comes easier. And when you see the results, you are motivated to make exercise a priority.

A positive attitude is positively empowering. Making the right decisions will help you feel more healthy, and will greatly increase your confidence and self-esteem.

Tips for Health

Health is self-love. Remember, your body is your temple. A temple is a structure in which spirit dwells. Are you being a good caretaker of your temple? Your earthly vehicle, the body you were born into, is a gift from the universe. Taking care of your body is a form of self-worship. Loving our bodies is a firm step in the direction of total self-love and higher self-esteem.

Make health, not looking good, your first priority. When Brazilian fashion model Ana Carolina Reston died in 2006 at the age of 23 from kidney failure linked to anorexia, the world took note. At five feet eight inches and eighty-eight pounds at the time of her death, Ana represented a common female malady: she needed to look thin at the expense of her overall health. Looking good, that is, looking fit and youthful, is the product of a healthy lifestyle. Unfortunately, many women associate looking good only with being thin, and they strive to achieve fashionable thinness by ignoring a healthy lifestyle. Instead of eating healthy food, these women may either not eat at all or take diet pills to lose weight. While they may achieve a thin body, they are doing so at the expense of their organs, hormones, and life-force energy. But the human body can endure under unhealthy circumstances for only so long. Eventually, it gives up.

When we make total health our priority, however, our body will naturally look good. It is healthier to strive to feel good, increase our energy, prevent disease, and strengthen our muscles than it is to be thin. A woman who is healthy, no matter what her weight, is more beautiful than a woman who sacrifices her health to be fashionably thin.

Everything in moderation. Good health doesn't mean deprivation. While the healthier choice is to avoid all alcohol, caffeine, sweets, and fatty foods, the occasional consumption of these things is not very harmful. We derive pleasure from simple things like food and drink. If we were to completely ban the things we enjoy, life would lose a dimension of joy. If you are a healthy person, an occasional, moderate serving of wine or chocolate is permissible. (That is, a couple of glasses of wine once a week, not a whole bottle of wine two or three times a week.) My philosophy is that if you put something less than healthy into your body, you should counter the negative affects with extra doses of good things like vegetables or water.

However, if a health professional has completely restricted alcohol or ice cream from your diet, for example, *please* follow the doctor's orders. Unhealthy substances can be dangerous, and recuperation from toxic substances, including sugar, fatty foods, and junk food, that do not promote health take much longer than the few seconds you enjoy the Coke or the truffle or the Big Mac.

Read books and magazines that teach health. There is so much to be said about health that I could write forever. Because there are brilliant health experts who say it better than I do, I recommend that you get your hands on as many health and fitness books and magazines as you can. I also recommend that you make learning about health a priority. Books and magazines on health and fitness are easy to find. Pick up a health magazine at the grocery store. Pick up health books at the library. Go on the Internet and explore "health" and similar subjects. Search Amazon.com for books on health to get a comprehensive look at what is available. A few books I recommend are these:

Back to Eden: The Classic Guide to Herbal Medicine, Natural Foods and Home Remedies, by Jethro Kloss. A time-tested health best seller originally published in 1972, this book will open your eyes to the power of health food and natural healing.

The Total Health Makeover, by Marilu Henner. An actor turned health advocate, Marilu Henner has devoted her life to promoting healthy lifestyle habits. Her books thoroughly explain the benefits of healthy living, and offer a program to get you on your way.

Get Healthy Now! A Complete Guide to Prevention, Treatment and Healthy Living and Gary Null's Ultimate Lifetime Diet: A Revolutionary All-Natural Program for Losing Weight and Building a Healthy Body, by Gary Null. Dr. Null is one of our country's greatest advocates of alternative medicine and natural healing.

Clarity of Gifts

Twenty-five hundred years ago, the words *Know Thyself* were inscribed on the wall of the Temple of Apollo at Delphi. While many attribute the aphorism to Socrates, other ancient sages have also been credited. That long ago, wise men and women knew that knowing ourselves is the key to success and a source of strength. When we know ourselves, we identify our gifts and purpose in life, which enables us to confidently move in the right direction to create our vision. Whether you decide you want to become a stay-at-home mother or President of the United States, knowing yourself is the first step to attaining your dreams. It is only after you have unlocked the treasure chest of YOU that you can discover the gifts that will help you live to your highest potential, be most effective in the world, and create interesting work and harmonious relationships.

Knowing ourselves is the foundation of high self-esteem, which is necessary to create a life that expresses who we are. If we don't know what we want or the kind of life we want to live, it will be difficult for us to achieve anything.

So who are you?

1. An energetic being composed of a divine soul and an earthly physical body
2. A being containing a mind, divine gifts, and talents with a purpose in your lifetime (your soul mission)
3. A life form possessing personal beliefs, values, and principles
4. An energetic force with a potential for action

Each of us is a unique combination of these components. In every single person, each component has its own special flavor, making each and every person on the planet a unique being. No one else in the world is a duplicate of you. Knowing yourself means recognizing and appreciating each and every unique quality of your being. The most joyful and successful people are those who remain true to who they are and committed to living a life that expresses their individuality. This is Strength in motion.

Some of us are born knowing ourselves. Oprah Winfrey says she practically emerged from the womb speaking to the public. At the age of three, she recited Bible verses to the congregation of her church. Others search for years to discover who they are. And some don't look at all. Back in the 1960s, it was common for people to abandon their conventional lifestyles to go "find themselves." To this day, people are still finding themselves. Many of us know ourselves, but then, because change is a natural human condition we change or experience a life-altering event that forces us to discover our new self. Knowing ourselves is thus a different journey for each of us, and comparing ourselves to others is a waste of energy. Focus on yourself.

After we come to know ourselves, a cosmic force within us drives us to do or express what is in us. As a gentle force drives us to move against all odds, it's almost as if it's out of our hands. We become almost giddy with excitement and passion as we move forward and touch every milestone along the way. When we know ourselves, we know our soul—our gifts, dreams, desires, and turn-ons, as well as our values and principles. Self-knowledge is the reference point we will return to time and time again to remind us of who we are and what we want to create as we travel through life. We are sure to make the right choices and decisions because the *right* ones feel *good* and the wrong ones don't feel so good. In addition, *trusting* ourselves will help us confidently live the life we want, no matter how unconventional it seems, and in spite of the doubt of our well-intentioned friends and family.

"Know Thyself" is your life's compass. At some point in her life, every successful woman will ask herself, "Am I on the right road?" When you know who you are and what you want, you will travel the correct road and quickly figure it out when you've taken a wrong turn. You can return to the right road

For many people, their life's mission is a single pursuit that endures for their lifetime. For others, their life's purpose changes and/or evolves, with the accomplishment of one goal acting as a stepping-stone to the next. I, myself, have had many different missions, from living as a full-time artist, to producing documentary films, to producing women's workshops, and now to writing a book. I know there is much more to come.

Developing Our Gifts and Life's Purpose

As a spiritual being in a physical body on the planet earth, you have a reason to exist. Your spirit is the expression of your soul. I believe our reason for existence is to discover our gifts and bring them forth to benefit the planet. Success means living life passionately by doing what you love. Expressing yourself by using your gifts creates a kind of spiritual high that stays with you every minute of every day and leads to a joyful life.

Your Life's Purpose

Your life's purpose, often referred to as your "mission" or "calling," is the specific reason you were born on earth. Of all of the definitions the Webster's New World College Dictionary gives to the word "mission," two are pertinent here: "a sending out or being sent out with authority to perform a special service," and "the special task or purpose for which a person is apparently destined in life; calling."[205] Author and theologian Frederick Buechner defines a calling as the "place where your deepest gladness meets the world's deepest need."[206]

According to the Gnostic *Gospel of Thomas*, Jesus Christ once said, "Bringing forth *that* within you, *that* will save you. If you do not, then *that* will kill you"[207] Jean-Yves Leloup, translator of the Gnostic texts, including *The Gospel of Thomas*, translates *that* as love, being, and self-knowledge. And without knowing *that* (the self), he writes, life becomes "stale and depleted."[208] Using your gifts and bringing them to fruition is almost an obligation. Knowing your self leads to self-love and goodness in the world. Not recognizing your gifts and ignoring your potential is a waste of your soul. It makes you feel unimportant and insignificant.

Some of us are born knowing our life's mission. Some of us feel a "calling" or inner urge to embark on a particular path. Some of us were programmed by our parents and society to do or become something that is not true to our soul. Others have been given no programming, hope, or help to find their life's purpose. Others discover it as they grow. Still others may make a conscious effort to pick a purpose after thorough self-exploration and research of options. Whatever category you fall into, make a conscious effort to discover your purpose.

For the past several millennia, two of the primary life purposes assigned to women were to marry a man and raise a family, whether they wanted to or not. However, as humans evolve and opportunities for women increase, the life's purpose of many women has expanded beyond wifedom and motherhood. Pulsating with abundant creative energy and a desire to contribute to the world, women are pursuing outlets that fulfill their souls. Following their callings, they use their gifts to express themselves, support themselves financially, and contribute to every field. Only in the last fifty years have opportunities once available only to men become available to women. And women are fully embracing them. It is no longer unusual for women to become astronauts, politicians, stockbrokers, and scientists. Freedom increases possibility, and when possibility is explored, our perceptions of ourselves expand and we feel more confident about our capabilities. As women grow into their most powerful selves, nothing can stop them.

Your life's purpose needn't be grand. It can be as simple as learning to become patient with your parents, or as instinctive as raising a healthy child. It can be as ambitious as you can imagine. You can start your own business, join the Peace Corps, or star in a movie. But even if your life's purpose doesn't take your full-time attention, just knowing what it is will make you feel better about yourself. Knowing your purpose and your gifts gives your life meaning and direction. As with knowing ourselves, knowing your mission will empower you to stay on track and make the right decisions for your life.

Discovering your life's purpose can be a mission itself. There are several methods that can help you unlock the expression of your soul. I offer a few here.

Our Gifts

What are our gifts? I define our gifts in this sense as the extraordinary personality and physical traits and developable talents, skills, and intellect that we are born with. A gift can be a sense of humor, an aptitude for leadership, natural charm, fantastic physical beauty, or psychic ability. If your gift is talent, it can be a magnificent singing voice, an artistic eye, or a way with words. An intellectual gift can be a proficiency in math or science or a knack for problem solving. Every human being is born with at least one gift, if not dozens. Some are obvious at an early age, whereas others emerge with maturity and introspection.

Our gifts may define our life's purpose and mission. If a girl is born with many gifts, she may be called to select one or two to create a life path that will bring her the greatest fulfillment. Her gift may become the focus of her life's purpose, her mission, to hone it to perfection. For example, a painter continually pushes herself to perfect her painting style so she can create a masterpiece worthy of exhibition in the Metropolitan Museum. The singer practices daily to increase her vocal abilities so that she can perform the solo in Carnegie Hall that will bring her audience to tears.

Gifts can also be the tools that support our life's purpose. A brilliant scientific mind, for example, is the gift that supports the scientist's endeavor to find a cure for cancer. The exotic and beautiful face is the gift that ensures that the model makes the front cover of *Vogue*.

Your gifts are the God/dess-given tools that help you forge a meaningful life. Acknowledge, appreciate, and perfect them, as bringing them forth will bring you joy, and will assure your success in your endeavors.

Journaling

Writing out your thoughts is as effective in knowing yourself and discovering your life's purpose as it is purging negative thoughts. Throughout my life and numerous career moves, I have kept journals. Journaling is highly valuable when embarking on the discovery of your life's purpose. When you identify your gifts, accomplishments, passions, and dreams and write them down, you can see clearly in black and white your uniqueness and value on the planet. The writing exercises below are powerful first steps.

Gift List

Writing often yields clarity. When you write a list of your gifts, you are on your way to discovering your purpose. In your journal, write down every single, tiny thing that you can think of that makes you who you are:

1. Your general abilities, such as walking fast, being good listener, smiling a lot
2. Your physical gifts, such as gorgeous hair, great breasts, powerful legs, well-groomed nails

3. Your trivial special talents that no one else knows about, such as wiggling your earlobes or singing *great* in the car
4. Your extraordinary skills and talents, such as writing winning proposals or sewing a gorgeous dress
5. Your gifts of character, such as kindness, courage, having an open heart and being nice to everyone, being able to get things done, always keeping your word

Take time to make your lists, as your gifts may continue to pop up in your mind for an hour or a day or longer. You may even devote an entire page to just one list so that you have plenty of room to write. Now look at this list and admire who you are. Most likely, your gifts are abundant and noteworthy. Your list not only helps you recognize them as potential tools for future missions, but also lets you see your magnificence.

Accomplishment List

On a new page in your journal, list every significant accomplishment you've achieved so far in your life. List the things that make you feel proudest, and that you think made a positive impact on your life. Your accomplishments can be as minor as hemming your pants by yourself to something as major as graduating from college *cum laude*. Give yourself plenty of time to think and write.

Now review your list and on a scale of 1 to 5, rate the ease or difficulty of your accomplishments, 1 being easy and 5 being very difficult.

Now look at your ratings and see how many of your accomplishments were easy. Look at the ones that were difficult. Were the achievements you are most proud of a 1 or a 2? Would the more difficult accomplishments be easier the second time around?

Usually, the things that come most easily indicate that we were using one of our gifts. The same goes for the difficult accomplishments you believe would be much easier a second time.

Often we don't accomplish our missions, but this doesn't mean we're failures or on the wrong track. Feeling joyful and alive while working toward something indicates that we are putting our gifts to work, and this is an achievement in its own right.

On your list, include those things you didn't accomplish, but had a blast working toward. And give them a 1. Every endeavor in which you express your gifts is an accomplishment.

Passion List

On a new page in your journal, list everything you love or feel passionate and excited about. This includes people, places, things, events, sensations, the pleasures of life. Give yourself plenty of time to think about it and extract and write every morsel of passion from your soul.

Dream List

On another new page of your journal, list your dreams. Go wild, baby! Describe the lifestyle you'd like to have, the people you'd like to be with, all the things you'd like to do for joy, pleasure, and thrills. Think big. Write until nothing else comes out.

Now review your Passion and Dream lists. What turns you on, excites you, drives you? When you have found your life's purpose, you will feel it in your bones. You will feel motivated to do whatever it takes to pursue it, from education to honing your skills or networking with the right people. It will feel very right and true to who you are. Congratulations.

Recommended Reading

I highly recommend *The Artist's Way: A Spiritual Path to Higher Creativity* by Julia Cameron. This guidebook offers a twelve-week program for self-discovery. It is filled with practices and exercises to help you identify your gifts and dreams, and the underlying beliefs that block them. *The Artist's Way* will help anyone, not just "artists," identify their soul's desires.

Another great book is *What Color is Your Parachute* by Richard Nelson Bolles. This classic asks that you do some serious soul searching and helps you pinpoint your skills and leads you in the right direction to your most fulfilling life

The Path: Creating your Mission Statement for Work and for Life, by Laurie Beth Jones, offers advice to help you write and fulfill your mission statement, a "brief, succinct and focused statement that can be used to initiate, evaluate and refine all of life's activities."[209]

Positive Mindsets and Expansion

A mindset is a mental attitude that is formed by one's life experiences. Starting in childhood, events and influential people form our perceptions of people, places, events, and ideas, and determine whether we're looking at a glass that is half-empty or half-full, and whether we perceive things as good or bad, important or frivolous, desirous or to be avoided, or positive or negative. A strong woman is guided through life and toward success by positive and empowering mindsets. Many of us don't realize that our negative opinions and perceptions are limiting, and often negate success and joy. Luckily, our mindsets are not set in stone and often change through life as we are introduced to new ideas and perspectives. We can even change our mindsets by being aware of them, and consciously replacing negative ones with positive.

Following are a mindsets held by strong and empowered women. By putting them into practice yourself, you will become empowered and in greater control of your life. You'll also experience more joy as you traverse life's rocky terrain and move toward success and fulfillment.

Be Fully Present

There is nothing but this moment. Being fully present is paying attention to a person or situation, engaging all of your senses to experience what is happening at the moment. It's "being here now." In fact, as Ram Dass, author of the classic *Being Here Now* says, "When you have quieted your mind enough, and transcended your ego enough, you can hear how it really is." As the characters in the musical play, *Rent*, sing, there is "no day but today."

The concept may sound New Agey, but it's really ages old. Being present means having absolute awareness, right here, right now, in this moment. Being present means really seeing what is in front of you and around you. It means listening to, and really hearing, what someone is saying to you. Being fully present is connecting energetically with a person, observing a person or event without judgment. Being fully present asks us to maintain awareness of the various mental and psychological filters that develop through our conditioning and influence our opinions. As we see our judgments arise, we can release or override them, so as to witness a situation with as much clarity as we can muster. In our typical American society, we dwell on everything *but* the present. We rehash old scenarios, especially the ones that hurt us, over and over and over again. We space out and mentally write our grocery list while our friend is telling us about her date. Some of us keep working while people are talking to us, not making eye contact and responding only to a particular trigger. It's easy to identify someone who is not fully present with you. It feels like the person isn't listening and doesn't care what you're saying.

Moving through our lives "in our heads" all the time will diminish our power. Yes, I know your head is the most important and exciting place on earth, but staying there all the time causes you to miss out on the details of life. Being fully present will make you a better friend and co-worker. You'll generally function more effectively in your life.

Here is a simple exercise in awareness. Give yourself fifteen minutes to take a walk. It can be anywhere—around the neighborhood, in the mall, wherever. For those fifteen minutes, maintain full awareness of everything around you. Be fully conscious of the sounds and smells that come to you. Maintain a sharp alertness to what you see. Keep your mind from wandering or judging. Notice any judgments you have of what you see or hear, and see if you can neutralize those judgments. For example, if you see graffiti or a homeless person, don't immediately label it as bad. Merely witness what you are seeing, as if you're watching a movie. Be here now. You may be startled at just how difficult it is to maintain full focus on the present moment without your mind wandering, but also to release all judgments. Practice this exercise whenever you can and make full presence a normal state of being.

Take Responsibility. Eliminate Victim Consciousness.

I know an unhappy woman who blames her husband for all of her misery. Unfulfilled and helpless, she blames him for holding her back from her dreams and not supporting her needs. In the meantime, her hard-working and devoted husband supports her financially, gives her cars, money, and encouragement to do what she wants to do. Fearful and devoid of inner strength, she points her finger at him and blames him for her lack of friendships and adventure. It's his fault she has no career. A classic victim, she is frequently depressed and resentful. She's powerless to create her own happiness.

You cannot be powerful without taking responsibility for your life and all that occurs in it. It's easy to take credit for your successes, but failure is a different story. The bad relationships, overdrawn bank account, misery on the job—these are the things you want to blame on the men, the bank, the boss. But get this. Barring an act of God like a tornado or earthquake or fire, *you* are fully responsible for your life and all of its successes and failures. You have more power over your life than you realize. Only *you* can make your life work the way you want it to. Only *you* can make yourself happy and bring yourself the fulfillment your soul desires. Adopting this philosophy will make you stronger and more powerful in the world.

Nothing is more disempowering than victim consciousness. Victim consciousness is the feeling of being wronged or kept down. It's not taking any responsibility for a situation, or even for your whole life. Victims say, "I didn't get that job because I'm a woman," rather than, "I didn't get that job because I probably don't have the skills they're looking for." The victim's "poor me" attitude creates a negative vibration, making her the perfect target for manipulative people. She's the first to be rejected or fired and often the one who others may wish to avoid. (Thus she creates what she blames and hates the most.) Victim consciousness gets you off the hook. It makes you right and the other person wrong. Victims see every situation as out of their control. They keep complaining about it, but never take action to correct it. Whining, complaining, blaming, and making excuses stunt your inner power and prevents you from growing. Victim consciousness leads to hopelessness and surrender.

When you always blame someone else for what happens to you, you are saying that the other person has more power over your life than you have. But we cannot blame other people for everything. Your rat of an ex-husband left you for another woman and you still have all that credit card debt? Blaming him for your unhappiness may make you feel that you are right, but, really, you're giving the power to him. When you take the responsibility yourself and admit that you married a rat-man, admit that you suspected he was running around but didn't confront him, admit that you watched him buy all that stuff but didn't say anything, you take back your power and become a responsible adult. Blaming diminishes you and gives your power away. Taking full responsibility will contribute to your greatness.

Here's a prime example. I was once in a relationship with a man who was very charismatic and intelligent, but also critical, dominating, and excessively powerful. In one moment he would demonstrate his love for me, then in the next disapprove of my work, my look, anything I did, often in front of other people, including women I felt he was seeing on the side. I wouldn't acknowledge those feelings. I was miserable, but I remained in the relationship in spite of my inner voice pleading with me to leave. I thought the relationship was an endurance test, that it was "good for me." I was living in a mental haze, abhorring his attitude toward me, hating his arrogance and manipulative ways, blaming him for my decreased joy and lowered self-esteem.

It wasn't until I checked myself into an intense healing program that I began to see that I had given away my power and allowed him to assert his. *I* had allowed *him* to make *me* miserable. I had all the power to leave the situation, but I had stayed and enabled him. I had let him control the relationship. Once I realized that I deserved better and was capable of controlling my own happiness, and that he wasn't responsible for my misery, I became more powerful. I took the time to repair my self-esteem. I completely ended the relationship.

"Why did *I* let that happen?" is much more empowering than, "He did that to me!" It's also admitting a mistake and saying, "It's my fault," and "I'm sorry," and doing what you can to correct a situation.

But taking responsibility doesn't mean we *blame* ourselves. Blame creates feelings of judgment and shame, and when we blame ourselves, we see ourselves as less than we are. Taking responsibility has an entirely different vibration. It is taking power over our own life. It means we've educated ourselves and entered a situation with full awareness. It means we have the information to make the right decisions. It means we set boundaries so others don't take advantage of us. It means acknowledging the breadth of our power and being able to admit to a mistake or misguided judgment. Accepting responsibility not only makes us greater humans, but it also offers opportunities for growth and increase of our personal power.

Quit Complaining. Be Proactive.

A complaint is a negative statement expressing dissatisfaction, annoyance, or displeasure. Complaining sends out negative vibes. Like the victim, a complaining woman feels she has no control over her life. Chronic complainers see everything though lenses of negativity and constantly criticize and whine. Complainers can poison any moment. You definitely wouldn't want a complainer on your team.

A strong, powerful woman doesn't complain. When she is unhappy with a situation, instead of wasting her time with negative talk, she comes up with a way to fix it, proposes her solution to the right person or people, and offers to take action. If the situation is beyond her control or is unchangeable, she changes her mindset and lives with it. If it's impossible to accept the situation, she removes herself from it altogether.

So. Do you hate your job because you're overworked? Feel like complaining? Here's what you can do:

1. Present the perceived problem *and your solution* to the person who has the power to change it.
2. If the problem is not changed and a compromise is not possible, change your mindset about it to make it less of a problem. Fully accept it and never complain about it again.
3. If, in your heart of hearts, you can't accept it and compromise isn't an option, leave the situation. Find a new job.

The biggest obstacle to change is fear. Until you feel confident in making changes or strong enough to endure your current situation, you will live a life of dissatisfaction.

Practice an Attitude of Gratitude

Strong and powerful women are grateful for every aspect of their lives. They see the good and the potential for goodness in their lives. When you really appreciate and feel grateful for what you've accomplished, acquired, possess materially and internally, and all of the wonderful things to come, you are in a place of power.

Gratitude is positive energy that attracts positive people and experiences to you. It puts you in a positive frame of mind and helps you to get through the rough times. It offers hope for the good things to come. Seeing the good in what you have, what you are, and what you can do will make it easier for you to move through your day and accomplish your goals. As you go through the day, from morning to night, therefore, be grateful for the people around you and for the lessons you learn. Rejoice in the miraculous body vehicle you inhabit. Celebrate your brains and give thanks for the opportunities that appear before you on a daily basis. Be grateful for the choices you have at work, at the grocery store, on the highway, and in friends and relationships.

Life isn't always the clichéd bowl of cherries, so it's important to be grateful even for the tough times. See the good in the challenges that make you uncomfortable or hurt you, and be grateful for the growth you experience. When we take the greatest leaps in our growth and maturity, we become stronger and wiser.

Positive Thinking

"Thoughts become things . . . choose the good ones," quips Mike Dooley, author of *Notes from the Universe: New Perspectives From an Old Friend*. The way we think about our health, weight, finances, relationships, self-worth, and self-esteem may influence our potential for success or failure. To become happy and empowered, we must think positively about our capabilities. Energetically, the universe responds to our every thought. In their book, *Ask and It Is Given*, authors Esther and Jerry Hicks likewise write, "Every thought that you give your attention to expands and becomes a bigger part of your vibrational mix. Whether it is a thought of something you want or a thought of something you do not want, your attention invites it into your experience."[210] Positive thoughts thus yield positive outcomes, and negative thoughts create negative outcomes.

Dr. Dean Radin of the Institute of Noetic Sciences and author of *The Conscious Universe: The Scientific Truth of Psychic Phenomenon*, appears in *What The Bleep Do We Know* and *What the Bleep: Down the Rabbit Hole* and compares human consciousness from the perspectives of classical mechanics and quantum mechanics. "The world is not this clockwork thing," he says, "but is more like an organism. It's a highly interconnected organistic thing of some type, which extends through space and time. And that kind of environment, what I think and the way that I behave, has a much greater impact, not only on myself, but the rest of the world."[211]

Dr. Masaru Emoto is famous for his experiments that demonstrate the impact of words on the molecular structure of drops of water. He tapes signs with a single word expressing a positive emotion, such as love, peace, or hope, on a container filled with water, and then freezes a single drop from each container. He does the same thing with a jar on which he has taped a negative word, such as hate, or anger. The crystallized droplets from the containers with a positive word form beautiful, symmetrical patterns similar to snowflakes. But the crystals from the containers bearing a negative word, such as hate and kill, are misshapen, asymmetrical blobs, or unattractive patterns.[212] Since the human body is composed of 60 percent water, and the brain 70 percent, if thoughts affect water, how might your thoughts be affecting your body?

Thoughts are the energy and vibrations that we project. We rarely think about what we think about, but if we did, we would think carefully and creatively. Carefully—we must avoid negative thoughts, because we invite a negative return of energy and create what we don't want. Creatively—we project positive energy and manifest what we *do* want. Madame H.P. Blavatsky, one of the founders (in 1875) of the Theosophical Society, an organization of advanced spiritual principles, is considered to be one of the first "New Age" thinkers. In her book *Isis Unveiled*, she wrote that when a thought "of good or evil import is begotten in our brain, it draws to it impulses of like nature as irresistibly as the magnet attracts iron filings. This attraction is also proportionate to the intensity with which the thought impulse makes itself felt in the ether...."[213] In his book *The Science of Mind*, Ernest Holmes writes, "Thoughts are things, they have the power to objectify themselves; thought lays hold of Causation and forms real Substance. Thoughts of sickness can make a man sick, and thoughts of health and perfection can heal him."[214]

Negative thoughts manifest as easily as positive ones. Persistent thoughts of dissatisfaction, disdain, and dislike manifest into negative situations. If you constantly feel annoyed by your coworker and think negative thoughts about her all the time, the universe will deliver a perpetually annoying coworker. Theologian Miceal Ledwith, Ph.D., says in an interview in *What the Bleep: Down the Rabbit Hole*, "Whatever way we observe the world around us is what comes back to us. If I am a victim, do I have a victim mentality? If so, perhaps my mentality is attuned to accepting that this is the way life is."[215]

Clearing away negative thoughts is as simple as shifting our thoughts from a negative perspective to a positive one. As simple as it may seem, though, it isn't easy. Negativity is an old habit that many of us have incorporated into our normal thought patterns. Like breaking any habit, awareness and commitment to change are paramount. Practice monitoring your thoughts and comments. Take note of the negative statements you make. Few of us are even aware of our thoughts at all, let alone whether they are positive or negative. You may be surprised at the subtle (or not so subtle) negativity that crosses your mind and your lips, but with this awareness comes the opportunity to make change. By replacing those negative thoughts with positive ones, we can affect our overall vibration and the messages that the universe receives from you.

Because we are highly energetic beings, our vibrations are transmitted into the universe. How can we create positive outcomes for ourselves? First, visualize what you desire and feel it as if it's already happened. Second, demonstrate that you really want it and take action. While your vibrations from your visualization will start the attraction process, proving that you are willing to work for it will strengthen the attraction and intensify your receptivity. (Some schools of thought say that only the first step of visualizing is necessary to activate attraction. Then we should step out of the way to let the universe do its work. I am a proponent of helping the universe along.)

Try this the next time you're looking for a place to live. Visualize the features you want exactly as you want them—the number of bedrooms, the layout of the living room and kitchen, wood floors or carpet, the backyard, the neighborhood. Imagine the feeling of living in that home, the peaceful, private haven for just you, or the party spirit with the coming and going of lots of friends. And imagine it is easily affordable. Magazine pictures may help solidify your visualization, and cutting them out for regular reference will further empower your vision. Now demonstrate that you really want this. Start looking. Be willing to look at a lot of places, and don't settle for less. (Although it is OK to change your mind and establish a new vision. You may see something that is more impressive than your wildest dreams!) Eventually your vision will manifest.

Winning athletes are famous for visualizing success. They see themselves performing the flawless dive, crossing the finish line first, lifting the heaviest weight. They imagine their every move performed in perfectly-honed style and feel the action in their muscles as if it were happening in real time. They feel the elation of accomplishing a 10 performance. They hear the applause and feel the satisfaction of breaking their own records. When they demonstrate a true desire for this dream through dedicated training, their chances for attracting their dream increases greatly.

Sometimes a mere thought will activate the attraction of a desired item or result. I've often had a fleeting desire for something—a special food, a phone call from a certain person, a particular item of clothing—only to have it appear magically in front of me without any effort on my part.

If you encounter an obstacle like a nasty coworker, try thinking more positively about her. Visualize her good qualities. See her helping you. Really feel appreciation for her. Feel the success of overcoming the obstacle. You may be surprised when that the nasty coworker becomes civil, possibly even helpful. (Affirmative Prayer, described in the Spirited chapter, is a similar practice.)

If you have trouble thinking positively, I recommend an old classic, *The Power of Positive Thinking*, by Norman Vincent Peale. Also watch *What the Bleep* and *The Secret*.

Kick Negative Habits and Addictions. Create Positive Habits.

A habit is a pattern or action that is performed frequently and automatically. Some habits can benefit us, such as the habit of stashing ten percent of every paycheck into a savings account. But others can harm us, such calling yourself a loser every time you make a mistake.

An addiction is a habit that has taken over your mental will. The Webster's New World College Dictionary defines addiction as, "to give (oneself) up (to some strong habit.)"[216] An addiction is thus actually a giving up your power. It's the outer sign of an internal weakness. Addictions to cigarettes, alcohol, drugs, food, sex, negative talk, and even television are much more than physical or chemical needs. You have given yourself up to these things that you think make you feel better. Negative habits and addictions will destroy your strength and power as a woman. They will destroy your connection with your own soul. You will disrespect yourself, people around you may take on feelings of pity, scorn or anger for you.

Serious addictions to such things as drugs and alcohol often require professional intervention and rehabilitation, which incorporates intense detoxification and psychological healing that few of us have the power to do on our own. If you are seriously addicted, please consider seeking help from twelve-step programs like Alcoholics Anonymous. Try the Betty Ford Center in Rancho Mirage, California, or similar rehabilitation centers where you live or other professional programs. Admitting you need to take control of your power and your life is the first step to recovery.

When it comes to less serious addictions to such things as negative talk, television, or sugar, I believe most of us the have inner strength to kick them on our own. One of the best ways to eliminate a bad habit or addiction is to replace it with a positive habit. Instead of settling in to watch bad television, turn on the radio or a good CD and pull out that art project you've been promising yourself for the past year to work on. Put your energy into your creative expression. Instead of eating a candy bar for your mid-afternoon boost, eat raisins or a banana and feel the energy from healthy, sweet foods. Notice the healthier sensations your body experiences. When breaking any habit, focus on the positive benefits of the healthy replacements and feel how good they are for you. Don't dwell on lack or feelings of deprivation. Instead, feel your inner strength and celebrate your will power. Observe yourself becoming stronger, healthier, and more empowered. It takes discipline, but we do have the will to overcome.

Become Courageous

Fear is our greatest enemy. Fear is our greatest obstacle to success. It stands in the way of living our life fully. Fear will keep us in the safety zone and prevent us from growing and succeeding. Fear is that feeling of anxiety that occurs in situations that we perceive as dangerous or painful. We have the ability to control and overcome fear, yet often its grip on us is immobilizing. People are fearful of many things: public speaking, death (a famous lists puts fear of public speaking above fear of death), loud noises, snakes, the boss, the opposite sex. Often our fears are the results of our conditioning. Our parents' powerlessness or paranoia may have crept into our young minds. Or perhaps an unpleasant experience in our past may cause us to feel trepidation or the need to avoid certain situations. Occasionally, our society and the media implants fear in us. We're taught to be afraid of terrorism, global warming, crime, et cetera. And occasionally, there is no rational explanation for these fears.

Low-level fear can serve us and keep us on our toes. It keeps us sharp and influences us to reach a level of excellence when we perform. For example, the fear of delivering a presentation to a group of people may inspire us to take extra care in preparing and practicing our speech. Adequate preparation yields a dynamic presentation. But chronic fear or fear of non-threatening people or events may completely block our next move. We freeze in our tracks or run the other way. We limit our expression of ourselves and possibilities for our lives.

Strong, powerful women are courageous. They may notice occasional twinges of fear, but they swiftly lay them to rest by tapping into their inner strength and courage. As Mark Twain said, "Courage is the resistance to and mastery of fear—not the absence of fear."

As Susan Jeffers, Ph.D., expert on fear and author of several books, including *Feel the Fear and Beyond*, writes "Feel the fear and do it anyway."[217] It's like the famous Nike motto, "Just Do It." Jeffers confirms that fear is a condition of the mind that we can take control over. No one holds us back more firmly than ourselves, and only we can push ourselves to conquer. "Whether it feels like it or not, you already have more power than you could have ever imagined. We all have," Jeffers assures us.[218]

Cynthia Kersey, author of *Unstoppable*, writes that being unstoppable "means finding the courage to make a change or achieve a goal in your life that may not remotely resemble your present circumstances. Regardless of your current situation, you don't allow fear, self-doubt, or someone else to stop you, and you consistently take one step forward, refusing to give up, until you achieve your goal."[219] She is advising us to be courageous.

Strong and powerful women know they have the courage it takes to face any challenge. Iyanla Vanzant's story is worth knowing. She is a remarkable woman whose resistance to fear helped her achieve greatness. She was born in 1953 in the back of a taxicab in Brooklyn, New York. When she was two years old, her mother died and she was sent to live with her grandmother, who beat her severely. Later, she was sent to live with her aunt and uncle. The uncle raped her repeatedly, and when Iyanla cried out for help or tried to talk about it, no one would listen. Iyanla married twice and bore three children, her first at the age of sixteen. She fled her abusive second husband in the middle of the night, kids in tow, with only one bag of clothing. They lived in poverty until one day Iyanla saw a sign that would change her life. It was an ad for a college. She enrolled and was accepted. Challenged by her children and her financial struggle, she received her Bachelor's degree in 1983, then continued her education and earned her law degree in 1988. She next practiced law in Philadelphia, where she worked as a public defender, providing aid to women on public assistance. Iyanla saw this as the perfect forum to help women who had challenges similar to hers. She spoke with such women to offer ways they could change their lives. In 1992, she wrote her first book, *Tapping the Power Within: A Path to Empowerment for Black Women*, which was based on spiritual principles that uplift and motivate women. This book inspired a new career for her, and she became a motivational speaker. Eventually, she left the field of law to devote herself full time to travel the country and speak. She has inspired thousands of women and has appeared on the *Oprah Winfrey Show* several times. With eighteen books published to date, she gives women positive, uplifting messages of hope. She also delivers valuable tips for improving our lives.

While it may seem easy to understand the fear of something tangible, like bosses, snakes, or bombs, fear of the intangible, such as fear of the unknown, of the dark, of being alone and death can be even more debilitating. Perhaps fear of failure is the greatest obstacle most people face. The negative concepts that are associated with failure, such as "unsuccessful," "incapable," "inadequate" and "loser," often paralyze people from taking action in the first place, much less becoming successful.

Strong women don't fear failure, and in fact perceive it as a means for success. To become courageous, you must change your perception of the word "failure." Think of failure as a "learning experience," as "practice," as an "experiment," as a "step toward success." Remember the powerful and brilliant people of the world who made numerous attempts at something before they succeeded. Napoleon Hill, who studied the qualities of the world's most successful people and wrote the classic *Think and Grow Rich*, observed that "Every adversity, every failure and every heartache carries with it the seed of an equivalent or a greater benefit." So important is failure to Charles C. Manz, author of *The Power of Failure: 27 Ways to Turn Life's Setbacks Into Success*, that he advises if you want to be more successful . . . "double your failure rate."[220]

Successful people learn from every attempt, even if it is not successful because their early failures taught them how to reach success. When you realize that there is no such thing as failure, it is easier to take risks. When you see the value of multiple attempts, you will become less fearful and bountiful with courage.

Courageous women take risks. They step into their fear and do things that are uncomfortable. But they grow from their risks. It gets easier the next time. Taking risks and doing what you fear most (not including thrill-seeking activities) will expand you as a person. When you confront your fears, you will be amazed how strong and powerful you really are. You may also discover how you created your fear and that the feared thing really was not a threat at all, except in your mind. Victory has a way of increasing self-esteem and building confidence. When you build up your courage and face your fear, you become stronger.

Educate Yourself. Never Stop Learning.

A strong woman loves to use her brain. Perpetually eager to learn, she seeks out information, soaks it up like a sponge, and uses it to support her professional endeavors, enrich her personal life, and increase her understanding of the world. She greatly values and invests in education and other intelligence-raising opportunities. Inspired by the teaching of other brilliant people, her knowledge of the world expands far beyond her own three-dimensional existence. Strong, intelligent women are leaders, thinkers, creators, teachers, givers, and doers. They are interesting, authoritative and often the Wise Women of our culture. They contribute to the advancement of civilization and the upliftment of the planet. For strong women, learning doesn't end at graduation, but at the end of life.

One of our greatest gifts is our brain. By continually feeding and cultivating it with knowledge, we actively honor ourselves. I feel that it is our obligation as Sexy, Spirited, and Strong women to continue to learn throughout our lives and in every area of our lives. As we learn, we improve our daily lives, enhance our power and strength, and increase our self-esteem. Intelligence cultivates positive energy.

Our life is a gift and the planet our playground. There is so much to learn and explore. By educating ourselves about other people, cultures, and disciplines, we broaden our perceptions of life on this planet. Whether you focus on one subject and become an authority, or dabble in many subjects of interest, you are positively activating your intelligence and expanding your consciousness. Your brain can potentially increase your overall strength as a Positive Energy Woman.

In the professional world, knowledge increases our worth, often justifying better pay and more advanced positions than our less educated co-workers. By being a sharpshooter in our fields and the top of our game, we are a valuable and desirable asset, which can increase our net worth in the earnings department. According to a 2007 study by the Bureau of Labor Statistics, the average weekly earnings of a person with an associate's degree is $604, while those with professional degrees (master's level) average $1,427. In 2007 the unemployment rate for those with a bachelor's degree was half that of high school graduates.[221]

Multiple skills are required in today's workplace, as specific jobs require the skills of several different disciplines. Business people need to be as skilled with PowerPoint as with human relations. Graphic designers are artists *and* computer technicians. The entrepreneurs and executives who rise to the top are excellent at their specialty, plus proficient as writers, speakers, number crunchers, and managers. To stay competitive and valuable in the work place, a diversity of skills and knowledge is becoming more and more necessary.

For those of you who are revamping your mission, discovering new gifts, and preparing for a new job or career, you may decide you need specialized training or a college education. While for some, going back to school may seem intimidating, if downright impossible, getting an education is essential to developing your skills and becoming the woman you have the potential to be.

If decide a college degree is necessary to help you accomplish your goals and mission, I encourage you to pursue it. Don't let the expense of a college education intimidate you. Your investment in yourself will assure a more fulfilling life with greater opportunities. Creative financing is possible, but research is necessary to find what works for you. And adjusting to a new lifestyle that includes classes and tests may be easier than you think. Your entire being may come alive with the stimulation of learning, connecting with like-minded people, and creating new possibilities.

Depending on your goal, it is not always necessary to enroll in a college degree program. Maybe you aren't interested in an academic degree but would like to be certified in teaching yoga, the healing arts, the performing arts, or some other specialty. Or maybe you are just interested in learning more about a subject for personal enrichment, such as investing, anthropology, or video production. You can often gain the knowledge and skills you need through classes and seminars offered by university extension programs, community colleges, specialty schools, and professional organizations. They are taught by highly accredited and respected pros of the field. Often these courses and programs are less expensive and take less time than an academic degree program. They can help leapfrog you to a higher level of mind expansion and value in your field, and even catapult you into a whole new career. Contact your local schools and universities for information about the courses they may offer. Check professional organizations to discover seminars that are available.

Many colleges and universities offer online classes. In fact, online education is fast becoming the most popular form of learning. One study indicate that in the fall of 2006, almost 3.5 million students were taking at least one online course; a nearly 10 percent increase over the previous year. Not only that, online enrollment rates grew 9.7 percent, while the growth for the overall higher education student population grew only 1.5 percent.[222] Learning from home is convenient for those who work full-time jobs and are raising families. Some colleges offer bachelor's and master's degrees through online programs. Students receive individual attention from accredited college teachers and can communicate with others in the course, making online learning as effective as classroom study. In some cases, online tuition is more expensive than regular classes, but the rate doesn't change for out-of-state students, so you can pursue education at your school of choice no matter where in the country (or world) it is. Some calculate that without the cost and time of commuting, the overall price of online learning is reduced to the cost of traditional classes.

School is, of course, not the only way to gain an education. Books can teach us almost everything we need to know. With proper self-discipline, we might, in fact, learn all that is taught in a class just by reading the books. While this method of learning may be less acknowledged by the professional world, it will nonetheless increase your knowledge and intelligence, and ultimately increase your value in the world. Reading also has a magically positive affect on our self-worth and self-esteem. Libraries welcome anyone with a library card and offer valuable resources to every interested patron. Inexpensive, used books of every title are easy to find and purchase through Internet stores such as Amazon.com.

Specialized magazines are another good resource. For every field, from photography to personal finance to science, a publication exists to deliver authoritative articles with the most current information of the subject. I consider magazines to be "education lite." They report on state-of-the-art developments and trends and expert insights. While they don't replace books and classes, magazines will satisfy your thirst for information without making you feel like you're studying.

I also consider the Internet a great resource. It's our newest frontier for learning. In fact, it has changed the face of learning, as now we are no longer limited to walking to the library. We can sit in our living rooms and do research on the Net and the Web. Millions of bits of information are available on every topic. Search engines, on-line encyclopedias and newspapers, university websites, blogs, and other tools make research much easier. Unless you don't have a computer, there's no reason to not expose yourself to the Net and the Web. Please note, however, that articles can be posted by anyone. Sometimes they are neither factual nor accurate, sometimes they're biased or misleading. If you're doing serious research, double-check your facts with reliable resources, such as encyclopedias and articles by accredited scholars.

Travel

Traveling is another way to get an informal education. Learn the geography, culture, and history of where you're going. Since the beginning of time, humans have had the drive to roam. Early humans walked across the continents to find new homes. Still today, traveling into the unfamiliar is exhilarating; your mind opens to new experiences and philosophies and your senses open to new stimuli, new smells, new sounds, and new sights. Foreign travel strengthens us. Each hurdle we overcome—getting around on the local transportation, communicating with people who don't speak our language, and eating strange food—helps us grow.

But travel to foreign countries isn't the only way to expand our minds. There is much to be seen at home. Taking day trips to cities or landmarks you haven't explored before will bring great pleasure and increase your confidence as you drive unfamiliar roads and interact with strangers.

12

▼

OUTER MANIFESTATIONS

A Positive Energy Woman is not passive. She takes action toward success and making her dreams come true. I made up this saying many years ago:

The only way a dream comes true is not when you dream, but when you do.

This is, basically, how dreams come true. You have to work at them.

Taking Action: Making Dreams and Goals Come True

Sadly, many a great dream has gone to dust because the big picture seemed so impossible to achieve and the dreamer did nothing to make it manifest in reality. She was so overwhelmed by how to start that she gave up before she even got started. Many people believe their dreams are so big they're impossible to fulfill. So they tuck their dreams away and settle for an easier life. And that's fine. It takes incredibly strong and committed people to work toward their dreams.

But we can manifest our dreams. People prove it every day. They don't expect their visions to come to life instantly. They take many, many small steps to reach their goals, all along the way holding a clear picture and a strong feeling about their dream.

The two key components to seeing an idea through to fruition are setting your goals and holding your vision.

Setting Your Goals

Only fifty years ago, most women's goals were to have all of the beds made by noon, dinner on the table by five when the hubby got home, and the kids in bed by eight. Today, our goals are multiplied by ten and span every category—career, relationships, personal growth, and special events. We set goals for projects at home and at work.

The Webster's New World College Dictionary defines "goal" as "the line or place at which a race, trip, etc. is ended. An object or end that one strives to attain; aim." Goals can be as simple and short-term as having the grocery shopping done by Saturday evening or as elaborate and long term as having a million dollars in the bank by the age of 65 or establishing a foundation to promote world peace. No matter how minor or major it is, a goal is the finish line in our sight as we move through life.

Goals are essential for happiness. Setting and reaching a goal can make us feel worthwhile in the world. Without our goals, we have no purpose in life, and life becomes one day floating into another. Reaching our goals, even the simple ones, makes us feel like we've accomplished something. Steadily accomplishing our goals builds self-esteem and inner strength.

Holding Your Vision

Visualization is the process of seeing your dream or goal as if it were happening now. You see yourself living it. More than that, you feel all of the accompanying emotions. Your senses are stimulated as if you were living at that moment. Some people call this fantasizing, others call if visualizing, but whatever you call it, holding your vision is the driving force behind making your dream come true. This process may happen without any special steps or exercises, but usually, it takes practice to realize a vision. In their book, *Ask and It Is Given*, Esther and Jerry Hicks write, "If there is something you desire that you currently do not have, you only need to put your attention upon it, and, by *the Law of Attraction*, it will come to you, for as you think about this experience or thing that you desire, you offer a vibration, and then by *Law*, that very thing or experience must come to you."[223]

Plan of Action

Reaching your goals requires a plan of action. Your plan of action is a written document in which you first record the details of your dream and all your feelings about it and then prioritize the steps you need to take to accomplish it. Your plan of action will become your best friend and touchstone as you move ahead in your life's mission. With a plan, you become focused on what you need to do and are less likely to become distracted by things that waste time and don't direct you to your goal. You'll refer to your plan several times every day to keep yourself on track. Without a plan of action, your destination will be unclear and undefined. Day after day will go by without solid action, and your final goal will take much longer to reach. To make a plan of action, pick up your pen and open your journal. Let's begin.

Holding the Vision Exercise

Write today's date on a clean page. Write your main goal as the heading. It can be getting a new job, completing a project, fulfilling your life's mission. Write whatever it is you want to create or achieve.

On a new page, describe yourself and your life as it will be when you've accomplished your goal. Imagine that you've already achieved it. If you want to be a singer, imagine yourself on stage in front of a cheering audience giving you a standing ovation. Imagine yourself at rehearsals, collaborating with cool musicians to perfect a song. Imagine the travel, the recording sessions, writing the songs. Feel yourself in your goal, as if it were real, and write the details. How do you feel? Excited? Happy? Think often about your goal and experience those feelings, for those feelings are the ingredient that will keep your dream alive. They keep you motivated to accomplish it.

On a new page, write down the reasons you want to accomplish your goal. Let the logical, practical side of your brain speak. Will it allow you to express who you are? Make you famous? Give you more authority? Make you wealthier? Write down everything you can think of.

Continuing to use your logical brain, on a new page, explore the ways your goal will change you, your lifestyle, your relationships. Will you make more money? Relocate? Develop new relationships? Change your current relationships? Will you work more or fewer hours? Travel? Write it all down and get a sense of the reality you'll be changing.

Now, put away the logic and bring out your emotional side. On a new page, write down your feelings about the goal. How do you feel when you imagine yourself at your goal? Do you feel happy and hopeful? Excited? At peace? Write down these feelings.

Finally, write your feelings about the changes that will occur as you move toward your goal and reach it. Do you feel sad? Frightened? Motivated? Relieved? Are you ready? Hesitant? Do you have any fears? Why? Explore every feeling and the source of each feeling. If you're feeling fearful, write down the source of that fear. How can you get over it? (You may need to do some inner work. Are you willing to do that?) Journal about your feelings until there is no more to write.

We are not robots mechanically moving toward a goal. We're human beings with human fears, beliefs, emotions, and drives, and it is precisely those human characteristics that will drive us to meet our goals or thwart our efforts. Acknowledging the logistics and feelings around your goal will help you to fully accept it and prepare to achieve it, transforming it from pipedream to very possible reality. Should you find that you are stuck in one place, you will have an understanding as to why, and you can take action to heal.

These pages in your journal mark the beginning of your journey to achieving your goal. Refer to your journal frequently. These pages serve as reminders of your purpose and commitment.

Creating Your Plan of Action: Setting a Goal

You won't reach your goal in one giant leap. You have to take many, many baby steps. Psychologically, breaking down a goal into steps will make the goal seem more easily reachable. With steps to check off as you take them, you'll more likely stick with your mission and see it through to your final destination. As you finish each step, your enthusiasm will remain high and motivate you to continue. You'll be amazed at how accomplishing each task, no matter how small, will boost your confidence and self-esteem.

The elements of goal setting that assure success are (1) putting the steps in writing, (2) giving each step a deadline, and (3) looking at the steps daily. Writing your list of steps makes them real. When you write your steps, you're writing your plan of action. It will become your best friend as you travel to your goal and become a frequent reference to remind you of the steps that you still need to take. Without a plan of action, you might forget about your main goal, sub-goals, and all of the intermediate steps, but eventually, your plan of action becomes your record of victory as you check off steps you've taken. It is a great feeling to check off all the steps.

It's important to break down each major goal into major sub-goals, then break down your sub-goals into steps. Each step is a minor action taken to reach your sub-goal. Some steps may even require sub-steps. This breakdown of action will clarify each and every step you need to take to accomplish you sub-goal and mission.

For example, in my mission to create and present Aphrodite's Secrets workshops, one sub-goal was to promote the workshop. This one sub-goal required several steps and sub-steps. This is what my list looked like:

Sub-Goal #1. Promote the workshop.
Step A. Create a brochure
  Sub-step # 1. Write the contents of the brochure
  Sub-step # 2. Find or create the art work, including a logo
  Sub-step # 3. Design the layout
  Sub-step # 4. Print the brochure.

Step B. Create flyers and distribute them
  Sub-step # 1. Using info and material from brochure, create a layout for a flyer
  Sub-step # 2. Print the flyers
  Sub-step # 3. Identify places to hang flyers
  Sub-step # 4. Drive around and hang them.

Step C. Place an ad in local publications
  Sub-step # 1. Write the ad
  Sub-step # 2. Call the publications' ad reps for info
  Sub-step # 3. Place the ad in local publications.

Your own list of sub-goals, steps, and sub-steps may seem intimidating at first, but your lists will actually create a calmness within you. You will see the clear reality of what you need to do to accomplish your goals, and this truth will empower you. If you don't write down each task, you will soon feel overwhelmed and chaos will fill your soul.

You'll feel nothing but stress. Listing your tasks in an organized way will help you to feel clear and even excited. Your vibration becomes activated by your enthusiasm for taking positive steps.

Now, give each sub-goal and task a deadline. Deadlines create a sense of urgency. They motivate you. Without deadlines, there is no pressure to achieve even the tiniest step, and it could be months or even years before you take the most preliminary action to achieving a goal. (I love the word "deadline," but if you prefer a less ominous word, you can use "completion date.")

In your plan of action, you will use a three-month timeframe for accomplishing your sub-goals and much earlier dates, such as a day or week from now, for accomplishing each step. In goal setting, three months is magical. It's a period of time that we can fairly easily comprehend, and it's also short enough to create a sense of urgency. An event scheduled six months from now seems far into the distant future, but three months from now seems real and *soon*. Even if it's not possible to accomplish your sub-goals in three months, you can most certainly take steps to get there.

Reasonably immediate deadlines for each step are surprisingly motivating. You will find that there *is* time to do the things you never thought you would have time to do. Your productivity will get you to your goal faster, and raise your self-esteem higher than you ever thought possible.

Drafting a Plan of Action

At the top of a blank sheet of paper, write your main goal, aka, *your mission*. On the next line down, write today's date and next to it the date three months from now. Beneath that, list your five sub-goals, which are to be accomplished or at least worked toward within the three months.

Now, write *#1*, and under this, list *A, B, C, D* and *E*, leaving space after each letter. Now write *#2*, and underneath that *A* through *E*. Continue to 5.

This is how it will look:

My Mission: _____

Today's Date: _____
Future Date: _____

Five main sub-goals (to be accomplished within three months):

    1._____
    2._____
    3._____
    4._____
    5._____

Sub-goals and Steps:
#1. _____

    A. _____
    (date of completion)

    B. _____
    (date of completion)

    C. _____
    (date of completion)

    D. _____
    (date of completion)

    E. _____
    (date of completion)

2. _____

    A. _____

    B. _____

C. _____

D. _____

E. _____

Continue to #5.

Now it's time to formulate your own, real plan of action. Spend time thinking about your mission and all the sub-goals and steps you need to take in order to achieve it. You may want to write in your journal and make preliminary lists. Think about all of the details. Get real with them. Accomplishing goals takes many, many steps, and only by being realistic will you be able to get where you want to go.

When you're ready, neatly write or type your plan of action. Turn it into a professional-looking document. Making your plan official will reinforce the importance of your goals. You are a Woman on a Mission, and your plan of action is as important as any corporate business plan.

Make copies of your plan of action. Carry one with you at all times. Tape one on the wall in your workspace at home. Refer to your list daily, if not several times a day. Seeing the steps in black and white will remind you of the tasks at hand and motivate you to take action. Check off each step and sub-goal as you accomplish it.

At the end of three months, pat yourself on the back for a job well done. You'll see that you have accomplished numerous steps toward your final goal. (Probably many more steps than if you hadn't created your plan of action.) Besides that, sticking to your plan takes discipline and strength, so you should feel good about yourself for taking such action. Making your plan of action part of your lifestyle will help you develop discipline and strength.

At the three-month mark, create a new plan of action, which will include new sub-goals and steps. Transfer incomplete tasks onto your new plan. Make your plan of action a part of your life and see how fast you achieve your dreams!

Adopt the Traits of a Role Model

Back in the 1980s and '90s, when singer/entertainer Madonna was rising in fame for her bold and brazen music and videos (and the famous sex book), she became an icon of power for many of us less-confident women. When faced with a challenging decision or move, we would put ourselves in Madonna's shoes, which magically allowed *us* to become bold, and ask, "What would I, as Madonna, do?" At times like these, Madonna was our role model, and by modeling her traits of clarity and self-assuredness, we successfully achieved our immediate goal of making a decision. We would more easily and confidently make the right decisions.

Modeling success is one course of action that has taken many people to stardom. When we study and adopt the traits of a strong and successful person we admire, we can actually absorb them into our own psyche, and use them to help us reach our highest potential.

As young women, we may have unconsciously chosen a role model from our immediate surroundings. Perhaps it was our mother or a sister or classmate. Whoever it was, for better or for worse, the impact she made on our life was profound. As we adopted and fully embodied her traits and habits, these helped make us who we are today. As human beings who are continuing to grow, we can consciously choose new role models and integrate their positive traits into our being.

As you work toward becoming a Strong and Powerful Woman, your assignment is to choose one or two people you admire, people who possess the traits of power and success you wish to have. Your role models can be female or male, living or dead, historical figures or celebrities, personal friends or mentors. Now study each person as if it were your job to portray her or him in a play. Read books about them, take notes on their personality traits. If you know or work with them, watch them in action and ask them questions. Who are they? What are their secrets to success? Are they pushy? Kind? Generous? Tireless? Find out what steps they took on their path to achievement. Were they workaholics? Did they work alone? Did they recruit people to help them? Did they walk the road of success slowly? Or did they sky rocket at a young age? Were they highly educated? Organized? Lucky? How did they face adversity and failure? Write everything you learn about your role model in your journal.

After doing this research, it's time for some introspection. Write down how you feel about your role model or models. Why do you like them? What traits impress you the most? What traits do you wish you could develop? How would your life be different if you became more like your role model? How do you feel about adopting those traits? Is it frightening? Motivating? Are you willing to adopt certain traits, even if they seem to be contrary to your nature? Once you decide to commit to integrating their traits into your psyche, you are on your way to increasing your strength and power.

When you act it, you will become it. Act and think like your role models. Adopt their attitudes about life. Dress like them. Put yourself in their shoes as you make decisions and take action in your life. At first, you may feel uncomfortable or silly, but eventually these powerful and positive traits will become a part of you. Don't mind that your immediate friends and family notice and make comments. Just explain what you're doing. "I'm doing what Oprah would do," is all you need to say, and they'll get it. Many will admire and support you in your adventure. Eventually, the positive traits of your role model will become permanent and positive parts of you, helping to catapult you toward success.

Networking

You're on your mission. Now it's time to work it! Get out there and meet the people who will recognize your gifts, potentially use them, and possibly help you on your mission. Find people who will stimulate you and help you grow, people to whom you can offer *your* support. It's time to network. Networking is connecting with people, individually and in groups, with whom you hold a common mission or interest. Life is made up of relationships, and networking can accelerate the speed with which you bring into your life the people who can help you on your mission. Many masters of empowerment claim that the best way to bring your gifts to the world is with the help of other people. The way to meet those people is through networking.

When you connect with people on a similar path to yours, you multiply your resources for information and support. Not only that, but the energy you receive from a person or group that shares your interests and goals is stimulating and motivating. You'll be more excited about your mission when you can compare notes with someone else on the path.

But networking isn't just about taking. It's also about giving. Networking is an exchange. It taking actions that can be mutually beneficial to you and the people you connect with. Your connections can be a great resource, and, likewise, you may have the information that others need. Sharing your gifts of support and information (as long as you're not taken advantage of) is a service that you will find greatly empowering. Your value as a human being increases when you are willing to give your energy to support others. You will be appreciated and noticed. Often you will be rewarded with opportunities you couldn't even imagine before.

To network, go to professional lunches and other club or organizational meetings and industry functions. Even parties are opportunities for networking. Even if you have to go alone, get your courage on and attend those meetings. I guarantee you won't be going alone for long. The Internet has become another primary networking tool, with on-line communities and e-mail listservs that connect people around the world. Engage everyone you know in sharing energy and expressing yourself. You will attract success.

Connection and Communication

Communication is how we send and receive information verbally, energetically, and through gestures and actions. The trademark of strong and powerful women is effective communication. She has excellent speaking and listening skills.

Fully Present Connection

Some people call it charisma, others call it love, but whatever you call it, when you engage with a strong and powerful woman, you feel an energetic connection. A powerful woman is fully present and gives her full attention to your conversation. She exudes the positive energy that assures you that you are important. She is empathetic and responds with the appropriate energy or support, whether it's gut-level advice, heart-filled sympathy, or a joyful *tête-à-tête*. The strong and powerful woman looks into the eyes of the person speaking and listens carefully. To really understand, she asks questions and listens deeply, making this person her number one focus. She waits until the person is finished with her thought before she responds.

When presenting to a group, the strong and powerful woman will catch the vibe of the group, and project confidence and caring through her positive energy. She makes eye contact with each and every person at some point during her presentation and sends positive energy to the Doubting Thomas in the group. She's empathetic to the group's needs and will respond accordingly. While she really listens to questions, she also has the authority and information to defend her point and keep the presentation on track if someone tries to seize control.

Your work from the Energy chapter will help you learn the power of connecting. This is the first step to powerful communication. With their open hearts, minds, and spirit, Positive Energy Women can be some of the greatest communicators on earth.

Learn the Art of Listening

Americans are generally so consumed by what is happening to them that they suffer from what I call SAS, or the Self-Absorbed Syndrome. A self-absorbed woman cares most about—you guessed it—herself and has little concern for anyone else, even in social situations. This self-absorption most obviously affects her mode of communication. The SAS woman talks about her favorite subject, herself, and no world event or exciting news from you will distract her from her verbal vomit about her new shoes, what the jerk at the office is doing to her, her feelings about love, how much she hates pink, etc. Your thoughts? Forget it. She doesn't care. Listening to you isn't an option, and even if you try to speak up, the SAS woman takes your thought and brings it back to herself again. Depth? Philosophy? Forget it. This woman is shallower than a blow-up swimming pool.

Sadly, a great number of women suffer from SAS. Or, rather, WE suffer from their superficial talk. We have all been afflicted by SAS ourselves, especially during our childhood and teenage years. Fortunately, most of us have matured and developed greater communication skills. SAS communication is the antithesis of the mode in which powerful women converse.

Powerful women know the art of conversation and find *listening* to be key to communication. Not only is listening a matter of common courtesy, but it is also critical in effective communication. Conversation is an equal-opportunity event of give and take. It's like volleyball (back and forth, back and forth), one person talks while the other listens, then vice versa. (The exception is, of course, when someone makes clear that they need to talk through a crisis.) Good conversation is an occasion to make an energetic connection with someone. It provides a forum in which we can express ourselves and work out our challenges. It is also a wonderful opportunity to learn and become wiser.

Talking is easy. Listening is the challenge. In fact, listening has practically become an art. Listening requires energy and focus, but it will give you the edge in the professional world and in your social life.

Here are the steps to becoming a better listener:

1. Offer your full attention.
2. Really hear what the other person is saying. As you take in the information, notice your immediate thoughts and feelings, but don't put a lot of thought into how you're going to respond. Listening is your focus.
3. Ask questions to get more information or to confirm that you understand what the other person is saying.
4. Be empathetic. Feel the other person's energy.
5. Give feedback to support the person and the conversation. Respond with supporting action, such as a nod or a quick comment ("yes, I get it") or sincere emotional energy (sympathy, joy).
6. Unless there is a crucial point you want to make and it doesn't appear that the other person will pause any time soon, don't interrupt until the person is finished speaking.
7. Staying focused on the subject at hand until the conversation naturally goes elsewhere.
8. Ask questions to take the conversation deeper.

Now, let's take a look at two conversations. See for yourself which is more satisfying.

Conversation #1: Conversation with a Nonlistener

      Elsie: Hi, Patty! How are you?

      Patty: Elsie! I'm so glad to see you! I can't wait to tell you about the project I just started! It all began when I went to the gym the other night, and I met a gallery owner who knows my boss's wife, and she said she was looking for a style of art that I've been dabbling in. I mean it's not *exactly* what she's looking for, but close enough so that I can emulate what she wants... [Fifteen minutes later] ...and THAT's how I was able to fix my refrigerator. So how are *you*, Elsie?

Elsie: Pretty good, except that I'm worried about my mother. She fell down the other day for no real reason. I'm worried that she may have had a mini-stroke. So, I—

Patty: That reminds me of when my mother had Alzheimer's. It was a tough time. But get this! I checked out a great apartment that I'm thinking about renting, and it has this great balcony where I can put my plant, you know, I've told you about that that big rubber plant.... [She continues *ad nauseam*.]

Notice Patty's disconnect, her lack of concern, her unwillingness to listen to anything Elsie has to say.

Conversation #2: Conversation with a Listener

Patty: Hi, Elsie! Long time, no see! How've you been?

Elsie: Excellent! Great to see you. How are *you*?

Patty: Pretty good, except that I'm worried about my mother. She fell down the other day for no real reason. I'm worried that she may have had a mini-stroke. So I think I need to think about putting her in assisted living.

Elsie: Oh my goodness! I'm so sorry to hear that. Do you have any family members in that area that can help?

Patty: I do, but they're all very involved in their own family situations and don't have time to take care of my parents. I'm thinking about moving back to the east coast for a while to help them.

Elsie: Man! That's drastic! Is this something you really want to do?

Patty: Well, yes and no. Yes, because I love my parents and

want to help them. But no, because I can't stand the east coast, and I'm afraid if I move back there, I'll get really depressed, the way I was when I lived there before.

Elsie: Patty, you are such an amazing woman and daughter to even consider going back. You know, maybe if you go back on a temporary basis to help set them up with certain things, it will work out OK. Also, don't you have friends there? Knowing they're there could make a temporary move more tolerable.

Patty: Thanks, Elsie. You're right. I do have incredible friends there. Also, I love my sweet parents, so a temporary move wouldn't be that bad. Have you ever dealt with this kind of situation?

This conversation illustrates excellent listening skills on Elsie's part. She is energetically connected to Patty, fully focused on the issue at hand, and deeply concerned. She digs deeper with questions and offers proper response with sympathy and insights.

Listening Exercise

Listening is a valuable skill that is applied by successful people in every kind of business and specialty. The next time you're with a friend, make it your intention to focus on her or him. Listen carefully and ask questions. Offer responsive insights and support. Avoid changing the subject unless your friend does so. Is it easy for you to listen? Or would you rather jump in and talk about yourself?

What to Do If You End Up With a SAS Talker

You may recognize that a SAS talker is in great need of communicating and sharing. Perhaps she doesn't have friends or a support system. At times, you may consider it a service to just listen to her and not expect to be asked to share. Some people are grateful for any opportunity to vent or express a fear or to talk about their growth or their goals. If you're confronted by a SAS talker, therefore, remain connected, listen attentively, and offer what you can. However, if it is clear that this person is superficial and unconcerned about anyone but herself and she is draining your energy, politely wrap up the conversation, excuse yourself, and leave. SAS talkers will feed on your positive energy and drain you.

Speak Honestly and Courageously

Strong and powerful women have confidence in themselves, their ideas, and their value. They are experts at expressing themselves, even if their message is radical, in opposition to the majority, or challenging to another person. The masterful communicator expresses herself clearly. Her thoughts are organized and she knows enough about the topic at hand to defend her ideas.

It is a fact that most women wish to please others. We often hold our tongues in exchange for social harmony. While this may seem to be honorable and noble, it is actually behavior that can defeat our self-esteem. When we discount our feelings and ideas and restrain our self-expression, we are chipping away at our integrity and our power.

As a strong woman with big plans in the world, get used to the idea of courageously expressing yourself whether you are in agreement with others or not. The way we were raised has much to do with our fear of expressing ourselves. Our parents, schools, and society have programmed us to believe we will get along better in life if we are liked and approved of. We learned very early that if we agree with someone (or everyone) and say what they want to hear, then we'll be better liked and more successful in life. We have thus learned to lie to make someone like us or to make someone feel comfortable. In our patriarchal culture, women have not been held in great value and our ideas have been ignored. To this day, many perceive as "feminine" a woman who is quiet and agreeable.

Women especially withhold their truth in relationships. A woman's "sometimes" boyfriend may do something that is totally against her values, like not call her for a week after an intimate evening. But she may tell herself or others that she is OK with it. She is willing to sacrifice her self-respect and value so she can avoid angering this man. It also happens at work. If a woman is ignored in a meeting or conversation with her male coworkers, she may just surrender and disconnect. Later, if the boss says, "Were you OK in that meeting?" she may say, "Oh, sure. I just had indigestion."

Get over this! Expressing our honest truth is the only way to become strong and powerful. As an effective communicator, it is your duty to express your honest viewpoint. Why?

1. Honest communication helps others to learn about you, your values and principles, your position, your ideas. They can relate to you on an honest level.
2. You will be respected for your courage. Knowing that you have integrity and are truthful, people will feel safe with you.
3. Your ideas are important. They can offer value to a situation. Offering your suggestions, even if they are unusual, off-beat, or unconventional, will inspire others to become more open. Your ideas may be the perfect solution to a problem.

Withholding your truth to make someone like you or to keep the peace is unhealthy and dangerous. It jeopardizes your power. Why?

1. Expressing an idea that is not truthful for you is telling a lie. A lie is the basis of a dishonest relationship.
2. Withholding your truth, especially at the beginning, will mushroom into a larger situation in which you are dishonest with the others and yourself, making a situation unbearable.
3. Not being truthful or withholding the truth creates in you negativity and resentment toward the person you withheld it from. Then you find yourself withholding these feelings of resentment. All of this withholding will affect your vibration.
4. People who are dishonest are fakes. Most people can detect fakery.

What does it take to speak honestly?

1. Courage and self-confidence
2. Positive energy
3. Well-thought-out ideas with enough information to back up any debate
4. Articulate expression of your ideas

Other traits of a strong and powerful communicator are:

1. She speaks in a positive way that is inspiring and influential. She is persuasive without threats or force.
2. She acknowledges and respects the ideas and opinions of others, even if she doesn't agree with them.
3. She communicates how she feels, but keeps her emotions under control, especially at work. She does not cry or yell.
4. She remains poised and confident, even under tremendous opposition. She speaks kindly but firmly and never attacks.
5. She gracefully stands firm on her convictions and doesn't back down.
6. She makes clear what her boundaries are and communicates when they have been crossed.

Expressing anger is an acceptable form of communication, but only in the right circumstances. It is OK, if not necessary, to express anger when your boundaries have been crossed or you've been deceived or betrayed or harmed in any way. Sadly, even under these circumstances many women will withhold their feelings. This dishonesty with themselves will destroy their self-esteem. It will eat at them for years. Withholding anger is also a lie to the perpetrator, who will believe you are someone that you really aren't. It may influence the idea that you are a pushover and easy to violate.

It is imperative to express your feelings about the violation with as much clarity and truth as possible. Remain as composed as possible when explaining what is inside you. Our emotions will indicate that we are upset, but if we're overly emotional, it may be difficult for the violator to understand the real issue. Refrain from screaming expletives and name-calling. While filling the air with negative words is a great way to vent, it may not make clear your feelings and perspective. The violator may get that you are angry, but may not really understand exactly why. Explaining your feelings about the injustice will help the person understand her or his role in your feelings, and may suppress future infringements.

Instead of yelling, "you creepy, lying bastard!" express your feelings about the actions of that person in a clearer way, such as, "I feel betrayed, disrespected, and hurt!" Calling someone a rude name, especially someone with whom you are in relationship, can cause long-lasting damage. Emotions may be fleeting, but the sting of a negative name can last a long time.

Remember, the purpose of effective communication is to create harmonious relationships. This includes impeccable honesty with them and with yourself.

Two excellent books on honest communication are:
Don't Be Nice, Be Real: Balancing Passion for Self with Compassion with Others, by Kelly Bryson
Non-Violent Communication: A Language of Life, by Marshall B. Rosenberg, Ph.D.

Learn to Speak in Public

Just say these two words—*public* and *speaking*—together, and most people break out in a sweat. Glossophobia is the scientific term for fear of public speaking (*glossa*, meaning "tongue," and *phobos*, "fear or dread"), and in our society, glossophobia is the most common phobia. Statistics indicate that some people would prefer death to giving a speech.[224] But if you are afraid to speak to a group, this can have a subtle, crippling effect in your life. When you stifle your self-expression, you may prevent advancements in your career and livelihood. You will also feel anxious in social situations with strangers. If you are gripped by the fear of public speaking, now is the time to overcome it.

I believe that public speaking is a most effective way to become a successful communicator. Speaking in public will help you become courageous and confident. It will teach you how to prepare your thoughts before you open your mouth and communicate what you mean to say. You overcome any doubts about expressing yourself, your ideas, and what is brewing inside you. Connecting and relating with others becomes easier and more joyful.

Why are so many people afraid to stand in front of an audience? They worry about messing up in front of a bunch of people, showing their imperfections, or looking like a fool. They fear their ideas will be rejected. Fear, that limiting emotion, is based in the mind, but while it may seem frightening to be on a stage in front of people with their attention fixed on you and you alone, it can also be an occasion of great joy. It feels wonderful to express your ideas to people who really want to listen. It's exciting to influence people and exchange positive vibrations. You feel victorious when you have made a positive impact on an audience that applauds when you finish.

Strong and powerful women are skilled public speakers. They connect with their audience and generously impart messages of inspiration, information, or entertainment. They are engaging and charismatic. With practice, you can attain this, too.

There are many ways to learn public speaking. One is to practice on your own at home, in front of a mirror, with friends, or with someone with a video camera. However, I highly recommend that you investigate Toastmasters, Intl. This professional organization teaches the skills of public speaking. Members practice with each other and offer support, feedback, and constructive criticism to guide each other to become the best public speakers they can be. You will learn how to write a speech, to present it, to stay within a time limit, to learn from your mistakes, and to give feedback to others. With its focus of empowering members, Toastmasters is a greatly supportive and loving community group where negativity is not tolerated. Toastmasters groups are everywhere. Some cities have several groups. Log onto the Toastmasters website (www.toastmasters.org), for more information and to find chapters in your area.

Self-Talk

Words carry a lot of energy. We know that complaints create negative energy. Keep this in mind as you flagellate yourself for making a mistake or call yourself a dummy, or stupid, or lame. What you say, your body believes. This kind of self-abuse is harmful to body and soul. The therapeutic community knows well that when others put us down, our self-worth is eroded. But so often the person putting us down is *us*! As kids, we're taught to avoid or ignore bullies who make fun of us. But we never learned to avoid our own put-downs.

No matter what the situation is, be gentle and loving to yourself. Speak to yourself only in kind words. Congratulate yourself when you have achieved something or when you completed a project. If you make a mistake or don't do as well on a task as you had planned, tell yourself, "It's OK. I've learned from this and I'll do better next time." Working toward being the best you can be involves challenging and competing with yourself, so it's beneficial to notice areas in need of improvement. But cursing yourself for not being perfect will diminish your self-esteem and tarnish your perception of yourself.

Remember, you are a miraculous creation, and an emanation of God/dess. Why would you be anything other than perfect, even when you make so-called mistakes? You would never call God/dess a loser, so don't think about doing that to yourself. Every person on the planet, including you, has gifts and value. When you feel like putting yourself down, remember those gifts and fantastic unique qualities that make you who you are, and that serve others.

Remember, thoughts become things. When you tell yourself that you're "lame" or "stupid," or that everything you touch "turns to crap," you will fulfill that prophecy. Your mind, body, and vibration respond to what they hear and activate that command. Knowing this, please tell yourself things that will feed the positive attributes of who you are. These positive words will only become stronger, increasing your confidence and self-love. Replace "I'm such a screw up," with "I am SO good at this!" And "I can't do that," with "Of course I can do that." Notice the kinds of miracles you can perform.

Service and Community

Becoming a strong and powerful woman is not a selfish undertaking. We are becoming the best we can be while we make contributions to people and things we care about. Most high-profile women don't ignore others. They are supportive of other individuals on their own journeys and active in community efforts. Strong and powerful women don't give away their energy, however; they invest their energy in people and issues they believe in. Thus their energy perpetuates itself and flows to a higher good. They selflessly give time, money, and energy, and this output of positive energy flows into the universe, which, of course, returns it to us. The rewards of service are great. They take the form of love, support, and personal satisfaction.

Volunteer

Giving your time to support something you believe in is an act of love. It is a selfless action that will not only contribute to the betterment of a person, cause, or organization, but will also strengthen you, yourself. Volunteering is being willing to *give* your time without the expectation of anything in return. This is, basically, opening your heart chakra and radiating positive energy; it is also known as *love*. Being in a state of giving is fulfilling and will increase your self-esteem and raise your vibration as a human being.

Many a benevolent soul has established an organization to solve a problem or create a better way of life on the planet. Non-profit organizations target issues of every kind—the environment, incurable diseases, world hunger, politics, you name it. Volunteers are the life-blood of such organizations. But non-profits aren't the only organizations that need our help. Large and small community organizations like churches, community centers, schools, hospitals, even individual families, also rely on volunteers. When you pitch in and offer a hand, you dive into a pool of volunteers who can make the impossible possible. The more energy you can devote to a mission, the sooner and more easily it will be accomplished.

Giving of yourself is rewarding in ways far greater than mere financial donations. You will feel tremendously positive about yourself and life. You may awaken dormant skills and develop new skills. You will make new contacts and friends. You may discover a new passion. Most of all, you will feel the delight of being of service to a person or organization in need.

Donate Money

But money is a form of energy, and when you give money, you are putting energy into circulation. Organizations need money just as much as they need your time, and any financial support you can offer is a positive statement of appreciation for the cause. Donate generously. It will come back to you in numerous forms of satisfaction. Like the energy of love, the more freely you circulate the energy of money, the more will be returned to you.

As we learned about the Law of Attraction in the Energy and Spirited chapters, the vibration you radiate is what you attract. By giving lovingly and generously of yourself, you position yourself to receive. In her book, *The Dynamic Laws of Prosperity*, Catherine Ponder writes, "True prosperity has a spiritual basis. God is the source of your supply.

Sharing is the beginning of financial increase. Systematic giving opens the way to systematic receiving."[225]

Believing you don't have extra money to donate is a practice of poverty consciousness. By not giving, you are telling the Universe you aren't able to receive and that you don't believe there is "enough" for you. Poverty consciousness, the fear that there isn't enough, will suck you into financial poverty. Until you understand that the Universe has a bountiful supply of every kind of wealth and that you are a part of the Universal energy and worthy of monetary support, you will not realize prosperity. Overcome this by demonstrating to the Universe that you are a willing participant in circulating the endless Universal supply, that you are open to wealth and abundance. Give what you can—if only a dollar—to your church, a food kitchen, or a charity or other worthy cause. This simple act of financial giving will diminish fear, boost self-esteem, and open you to financial abundance.

Become an Activist

When you devote yourself more actively and fully to a mission you feel passionately about, your volunteering can evolve into activism. Activism is energy expressing a sense of urgency. Activism opens the mind of the public and can shift consciousness worldwide. It can change paradigms. The world evolves when proactive people enforce change. Some of our most powerful activists have been women. In the mid-1800s, for example, Harriett Tubman led hundreds of slave families to freedom along the Underground Railroad. At the same time, Susan B. Anthony was a leader for women's right to vote. In the 1960s, at the beginning of the third wave of feminism, women like Betty Friedan, who wrote the landmark book, *The Feminine Mystique*, and Gloria Steinem, founder of the National Women's Alliance and *Ms. Magazine*, were activists who worked to gain equal rights for women. Recognizing the need for spirituality in the feminist movement in the 1970s, Z. Budapest founded the women's spirituality movement. Starhawk, an activist for the global justice movement, tirelessly protests the actions of the World Trade Organization and other globalization efforts. From 1997 to 1999, Julia Butterfly Hill sat in an ancient redwood tree to prevent loggers from cutting it down. Such activists are passionate for their causes. They are committed against all odds. The mission of the activist is often her life's mission. The activist's soul drives her to forge ahead.

Great strength of character and will are needed in activism. Opposing forces will attempt to separate the activist from her mission. But the passion that arises from activist energy for a cause will inspire others to take action. The results of activism are thus not only an expression of your own power and an opportunity to work with kindred spirits, but also tremendous personal fulfillment. Knowing you are making a positive difference on earth is the greatest reward.

Suggested Reading to increase your strength and power:

Power Versus Wisdom: The New Path for Women, by Priscilla V. Marotta, Ph.D.
Now It's Our Turn: How Women Can Transform Their Lives and Save the Planet, by Alana Lyons
What the Bleep Do We Know? (DVD)
Ask and It Is Given, by Esther and Jerry Hicks
Three Steps to Wealth and Power: Unleash Your Potential for Unlimited Achievement, by Chris Howard
Awakening the Giant Within, by Tony Robbins
The Secrets of the Millionaire Mind, by T. Harv Eker
Think and Grow Rich, by Napoleon Hill
You Can Heal Your Life, by Louise Hay
How to Win Friends and Influence People, by Dale Carnegie
Infinite Possibilities: The Art of Living Your Dreams (CD series) by Mike Dooley

AFTERWORD

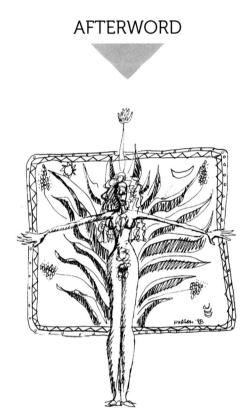

You already have in you everything you need to be a Positive Energy Woman. Perhaps the exercises in this book have helped you become the sexy, spirited, strong woman you've always dreamed of becoming. Now go spread your beautiful energy. The world will be a better place for it.

Love and blessings.

Meloney
Spring, 2008

ENDNOTES

Chapter 2, Self-Esteem

[1] Brody, Jane E. "Personal Health: Girls and Puberty: the Crisis Year." New York Times on the Web, November 4, 1997.

[2] National Institute of Mental Health, "Eating Disorders," <www.nimh.hih.gov>.

[3] Roy, Neal and Kendler. "The genetic epidemiology of self esteem," The British Journal of Psychiatry 166 (1995): 813-820.

[4] Steinem, Gloria. *A Revolution From Within: A Book of Self Esteem.* Little, Brown and Company, 1992. p. 21.

[5] Ibid., pp. 124-5.

[6] Ibid., p. 123.

[7] Ibid., p. 122.

[8] Ibid., p. 120.

[9] Ibid., p. 120.

[10] Ibid., p. 122 .

[11] Young, Iris Marion. *Throwing Like a Girl and Other Essays in Feminist Philosophy and Feminist Theory.* Indiana University Press, 1990. pp. 154-5.

[12] Hasbrook, C.A. "Young Children's Social Construction of Physicality and Gender." *Inside Sports.* Eds. J. Coakley and P. Donnelly, 1999. pp. 7-16.

[13] Brody, Jane E. "Personal Health: Girls and Puberty: the Crisis Years." New York Times on the Web, November 4, 1997.

[14] "Only Two Percent of Women Describe Themselves as Beautiful: New Global Study Uncovers Desire for Broader Definition of Beauty," The Real Truth About Beauty: A Global Report, conducted by research firm Strategy One in collaboration with Dr. Nancy Etcoff. Sept 29, 2004, <www.campaignforrealbeauty.com>.

[15] Social Issues Research Centre (SIRC). "Mirror, mirror: A summary of research findings of body image." 1997.

[16] Brown, Brene, Ph.D. LMSW, "No Body Is Perfect: Body Image and Shame." 2007. <www.surewoman.ca>.

[17] Stone, Merlin. *When God Was A Woman.* A Harvest Book, Barcourt Brace & Company, 1976. p. 3.

[18] Ibid., pp. 35-36.

[19] Ibid., p. 43.

[20] Ibid., p. 44.

21 Gimbutas, Marija. *The Living Goddess.* Ed. Miriam Robbins Dexter. University of California Press, 2001. p. xvi.

22 Eisler, Riane. *The Chalice & the Blade.* Harper San Francisco, 1987. p. xvii.

23 Holy Bible, Revised Standard Version. Deuteronomy 12:2-3 (The Asherim mentioned in verse 3 refers to the pillar or tree representing the goddess Ashera.) Deuteronomy 23:17-18, 2 Kings 18:3-4. Thomas Nelson & Sons, 1952.

24 Exodus 22:18, Leviticus 20:6 & 27.

25 Proverbs 2:16-20, Koran, 24:31, 2:282.

26 Deuteronomy 22:23.

27 1 Timothy 2:11-15, Ephesians 5:22, Colossians 3:18-19. 1 Corinthians 14:33-35, Koran, 4:38.

28 Leviticus 15:19-30, 20:18.

29 Genesis 3:12-13, 3:16.

30 Kramer, Heinrich and James Sprenger. *The Malleus Maleficarum.* Translated by the Reverend Montague Summers. Dover Publications, Inc. 1971.

31 Shlain, Leonard. *The Alphabet Versus the Goddess.* Penguin Compass, 1999. p. 373.

32 Brizendine, Louann. *The Female Brain.* Broadway Books, 2006. p. 5.

33 Ibid., p. 8.

34 Ibid., pp. 21, 129-131.

35 Ibid., p. 8.

36 Ibid., p. 5.

37 Ibid., p. 5.

38 Ibid., p. 29.

39 Biaggi, Cristina. "The Roots of Patriarchy in Europe, The Middle East, and Asia (or) Why Did The Kurgans Become Warlike?" *The Rule of Mars.* Ed. Cristina Biaggi. Knowledge, Ideas & Trends, 2005. p. 86.

40 Brizendine, Louann. *The Female Brain.* Broadway Books, 2006. pg. 42.

41 Davis-Kimball, Jeannine. "Nomads and Patriarchy." *The Rule of Mars.* Ed. Cristina Biaggi. Knowledge, Ideas & Trends, 2005. pp. 134-135.

42 Kneller, Tara. "Neither Goddesses Nor Doormats: The Role of Women in Nubia." April 5, 1993. <www.historicaltextarchive.com>.

43 Amdur, Ellis. "Women Warriors of Japan: The Role of Arms-Bearing Women in Japanese History." *Journal of Asian Martial Arts* Vol. 5, No. 2, 1996.

44 Sefscik, Sue M. "Zenobia." About.com: Women's History. <www.about.com>.

45 "The National Crime Victimization Survey." U.S. Department of Justice, 2005.

46 "National Crime Victimization Survey." U.S. Department of Justice, 2000. "Violence by Intimates: Analysis of Data on Crimes by Current or Former Spouses, Boyfriends and Girlfriends." March, 1998.

47 "Sexual Violence: Fact Sheet." National Center for Injury Prevention and Control, Center for Disease Control, 2004.

48 "Youth Victimization: Prevalence and Implications," U.S. Department of Justice, National Institute of Justice, 2003.

49 "Sexual Violence: Fact Sheet," National Center for Injury Prevention and Control, Center for Disease Control, 2004.

[50] Hofford, M. and Harrell A. *Family Violence Interventions for the Justice System.* Washington D.C., U.S. Bureau of Justice Assistance, 1989.

[51] Walrath, C., M. Ybarra, E. Holden, et. al. "Children with reported histories of sexual abuse: Utilizing multiple perspectives to understand clinical and psychological profiles." *Child Abuse and Neglect.* 27, pp. 509-524.

Chapter 3, A Return to Self-Esteem

[52] Dooley, Mike. "TUT's Adventurer's Club." 2003-2008, TUT Enterprises, Inc. www.tut.com

Chapter 4, It's All About Energy

[53] Webster's New World College Dictionary, 3rd ed, 1988.

[54] Fellner, Tara. *Aromatherapy for Lovers.* Charles E. Tuttle Company, Inc., 1995. pp. 75-77.

[55] Gardner, Joy. *Color and Crystals: A Journey Through the Chakras.* The Crossing Press, 1996.

Chapter 5, Female Sexual Energy

[56] Chia, Mantak & Manweewan. *Healing Love Through the Tao: Cultivating Female Sexual Energy* Felix Morrow Publisher. 1986. p. 28.

[57] Saraswati, Sunyata and Bodhi Avinasha. *Jewel in the Lotus: The Tantric Path to Higher Consciousness.* Third Edition. Ipsalu Publishing. 1994. p. 178.

[58] Chia, Mantak & Maneewan. *Healing Love Through the Tao.* p. 28.

[59] Shlain, Leonard. *Sex, Time and Power: How Women's Sexuality Shaped Human Evolution.* Penguin Books. 2003. p. 19.

[60] Morris, Desmond. *The Naked Ape: A Zoologist's Study of the Human Animal.* Second edition. Delta Trade Paperbacks. 1999. p. 66.

[61] Ibid., p. 65.

[62] Ibid., p. 66.

[63] Shlain, p. 73.

[64] Brizendine, Louann. *The Female Brain.* Broadway Books. 2006. pp. 67-8.

[65] Ibid., p. 60.

[66] Ibid., p. 59.

[67] Morris, p. 90.

[68] Maines, Rachel P. *The Technology of Orgasm: "Hysteria," The Vibrator, and Women's Sexual Satisfaction.* Baltimore: The Johns Hopkins University Press. 1999. Cited on Electronic Journal of Human Sexuality, Volume 3, October 12, 2000. < http://www.ejhs.org/volume3/book11.htm>.

[69] Sarawati, Avinasha, p. 20.

[70] *The Upanishads: Breath of the Eternal.* Trans. Swami Prabhavananda, Frederick Manchester. Vedanta Press. First edition paperback, 1983. "Prasna." pp. 43-45.

[71] Ibid., p. 45.

[72] Shaw, Miranda. *Passionate Enlightenment: Women in Tantric Buddhism*. Princeton University Press, 1994. p. 21.

[73] Ibid., p. 21.

[74] Ibid., p. 32.

[75] Ibid., p. 28.

[76] Ibid., p. 24.

[77] Ibid., p. 11.

[78] Ibid., p. 37.

[79] Avinasha, Bodhi. "Mastering Kundalini." Ipsalu Tantra Correspondence Course, Lesson six. p. 1

[80] Saraswati, Sunyata and Bodhi Avinasha. *Jewel in the Lotus: The Tantric Path to Higher Consciousness*. Third Edition. Ipsalu Publishing, 1994. p. 20.

[81] Chia, p. 29.

[82] Chia, Mantak. *Taoist Secrets of Love: Cultivating Male Sexual Energy*. Aurora Press, 1984. p. xvii.

[83] Steinem, Gloria. *Revolution from Within*. Little Brown and Company, 1989. Citing "Growing Up Creative: Nurturing a Lifetime of Creativity." by Teresa M. Amabile." p. 278.

[84] Hill, Napoleon. *Think and Grow Rich*. Fawcett Books. First Ballantine Books Trade Edition: August, 1996. pp. 182-5.

[85] Hill, p. 185.

[86] Brizendine, p. 5.

[87] Oesterley, W.O.E. *Sacred Dance in the Ancient World*. Dover Publications, Inc., 1923. p. 4.

[88] Lang, Andrew. *Myth, Ritual, and Religion*. Volume I. Chapter 9: Greek Myths of the Origins of the World and Man. Originally published by Longmans, Green & Company, 1913. <http://classiclit.about.com/library/bl-etexts/alang/bl-alang-myth-9.htm>.

[89] Natale, Frank. *Trance Dance: The Dance of Life*. Element Books Limited, 1995. p. 2.

[90] Noble, Vicki. *The Double Goddess: Women Sharing Power*. Bear & Company, 2003. p. 122.

[91] Steinem, Gloria. "Survey: Sex and Self-Esteem," *Medical Aspects of Human Sexuality*, vol. 17, no. 5, May, 1983. *Revolution From Within*. p. 202. Noted in the article, choice is key, as some people were intentionally celibate and happy.

Chapter 6, Yoni Magic

[92] Camphausen, Rufus C. *The Yoni: Sacred Symbol of Female Creative Power*. Inner Traditions International, 1996. p. 2.

[93] Ibid., p. 14.

[94] Shlain, Leonard. *Sex, Time, and Power: How Women's Sexuality Shaped Human Evolution*. Penguin Books, 2003. p. 17.

[95] Ibid., p. 63.

[96] Ibid., p. 137.

[97] Birnbaum, Lucia Chiavola. *Dark mother: african origins and godmothers.* Authors Choice Press, 2001. p. xxv.

[98] Ibid., pp. 44-45.

[99] Camphausen, pp. 10-11.

[100] Ibid., p. 10.

[101] Ibid., p. 17.

[102] Ibid., p. 11.

[103] Gimbutas, Marija. *The Living Goddesses.* Ed. Miriam Robbins Dexter. University of California Press, 2001. pp. 117-8.

[104] Rawson, Philip. *The Art of Tantra.* Thames & Hudson, 1985. pp. 54-5.

[105] Camphausen, p. 60.

[106] Tate, Karen. *Sacred Places of the Goddess: 108 Destinations.* Consortium of Collective Consciousness, 2006. p. 73.

[107] Camphausen, p. 57.

[108] Qualls-Corbett, p. 68.

[109] Qualls-Corbett, Nancy. *The Sacred Prostitute: Eternal Aspect of the Feminine.* Inner City Books, 1988. p. 32.

[110] Tate, p. 146.

[111] Qualls-Corbett, pp. 34-5. She cites her source as *Woman's Encyclopedia of Myths and Secrets* by Barbara Walker, p. 820.

[112] Ibid., p. 34.

[113] Holy Bible, Revised Standard Version. 1 Corinthians 6:15-18. Thomas Nelson and Sons, 1952.

[114] Shlain, pp. 15-20.

[115] Ibid., pp. 336-37.

[116] "Women call off Columbia sex ban." BBC News, Sept 22, 2006 <http://news.bbc.co.uk>.

[117] Proverbs 2:16-20.

[118] Interview with Camille Paglia. *Playboy.* Issue 483. May 1995.

[119] Camphausen, Rufus C. *The Yoni: Sacred Symbol of Female Creative Power.* p. 66.

[120] Chia, Mantak & Maneewan. *Healing Love Through the Tao.* p. 28.

[121] Ibid., pp. 39-40.

[122] Ibid., pp. 27-8.

[123] Brizendine, Louann. *The Female Brain.* Broadway Books, 2006. p. 34.

[124] Ibid., p. 19.

Chapter 8, Spirited

[125] *Webster's New World College Dictionary.* Third Edition. Macmillan USA, 1996.

[126] Ibid.

[127] Hawkins, David R. *Power vs. Force: The Hidden Determinants of Human Behavior.* Hay House, Inc., 2002. pp. 75-94.

[128] Holmes, Ernest. *The Science of Mind: A Philosophy, A Faith, A Way of Life.* Penguin Putnam, Inc. First Trade Paperback Edition, 1998. p. 309.

[129] Stanford Encyclopedia of Philosophy, The Uncertainty Principle. <http://plato.stanford.edu>.

[130] "What is Quantum Physics?" Oracle ThinkQuest Library <www. thinkquest. org/3487/qp.html>. Referenced: Rae, Alastair. *Quantum Physics: Illusion or Reality?* Second Canto Edition, 2004. p. 50.

[131] Vergano, Dan. "Quantum Physics: It's all about me, me, me. Isn't it?" March 11, 2007. <USA Today.com>.

[132] Democritus. Wikipedia.com <www.wikipedia.com> and Democritus. Stanford Encyclopedia of Philosophy. First published Aug. 15, 2004. <www.plato. stanford.edu>.

[133] Ibid.

[134] "Soul Man." Urban Legends Reference Pages. www.snopes.com. Barbara and David Mikkelson. July 17, 2007. <www.snopes.com/religion/soulweight.asp>.

[135] Hagelin, John S., Maxwell V. Rainforth, et. al. "Effects of Group Practice of the Transcendental Meditation Program on Preventing Violent Crime in Washington, D.C.: Results of the National Demonstration Project, June-July 1993." Institute of Science, Technology and Public Policy.

Chapter 9, Tools to Connect Soul and Universal Spirit

[136] "Cosmic Consciousness." Encyclopedia of the Unusual and Unexplained. <www.unexplained stuff.com>.

[137] Hicks, Esther and Jerry. *Ask and It Is Given.* Hay House, Inc., 2004. p. 25.

[138] Moon, Xia. "Ritual As Worship: Temple of the Goddess Handbook." Temple of the Goddess, Arcadia, California.

[139] Campbell, Joseph. *Primitive Mythology: The Masks of God.* Penguin Books, 1991. pp. 299-312.

[140] Ibid., p. 313.

[141] Lang, Andrew. *Myth, Ritual, and Religion.* Volume I, Chapter 9: Greek Myths of the Origins of the World and Man. Originally published by Longmans, Green & Company, 1913. <http://classiclit.about.com/library/bl-etexts/alang/bl-alang-myth-9.htm>.

[142] Campbell, Joseph. *Primitive Mythology: Masks of God,* pp. 300-304.

[143] Ibid., pp. 313-314.

[144] Braden, Gregg. *The Isaiah Effect: Decoding the Lost Science of Prayer and Prophecy.* Random House, 2000. pp. 186.

[145] Holmes, Ernest. *The Science of Mind: A Philosophy, A Faith, A Way of Life.* Penguin Putnam, Inc. First Trade Paperback edition, 1998. p. 152.

[146] Mark 11:23-24.

[147] Holmes, pp. 184-5.

[148] Ibid., pp. 186-7.

[149] Ibid., p. 186.

[150] Ibid., p. 188.

[151] Ibid., p. 188.

[152] "What is Karma?" Soka Gakkai International USA. Buddhist Association for Peace, Culture and Education. Jeff Kriger, SGI-USA Vice Study Department Leader, based on the book *Yasashi Kyogaku.* <www.sgi-usa.org>.

[153] Dasa, Drutakarma (Michael A. Cremo), Goswami, Mukunda, Dasa, Bhutatma (Austin Gordon), et. al. *Chant and Be Happy: The Power of Mantra Meditation.* Based on the teachings of A.C. Bhaktivedanta Swami Prabhupada. The Bhaktivedanta Book Trust, 1977. p. 107.

[154] Prabhupada, A.C. Bhaktivedanta Swami. *Bhagavad-Gita: As It Is.* The Bhaktivedanta Book Trust. Eighth printing, 1997. p. 283.

[155] Ashley-Farrand, Thomas. *Shakti Mantras: Tapping into the Great Goddess Energy Within.* Ballantine Books, 2003. p. 209.

[156] Chopra, Deepak. *The Seven Spiritual Laws of Success: A Practical Guide to the Fulfillment of Your Dreams.* Amber-Allen Publishing and New World Library, 1994. p. 17.

[157] *The Mudras in SpiritProject.* SpiritProject, © 2000-2007 <http://www.spiritproject.com/medicus/mudras/index.htm>.

[158] Mesko, Sabrina. *Power Mudras: Yoga Hand Postures for Women.* Ballentine Books, 2002. p. 8. Das, Dipankar. *Mudras: Graceful Gestures.* Positive Life Foundation, Dec. 1996. <http://www.lifepositive.com/spirit/traditional-paths/rituals/mudra.asp>.

[159] Biography. Vivekananda Vedanta Network. Ramakrishna Vedanta Society of Boston. Copyright 2003-2008. <www.vivekananda.org>.

[160] *The Life of Paramahansa Yogananda.* The Self Realization Fellowship, 2003. <www.yogananda-srf.org>. For more information on Yogananda and Self Realization Fellowship, read *Autobiography of a Yogi*, by Paramahansa Yogananda.

[161] McGirk, Jan. Obituary: "Indra Devi." *The Independent* (London), April 30, 2002. <www.Bnet.com>.

[162] Janakananda, Swami. *Yoga, Tantra and Meditation in Daily Life.* Samuel Weiser, Inc. Fourth printing, 1988. p. 14.

[163] Ibid., pp. 15-16.

[164] Ibid., pp. 16-17.

Chapter 10, Strong

[165] Bae, Yupin, Susan Choy, Claire Geddes, et. al. "Trends in Educational Equality of Girls and Women." March, 2000. National Center for Education Statistics. U.S. Department of Education, Office of Educational Research and Improvement.

[166] "College Enrollment and Work Activity of 2006 High School Graduates." April 26, 2007. News: Bureau of Labor Statistics. U.S. Department of Labor, Bureau of Labor Statistics.

[167] Fields, Jason and Lynne M.Casper. Current Population Reports. "America's Families and Living Arrangements: Population Characteristics." 2000. U.S. Census Bureau.

168 "Employment and Earnings. Annual Averages." 2007. U.S. Department of Labor, Bureau of Labor Statistics. Table 11. "Employed persons by detailed occupation, sex, race and Hispanic or Latino ethnicity <www.bls.gov/cps/cpsaat11.pdf > Found in article," Professional Women: Vital Statistics, Fact Sheet 2007. Department for Professional Employees, AFL-CIO. <www.dpeaflcio.org>.

169 Gogoi, Pallavi. "I Am Woman, Hear Me Shop." Edited by Patricia O'Connell. BusinessWeek. February 14, 2005. <www.businessweek.com>.

170 Fields, Jason and Lynne M. Casper. Current Population Reports. "America's Families and Living Arrangements: Population Characteristics." 2000. U.S. Census Bureau.

171 "Childless by Choice - survey of women on having children - Statistical Data Included." American Demographics, October 1, 2001. Bnet.com. <http://findarticles.com/p/articles/mi_m4021/is_2001_oct/ai_79052844/pg_1>

172 "Fertility of American Women: June, 2004." Current population reports by Jane Lawler Dye. Issued December, 2005. U.S. Census Bureau. Department of Commerce. <www.census.gov>.

173 "U.S. Adults Postponing Marriage, Census Bureau Reports." June 29, 2001. U.S. Department of Commerce News. U.S. Census Bureau, Public Information Office.

174 Bumpass, Larry and Lu Hsun-Hen. "Trends in Cohabitation and Implications for Children's Family Contexts in the United States." 2000. *Population Studies*. 54:29-41. Found on <www.unmarried.org/statistics.html>.

175 Eckel, Sara. American Demographics: "Single Mothers Many Faces." Bnet.com. 1999. <findarticles.com/p/articles/mi_m4021/is_issn_0163_4089/ai_54624902>.

176 Quote found in book: Marotta, Priscilla V. *Power and Wisdom: The New Path for Women*. Phelps & Associates, 1999. p. 24.

177 Ibid., p. 32.

178 Lyons, Alana. *Now It's Our Turn: How Women Can Transform Their Lives and Save the Planet*. Jaguar Books, 1998. p. 97.

179 Marotta, p. 32.

180 Starhawk, *Truth or Dare: Encounters with Power, Authority and Mystery*. Harper San Francisco. First Paperback Edition, 1990. p. 9.

181 Ibid., p. 14.

182 Ibid., p. 15.

183 Ibid., p. 10.

184 Ibid., p. 15.

185 Ibid., p. 15.

186 Ibid., p. 9.

187 Ibid., p. 15.

188 Ibid., p. 11.

189 Eisler, Riane. *The Chalice & The Blade: Our History, Our Future*. First HarperCollins Paperback Edition, 1988. pp. 192-3. Here, Eisler quotes Jean Baker Miller, author of *Towards a New Psychology of Women* (1976), a study of human relationships.

190 Ibid., p. 188.

191 Ibid., p. xvi.

192 Ibid., p. 191.

193 Ibid., p. 192.

Chapter 11, Inner Expansion

194 The Dalai Lama, and Victor Chan. *The Wisdom of Forgiveness: Intimate Conversations and Journeys.* Riverhead Books, 2004. p 73.

195 The Key to Theosophy, p. 198. Reference found on <http://www. teosofia.com/ Mumbai/7311light.html>.

196 Ponder, Catherine. *The Dynamic Laws of Prosperity.* DeVorss Publications. Eleventh printing, 2003. pp. 44-47.

197 Jampolsky, Gerald G. *Love Is Letting Go of Fear.* Celestial Arts, 1979. p. 35.

198 Hay, Louise E. *You Can Heal Your Life.* Hay House, Inc., 1997. p. 8.

199 Gray, John. *Mars and Venus on a Date.* Perennial Currents, 2005. p. 10.

200 The Dalai Lama, and Victor Chan., p. 74.

201 Arias, Elizabeth, Ph.D. "U.S. Life Tables, 2002." National Vital Statistics Report. Volume 53, Number 6. Center for Disease Control. <www.cdc.gov/ nchs/data/nvsr/nvsr53/nvsr53_06.pdf>.

202 "US Obesity at an All-Time High." Medical College of Wisconsin. 11/26/2002. <http://healthlink.mcw.edu/article/1031002183.html>.

203 Reyes, Maridel. "Psyched! Think yourself thin." Eat-right update. *Self Magazine.* June, 2007. p. 116.

204 The Mayo Clinic Staff. "Depression and anxiety: exercise eases symptoms." October 23, 2007. <www.mayoclinic.com/health/depression-and-exercise/ mh00043>.

205 Webster's New World College Dictionary. Third Edition. MacMillan, 1996.

206 Buechner, Frederick. *Wishful Thinking: A Theological ABC.* HarperOne. Rev Exp edition, 1993. p. 95.

207 Leloup, Jean-Yves. *The Gospel of Thomas: The Gnostic Wisdom of Jesus.* Inner Traditions. First U.S. Edition, 2005. p. 41.

208 Ibid., p. 168.

209 Jones, Laurie Beth. *The Path: Creating Your Mission Statement for Work and for Life.* Hyperion, 1996. Front cover, inner flap.

210 Hicks, Esther and Jerry (The Teachings of Abraham). *Ask and It Is Given, Learning to Manifest Your Desires.* Hay House, Inc., 2004. p. 41.

211 *What the Bleep: Down the Rabbit Hole.* Quantum Edition. Lord of the Wind Films/20th Century Fox, 2006.

212 Ibid.

213 Blavatsky, Helena P. *Isis Unveiled: Secrets of the Ancient Wisdom Tradition. Madame Blavatsky's First Work, A New Abridgement for Today* by Michael Gomes. Quest Books. First Quest Edition. 1997. p. 43.

214 Holmes, Ernest. *The Science of Mind: A Philosophy, A Faith, A Way of Life.* Penguin Putnam. First Trade Paperback Edition, 1997. p. 144.

[215] *What the Bleep: Down the Rabbit Hole.* Quantum Edition. Lord of the Wind Films/20th Century Fox, 2006.

[216] Webster's New World Dictionary.

[217] <www.susanjeffers.com>.

[218] Jeffers, Susan. *Feel the Fear and Do It Anyway.* A Fawcett Columbine Book, 1987. Quote found on <http://brian.gaia.com/blog/2008/1/quotes_from_ susan_jeffers_feel_the_fear_and_do_it_anyway>.

[219] Kersey, Cynthia. *Unstoppable Women: Achieve Any Breakthrough Goal in 30 Days.* Rodale, Inc., 2005. pg. 3.

[220] Manz, Charles C. *The Power of Failure: 27 Ways to Turn Life's Setbacks Into Success.* Berrett-Koehler Publishing, Inc., 2002. p. 15.

[221] *Education pays...* U.S. Bureau of Labor Statistics, Office of Occupational Statistics and Employment Projections, modified April 15, 2008. <http://www.bls.gov/emp/emptab7.htm>.

[222] Allen, I. Elaine and Jeff Seaman. *Online Nation: Five Years of Growth in Online Learning.* October, 2007. Babson Survey Research Group and The Sloan Consortium. < http://www.sloan-c.org/publications/survey/index.asp>.

Chapter 12, Outer Manifestation

[223] Hicks, Esther and Jerry (The Teachings of Abraham). *Ask and It Is Given: Learning to Manifest Your Desires.* Hay House , Inc., 2004. p. 26.

[224] "Do You Suffer from Glossophobia?" Glossophobia.com <www.glossophobia.com>.

[225] Ponder, Catherine. *The Dynamic Laws of Prosperity.* DeVorss Publications. Eleventh printing, 2003. p. 175.

INDEX

CPSIA information can be obtained
at www.ICGtesting.com
Printed in the USA
FSOW01n1402090216
16746FS